E/ESCWA/SDPD/2015/3

Economic and Social Commission for Western Asia

Arab Sustainable Development Report

First Edition, 2015

UNITED NATIONS
Beirut

E-mail: publications-escwa@un.org; website: www.unescwa.org

United Nations publication issued by ESCWA.

Photo credits:
Cover: © Fotolia.com
Page 15: © Shutterstock/Thomas Koch
Page 45: © Arab Network for Environment and Development (RAED)
Page 87: © UNEP
Page 121: © Fotolia.com
Page 151: © ESCWA
Page 181: © UNHCR/S. Baldwin

Acknowledgements

This report is the result of the combined efforts of the Economic and Social Commission for Western Asia (ESCWA) and the United Nations Environment Programme (UNEP). Contributions came from United Nations member agencies of the Regional Coordination Mechanism, the League of Arab States, and sustainable development experts and practitioners. Special thanks go to the individuals listed below, as well as to ESCWA division directors, publications committee and staff from substantive divisions for their comments and feedback.

ESCWA Core Project Team (Sustainable Development Policies Division)

Roula Majdalani, *Director*

Reem Nejdawi, *Chief*

Monia Braham, *Economic Affairs Officer*

Jana el-Baba, *Research Assistant*

UNEP Project Team (Regional Office for West Asia)

Iyad Abumoghli, *Director and Regional Representative*

Melanie Hutchinson, *Programme Officer*

Lead Authors

Reem Nejdawi

Monia Braham

Jana el-Baba

Susan Razzaz

Cameron Allen

ESCWA Focal Points and Contributing Authors

Fathia Abdel Fadil

Khaled Abu Ismail

Lana Baydas

Carol Chouchani Cherfane

Habib el-Andaloussi

Karima el-Korri

Lara Geadah

Naela Haddad

Khaled Hussein

Adib Nehmeh

Atsuko Okuda

Niranjan Sarangi

George Younes

Authors of Background Papers

Odeh al-Jayyousi, *Technology*

Cameron Allen, *Integrated planning and statistical trend and gap analysis*

Sherif Arif, *Green economy*

Fateh Azzam, *Human rights*

Sherine El Sharkawy, *Finance*

Kamil Hamati, *Statistical trend and gap analysis*

Kinda Mohamadieh, *Gender*

Lamia Moubayed, *Governance*

Nadine Naber, *Social development*

Robert Smith, *Measuring sustainable development*

Statistical Support

Kamil Hamati

Ali Alsamawi

Rita al-Ashkar

Leonore Lekkerkerker

United Nations Regional Coordination Mechanism Focal Points and Contributing Authors

Mohamed Abdel-Ahad, *United Nations Population Fund - UNFPA*

Luna Abu-Swaireh, *United Nations Office for Disaster Risk Reduction - UNISDR*

Walid Ali, *United Nations Development Programme - UNDP*

Mohamed al-Shamlan, *UNEP*

Mohamed Aw-Dahir, *Food and Agriculture Organization of the United Nations - FAO*

Dony El Costa, *ESCWA consultant*

Wadid Erian, *Advisor to the League of Arab States*

Tarneem Fahmi, *United Nations World Food Programme - WFP*

Shaza Ghaleb Al Jondi, *International Labour Organization - ILO*

Stephen Gitonga, *UNDP*

Fadi Hamdan, *UNISDR consultant*

Robert Hamwey, *United Nations Conference on Trade and Development - UNCTAD*

Melanie Hutchinson, *UNEP*

Ali Karnib, *ESCWA consultant*

Kishan Khoday, *UNDP*

Nathalie Milbach-Bouché, *UNDP*

Azza Morssy, *United Nations Industrial Development Organization - UNIDO*

Mohammad Naciri, *United Nations Entity for Gender Equality and the Empowerment of Women - UN-Women*

Katja Schaefer, *United Nations Human Settlements Programme - UN-Habitat*

Shahira Wahbi, *League of Arab States*

National Reports

	Report author	Country focal point
Jordan	Mohammad Khasawneh	Mutasim al-Kilani *Ministry of Planning and International Cooperation*
Lebanon	Jana el-Baba	Youssef Naddaf and Lamia Mansour *Ministry of the Environment*
Morocco	Meriem Houzir	Mohammed Maktit *Ministry Delegate for the Environment*
Tunisia	Mohammed Adel Hentati	Chokri Mezghani *Ministry of the Environment*
Yemen	Yahya Almutawakel	Abdo Almohaya *Ministry of Planning and International Cooperation*

External Peer Reviews

Yahya Almutawakel, *former minister of industry and trade, Yemen*

Mounir Majdoub, *former secretary of State in charge of sustainable development, Tunisia*

Administrative Support

Rita Wehbe

Abdul Halim Maarouf

Manal Tabbara

Moneem Murrah

Contents

List of Tables

List of Figures

List of Boxes

Foreword

In September 2015, Governments worldwide adopted the 2030 Agenda for Sustainable Development, with 17 ambitious goals (SDGs) at its core. Many see in this historic moment a cause for hope. That hope, however, may dwindle before the stark contrast between the transformative vision and aspirations set forth in the agenda, and the current state of affairs in the Arab region. The Arab Sustainable Development Report depicts a situation that warrants serious concern: dramatic increases in conflict, violence and terrorism; rising numbers of refugees and internally displaced persons (IDPs); persistent injustice; mounting frustration over unemployment and rising rates of poverty; unequal access to, and overexploitation of, scarce water and other natural resources.

This report explores a number of reasons for this apparent development impasse. It contends that, despite the significant progress made, especially in education, health and gender equality, the region still faces a number of persistent challenges. Education systems fail to prepare youth to participate in the modern economy. The vast majority of women are denied opportunities to contribute to economic and public life. The rentier structure of the economy in some countries prevents growth from translating into the well-being of citizens. Accountability and governance deficiencies undermine the legitimacy of Governments. Opportunities for regional integration, resource mobilization and the use of science and technology continue to be missed. Moreover, brutal political forces continue to plague the region, including the only remaining physical occupation in the twenty-first century, that of Palestine.

In a globalized world, countries do not suffer alone. Troubles in the region affect neighbouring countries and regions and even those further away. Solidarity is essential: we all have an interest and the obligation to act, and we have the means to do so. The 2030 Agenda is first and foremost a guide for national action, but its main value is in stimulating a new phase of global cooperation.

The Arab region is at a crossroads. It could continue to be mired in the status quo of occupation, conflict, inequality, division, frustration, development stagnation and, ultimately, disintegration. Or it could heed the aspirations of people in the region and embark on the path of sustainable development, ending the occupation of Palestine, achieving peace, providing quality education and empowering women. That is the path that will ensure dignity and well-being for all, men and women alike, irrespective of age, origin, religion, ability, or social and economic background.

We at the Economic and Social Commission for Western Asia (ESCWA) and the United Nations Environment Programme (UNEP) support those who are striding out along that second path towards the future we want. We hope this report will provide a useful contribution to that noble pursuit.

Rima Khalaf

Under-Secretary-General

Executive Secretary

Economic and Social Commission for Western Asia

In 2015, almost 200 nations agreed on an ambitious new agenda to secure a healthy planet with healthy people in the next 15 years. As a result, the 17 SDGs offer a prism through which we can focus on the changes, challenges and choices that arise from balancing finite resources with a growing population. However, delivering that agenda requires bold, evidence-based policies and decisions, which is why this report provides a timely snapshot of development progress across the Arab world over the past two decades.

Mismanagement of the planet and its natural resources during that time has increasingly come to affect our lives. It threatens to escalate human migration and conflict, short-circuit development and trap the most vulnerable in poverty; it is for that reason that each of the 17 goals integrates so many aspects of the environment, security and human rights, drawing on the data revolution to monitor progress.

As this first Arab Sustainable Development Report shows, the region's approach to sustainable development already encompasses an understanding of the relationship between key issues such as food, water and energy, while embracing the transition to the inclusive green economy that underpins the entire 2030 Agenda. Thanks to trusted experts and partners, this work outlines the state, trends and trajectories of the region against the 17 goals, highlighting achievements, best practice and gaps to be addressed. In particular, it includes the vast body of research coordinated by ESCWA.

UNEP is proud to have partnered with ESCWA on this flagship report and is committed to working together to build on its findings. We hope it will equip both public and private decision makers with key data to make informed choices that advance sustainable development nationally, regionally and globally.

Achim Steiner

Under-Secretary-General
Executive Director
United Nations Environment Programme

Preface

The Arab Sustainable Development Report 2015, being launched on the start date of the 2030 Agenda for Sustainable Development in early 2016, comes at an opportune time: it provides a comprehensive review of sustainable development progress and trends in the Arab region over the past two decades and analyses the current situation, looking at how sustainable development might be achieved and the obstacles that must be overcome.

By March 2016, Member States of the United Nations are expected to agree on a set of global indicators to measure progress in implementing the agenda. This first edition of the report relies on published data relevant to the themes of the 17 Sustainable Development Goals (SDGs). Future editions will be realigned with the global indicator set. People are placed at the heart of this report's integrated framework of analysis, which highlights the links between the five Ps of the agenda: people, planet, prosperity, peace and partnerships.

The report illustrates the extent to which human dignity and well-being have been secured in the region, and assesses Arab societies and their modes of living through the lenses of sustainability and resilience. Cross-cutting prerequisites and means of achieving sustainable development are examined. The report sheds light on a blend of factors: the occupation of Palestinian and other Arab lands, the prevalence of conflict, and governance, human rights and institutional deficits. It also examines gaps in the areas of financing, science and technology, trade and statistical capacity.

The report reveals that, although significant progress has been made in some sectors and subregions, complex and interlinked economic, social, environmental and governance challenges remain. Urgent action is needed at the national and regional levels, in the context of a more effective global partnership. The report concludes that the path to sustainable development necessarily passes through integrated, long-term and evidence-based planning and investments that take into account the risks and consequences posed by the turmoil in the region, and address its root causes.

Preparation of the report was challenging in two ways. Data covering the 22 Arab countries and spanning the past two decades are incomplete. In some instances, significant data gaps prevented the identification of trends and the calculation of averages for all country groupings. That raises questions about the capacity of Arab countries to make the best use of evidence in policymaking, and about future reporting on the 2030 Agenda. The second difficulty was how to accurately depict the situation in a region that is in constant flux. For example, no data seemed up-to-date enough to capture population movements due to instability and their impact on key development indicators. Nevertheless, we believe that the analysis provides a solid basis for assessing sustainable development in the Arab region in future issues.

The report is the outcome of a joint effort involving a wide range of United Nations agencies in the Arab region, regional and international experts and stakeholders, and national Governments. We would like to thank all contributors for their input. Our appreciation also goes to the core team members, who showed the utmost commitment in preparing a report that, we hope, will reflect global momentum and stimulate a frank dialogue on how to fulfil the aspirations of this region's people.

Roula Majdalani

Director
Sustainable Development Policies Division
Economic and Social Commission for Western Asia

Iyad Abumoghli

Regional Director and Representative
United Nations Environment Programme
Regional Office for West Asia

1. Overview

"The interlinkages and integrated nature of the Sustainable Development Goals are of crucial importance in ensuring that the purpose of the new Agenda is realized. If we realize our ambitions across the full extent of the Agenda, the lives of all will be profoundly improved and our world will be transformed for the better."

Preamble of the 2030 Agenda for Sustainable Development

1. Overview

The people of the Arab region face an uncertain future. Millions are fleeing their homes to escape violence and millions more remain trapped by conflict or in occupied territory. The expanding population is placing increasing strain on the environment through unsustainable consumption of limited water supplies and abundant energy resources. The rentier economy that prevails in many countries has proven unable to adapt to new realities or absorb the growing and increasingly youthful labour force.

Nevertheless, the region has a solid base on which to build a better future. Improvements in health care have lead to a life expectancy well above the global average. The population is increasingly educated; school enrolment and adult literacy have improved considerably, especially in the least developed countries (LDCs) and for females. Those accomplishments mean that the region is well placed to meet the challenges of sustainable development that lie ahead.

The region's challenges and priorities are well reflected in the 2030 Agenda for Sustainable Development and its 17 Sustainable Development Goals (SDGs).[1] The SDGs maintain the focus of the Millennium Development Goals (MDGs) agenda on eradicating poverty in all its forms, emphasizing the interdependence of development issues and covering themes not fully addressed in the MDGs, including equality, governance and promoting peaceful and inclusive societies. In the agenda, it is recognized that, although the goals are universal, each country has its own realities, capacities and policies: each country is firmly in the driver's seat in terms of setting targets, designing policies and monitoring and reporting progress.

At this juncture, the authors of the Arab Sustainable Development Report asked: Where does the Arab region stand with regard to the SDGs and what were the trends over the past two decades? What is hampering sustainable development? Where is the region heading and what alternatives are available in order to bring the SDGs to fruition? This report attempts to provide answers within an integrated framework that places the dignity and well-being of people in the region at the heart of its analysis.

A. Purpose of the document

This report reviews the current situation in the Arab countries in relation to sustainable development. In particular, it uses regional and global benchmarks to aid in examining progress over the past two decades, trends, and remaining gaps and opportunities. It also includes examples and cases from the region. In the absence, at the time of writing, of globally adopted SDG indicators, authors selected a set of indicators guided by a number of criteria, including data availability for Arab countries, with preference given to the Sustainable Development Indicators for the Arab Region adopted by the League of Arab States.[2] Although the report covers the themes of the 17 global SDGs, it emphasizes the issues of highest priority to the Arab region.

One aim of this report is to provide national stakeholders with evidence-based information to be used for establishing targets, designing policies and monitoring/reporting progress.

It should also help regional stakeholders to advocate for change.

B. Scope and methodology

This report has been produced at the request of Arab Governments.[3] In addition to input from experts and United Nations agencies, five Arab countries conducted national sustainable development assessments that provided a wealth of examples. The Arab Forum on Sustainable Development, which met in April 2014 in Jordan and in May 2015 in Bahrain, constituted important milestones in the preparation of this report. See annex I for the participatory methodology for preparing the report.

The report focuses on the Arab region. As far as possible, it includes data on all 22 Arab countries and provides comparisons between the Arab region and other regions, while benchmarking with global averages. Due to lack of data, not all countries are included for all indicators.

The region's considerable diversity makes it indispensable to break it down into the following subregions: the Gulf Cooperation Council countries (Bahrain, Kuwait, Oman, Qatar, Saudi Arabia and the United Arab Emirates); the least developed countries (the Comoros, Djibouti, Mauritania, Somalia, the Sudan and Yemen); the Maghreb countries (Algeria, Libya, Morocco and Tunisia); and the Mashreq countries (Egypt, Iraq, Jordan, Lebanon, Palestine and the Syrian Arab Republic). This breakdown has its limitations, but it enables the consideration of geographical proximity and development level criteria at the same time. It is also in line with the methodology adopted in previous Millennium Development Goals Reports.

Because international agencies use different country classifications, some parts of the analysis could not be presented using the Arab regional focus. For example, analysis from the World Bank and some United Nations agencies is based on the Middle East and North Africa regional classification, while analysis from the United Nations Environment Programme (UNEP) divides the Arab countries between the regions of Africa and Western Asia.

While acknowledging the limitations of non-nationally sourced statistics, data in this report were collected from a range of official databases, mainly from the United Nations system (see annex II). They cover the period from 1990 until 2015. A review of country experiences on monitoring and evaluation for the post-2015 period by the Economic and Social Commission for Western Asia (ESCWA) identified significant gaps in data for MDG national reporting.[4] Official country data was therefore not sourced directly from national statistics offices owing to problems concerning comparability, quality and the availability of time series in most of the 22 countries.

C. Framework of analysis and organization of the document

In the report, issues are analysed in clusters in a way that highlights links between them. The

Figure 1.1. Framework of analysis

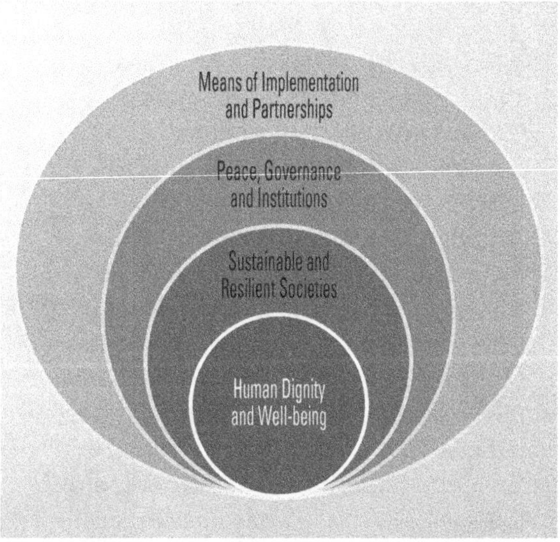

Source: Authors.

report starts with a snapshot of trends in the Arab region today using the themes of the 17 SDGs. The remainder of the report is organized in accordance with a framework developed in consultation with Governments, experts, civil society and other stakeholders. Five other frameworks considered for the report are presented in annex III.

The adopted framework (figure 1.1), with its four nested areas, recognizes:

- The need to place human dignity and well-being at the core of the analysis, so that all people in the Arab region might fulfil their potential and achieve their aspirations.
- The link between those core objectives and the natural resource base. Achieving well-being of populations will depend upon, and have a significant impact on, the environment and natural resources. For societies to be resilient and sustainable, economies will need to be transformed and decoupled from environmental decline, and ecosystems will need to be sustainably preserved.
- The importance of peace, governance and effective institutions as goals in themselves and as cross-cutting factors contributing to sustainable development.
- The role of the means of implementation, such as finance, technology, trade and data,

Figure 1.2. Correspondence of chapters and sections in the report with the SDGs

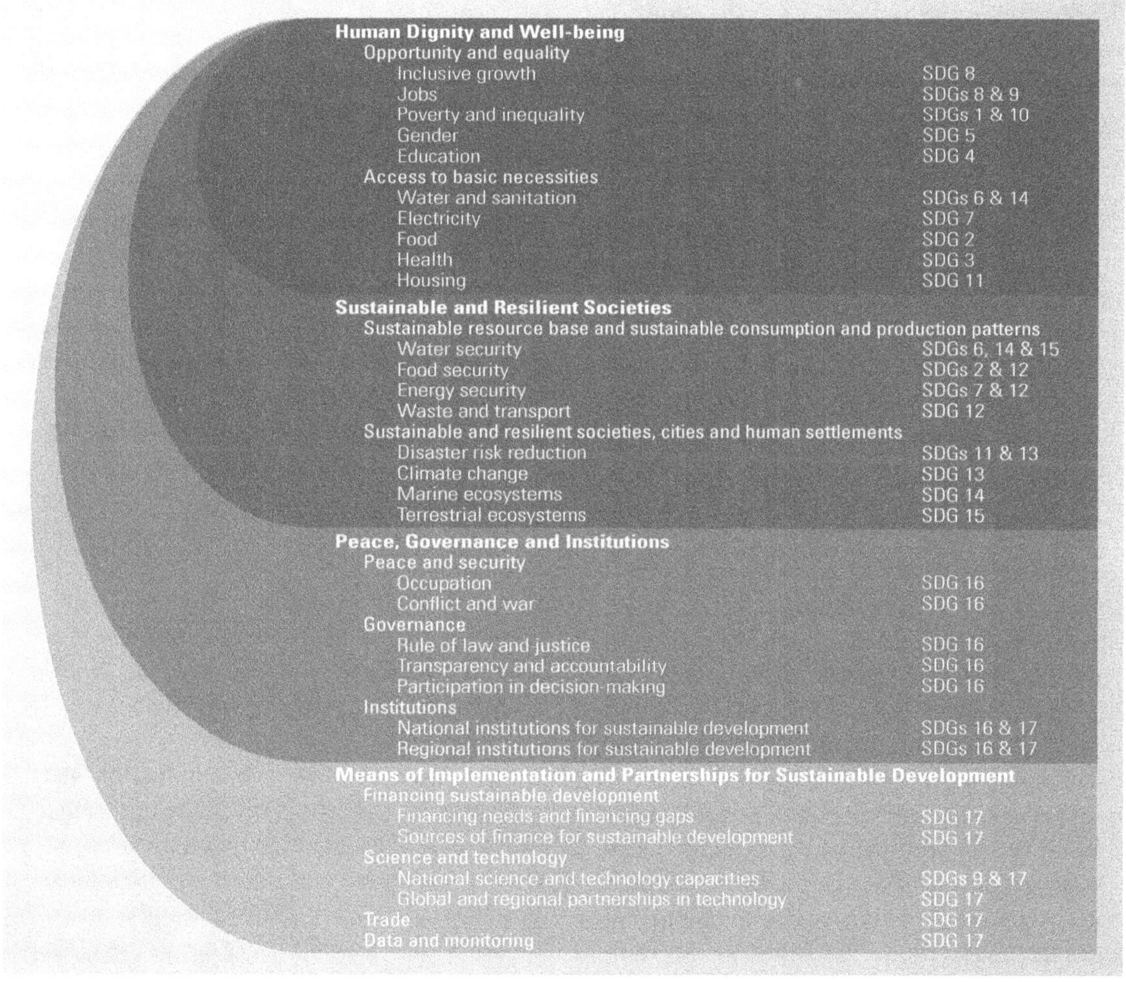

Source: Authors.

and the importance of partnerships, for addressing existing gaps.

Based on this framework, the report includes four core chapters (3 to 6) on human dignity and well-being; sustainable and resilient societies; peace, governance and institutions; and means of implementation and partnerships for sustainable development. Figure 1.2 shows the relationships between the framework, the report's core chapters and sections, and the 17 SDGs. A thorough regional reading of the SDGs and their corresponding targets took place ahead of their inclusion under one of the four nested areas. The framework reflects in part the outcome of negotiations on the global agenda in early 2015 and regional priorities. The principle challenges facing the region concern occupation, conflict and instability, and governance and institutional deficits. Those issues constitute the main elements of this report.

D. Summary of analysis

1. Human dignity and well-being

Although significant progress was made on some MDGs, it was uneven across the Arab region. Some goals have remained elusive and new challenges have emerged.

Growth has remained relatively high but there has been little change in economic structure over the past two decades. The rentier structure of the economy in most countries means that growth has little impact on human well-being. Productivity growth rates have been low and wages as a share of gross domestic product (GDP) have declined. Economic opportunities have expanded too slowly to fully employ the growing labour force. Unemployment remains the highest in the world, with moderate gains for women offset by commensurate losses for young people.

The region is well below the global average in terms of poverty incidence (based on the international poverty line), but inequality of opportunities and income has fuelled conflict in several countries, unleashing waves of refugees and internally displaced persons (IDPs) who have thus been plunged deeper into poverty.

Gender equality has increased in several important respects, including employment and political representation. Nevertheless, shortfalls remain significant relative to global benchmarks, especially considering the high levels of educational achievement in the Arab region. The failure to match educational achievement with analogous employment and gender outcomes is due in large part to the incapacity of the region's economies to generate employment, in addition to problems regarding the quality of education and its relevance to the labour market.

Across the Arab region, up to 195 million people gained access to improved sources of water and sanitation between 1990 and 2015. However, growth in the provision of water has not kept pace with population growth in the LDCs, where the share of the population with access to water has fallen. Access to electricity is almost universal in three of the four subregions. In the LDCs, however, the degree of access is less than half the regional average and has seen little improvement since 2000. There has been significant progress in eliminating slums, except in the LDCs. The existing housing shortfall (estimated at over 3.5 million units) is being aggravated in several countries by war, occupation and conflict.

Hunger and malnutrition in Arab countries is not a problem of food availability, but rather affordability. Despite significant progress in some subregions, undernourishment has remained constant in the Arab region and the nutritional status of children in the LDCs has deteriorated. Access to health care has generally improved, reflected in favourable trends in child and maternal mortality rates. As communicable diseases become less of a problem, non-communicable illnesses such as heart disease, diabetes and mental disorders are becoming more of an issue. Violence and conflict are creating additional health concerns for the region.

2. Sustainable and resilient societies

The population of the Arab region has grown significantly in the past decades and exceeded 377 million in 2014. The urban population of Arab countries accounted for 57 per cent of the total, slightly above the global average of 53 per cent.[5] The 215 million people living in Arab cities and urban areas require large public investments in infrastructure to provide essential services such as housing, roads, energy, water, waste and wastewater management, and other utilities.

Nowhere more than in the Arab region, where the scarcity of water is a defining characteristic, is the link between water, food and energy so keenly felt. Per capita water resources available in the Arab region represent 10 per cent of the global average.[6] The scarcity and degradation of water and arable land, the arid climate and the erosion of genetic resources all place limits on food production. The agricultural sector is by far the largest consumer of water in the region - a common occurrence in arid regions - while water productivity and irrigation efficiencies are well below global averages.

Water scarcity has led some Arab countries to invest heavily in desalination, and the region now accounts for more than half the world's desalination capacity. This has implications for energy security and carbon emissions (unless renewable energy desalination is considered)[7] and contributes to the deterioration of marine ecosystems. Energy is also needed to lift, move, process, and treat water at every phase, and water is used in power generation and oil exploitation.

The consumption of resources such as water and energy in the region is increasing at rates that cannot be sustained, and new approaches are urgently needed. A water-food-energy nexus approach could "ensure coherence across policies, initiatives and projects at the national and regional levels, taking into consideration differing natural resource endowments across countries of the region, with a view to minimizing negative trade-offs across sectors".[8]

Over the past several decades, the region has seen an increase in droughts, storms and floods. Droughts affect the largest number of people and earthquakes, followed closely by floods and storms, which cause the worst damage to infrastructure. Expanding cities have become concentrated hubs for economic development and are increasingly vulnerable to the risk of natural disasters.

Climate change is exacerbating the intensity and frequency of extreme weather events and the region is more likely than others to be affected by rising temperatures. It is predicted that it will experience growing variability in precipitation, which may have detrimental consequences, especially for agriculture-based communities. The impact of climate change on environmental migration and shared water resources has been found to fuel conflict.[9]

Although Arab countries are considered under annex II of the United Nations Framework Convention on Climate Change and are not formally bound to greenhouse gas emission reductions, some are making voluntary efforts to reduce emissions. Several Arab countries have prepared statements of their Intended Nationally Determined Contributions. However, the increase in per capita greenhouse gas emissions and the regional economy's carbon intensity is worrying.

Marine and terrestrial ecosystems are facing significant pressures due to misuse and biodiversity degradation. Vegetation cover is shrinking and the sharp rise in average annual fish-catch rates for Arab countries over the past two decades has put a strain on fish stocks. On the positive side, Arab countries have acted to preserve their biodiversity, including through the expansion of protected areas.

3. Peace, governance and institutions

The links between peace, governance and effective institutions for development are evident. By 2015, the Arab region had overtaken South Asia as the least peaceful part of the world. The Israeli occupation of Palestine continues and conflicts have worsened in Iraq, Libya, the Syrian Arab Republic and Yemen. Conflict and criminality have led to hundreds of thousands of fatalities and massive displacement. In 2015, about 7.6 million Syrians were IDPs and 4.1 million were living as refugees, mostly in neighbouring countries.[10] More than 2 million Somalis are displaced within or outside their country.[11] These numbers are in addition to the 5.2 million Palestinian refugees.[12]

A major cause of the Arab uprisings was the desire of citizens for a greater say in political decision-making and more accountability. In certain cases, their demands led to change. Improvements came in some cases, such as with free and fair elections, but in some respects matters have deteriorated, such as with freedom of expression. Variations between countries are considerable. The recent record of fairness and justice has been similarly mixed: although improvements have been made in the majority of Arab countries with regard to the separation of powers, things have worsened in terms of misuse of public funds and cronyism. Legal identity continues to be a concern. Many Palestinians, the Bidun and children whose fathers are not citizens of the relevant country are often considered stateless. The increase in the number of refugees across the region has highlighted the need for a unified regulatory framework for refugee status and asylum in Arab countries.

Several countries in the region are showing the way with examples of good practice that may serve as models for others. Indeed, some countries have demonstrated growing capacity to implement strategies with a broad ownership, harmonize short-term actions with long-term priorities, coordinate across sectoral ministries, and make full use of evidence. At the regional level, institutional mechanisms are being established and strengthened in order to support national stakeholders in this work.

4. Means of implementation and partnerships for sustainable development

Estimating the finance needs in the Arab region for achieving sustainable development is difficult. Based on the methodology used in this report, and acknowledging its limitations, it would appear that the LDCs have, contrary to expectations, lower financing needs than middle-income countries. The financing gap can be narrowed through tax and subsidy reforms and by rationalizing military expenditure. International flows are significant sources of finance for the region.

Official development assistance (ODA) received by the Arab countries, including from Arab development funds, peaked in 2005, decreased thereafter, and picked up again in 2012. Foreign direct investment peaked in 2008 at $97 billion and has declined since, reflecting the need to restore stability, reduce risks and improve the investment climate. Similarly, intraregional investments have been decreasing since the 2008 peak of $35 billion. Remittances constitute a sizeable source of finance in some countries (Egypt, Lebanon and Morocco). Public-private partnerships are concentrated in energy and transportation projects and require adequate legal and institutional frameworks to ensure their sustainability. Only a few Arab countries have tapped into green finance opportunities.

The Arab countries have strived to develop their national systems of science, technology and innovation over the past decades. Most have increased access to information and communications technology at rates exceeding the global average. However, the Arab region remains mostly a user of technology, with knowledge generation remaining very low relative to the rest of the world and even to developing countries. The little knowledge generated is not benefiting the productive sectors due to weak and undiversified economies.

The region's share of the world's non-oil exports remains modest and it is less economically integrated than other world regional groupings. Bilateral and other trade agreements with non-Arab countries and groups have been signed much faster than intraregional agreements, which remain stalled mainly for political reasons.

Statistical capacity in the Arab region remains limited. Many Arab countries were unable to report fully on the 45 MDG indictors using their national official data. The situation will be exacerbated with the anticipated 100+ global indicators to be used for monitoring the SDGs. The data gap has prevented Governments from fully benefiting from evidence in replacing failed policies. The success of statistical capacity development efforts will depend on the willingness of Governments to improve transparency and accountability.

2. Snapshot of Trends and Status in the Arab Region

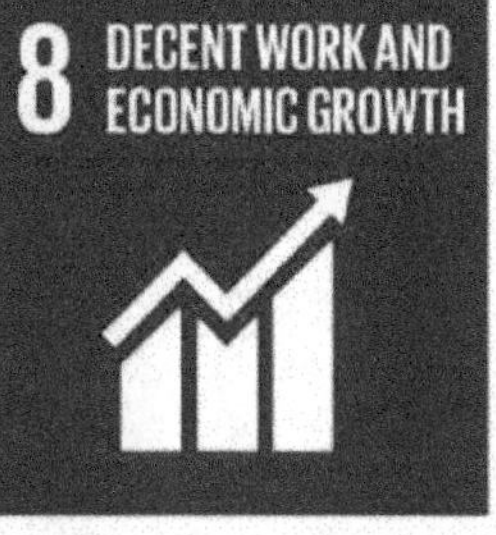

"Never again should it be possible to say "we didn't know". No one should be invisible. This is the world we want – a world that counts."

The United Nations Secretary-General's Independent Expert Advisory Group on a Data Revolution for Sustainable Development, 2014

2. Snapshot of Trends and Status in the Arab Region

This chapter provides information covering a range of indicators structured along the themes of the 17 SDGs (table 2.2). Many crucial issues could not, however, be included due to lack of data. The remainder of the report elaborates on these and many other issues. Weather symbols are used to characterize sustainable development trends over the past two decades (table 2.1). Such symbols are often used to benchmark progress against a specified quantitative target. Given the absence of such targets in the Arab region in most of the thematic issues reviewed, the symbols were usedhere to highlight whether regional or subregional trends could be considered favourable or unfavourable. The regional average value for each indicator is benchmarked against the MDG target or world average, where these are available or applicable, using traffic lights (RED or GREEN) to indicate how the Arab region compares against world averages and MDG targets. In future reports, evaluations for the SDGs should focus on progress with regard to quantitative targets.

The use of such symbols in the evaluation of trends and progress is limited by the absence

Table 2.1. Use of weather symbols and traffic lights

Symbol	Explanation
	Trend is clearly favourable in relation to SDGs (>30% positive)
	Moderately favourable changes in trend in relation to SDGs (10%-30% positive)
	Moderately unfavourable changes in trend in relation to SDGs (10%-30% negative)
	Trend is clearly unfavourable in relation to SDGs (>30% negative)
	No clear trend or little change (-10% to +10%)
!	Insufficient data available for a trend analysis
	Indicates that the Arab region met the MDG target. If no MDG target exists, the symbol indicates that the region's average is equal to or better than the world average for the indicator
	Indicates that the Arab region did not meet the MDG target. If no MDG target exists, the symbol indicates that the region's average is worse than the world average for the indicator

of quantitative targets in most instances. The evaluation represents the views of the authors and is primarily aimed at promoting discussion on sustainable development between stakeholders.

Data were collected from official databases of the United Nations and other international and regional organizations. Trends were reviewed for the Arab region as a whole and the four subregions. Due to considerable data gaps, the methodology relied on only two data points (one for the early 1990s and another for the late 2000s, unless otherwise specified), which provided a basic inter-decadal trend analysis for each indicator. The evaluation of each indicator was based, as far as possible, on the evolution of the indicator between 1990 and the latest year of data available for the Arab region. The methodology and data sources are detailed in annex II. Each indicator was graphically represented to show its trend for the Arab region and each of the four subregions, and trends were then interpreted using the weather symbols and rules provided in table 2.1.

For each indicator in table 2.2, traffic symbols show the current regional status compared to the world, whereas weather symbols reflect past trends in the region and subregions. However, these need not be correlated. For example, a red traffic light with a sunny weather symbol implies significant progress, but the situation is still below the world average or the MDG target has not been met, and further improvement is needed. Furthermore, while individual indicators are provided under each SDG, it is often necessary to look at a cluster of indicators in order to get the full picture of the situation and prospects for achieving the SDG under consideration.

Table 2.2. Snapshot of progress and trends for selected sustainable development indicators

Sustainable Development Goals	Subthemes	Indicator	Status of Arab region compared to world	Trend in Arab region	Trend in subregions				Comments
					LDCs	Mashreq	Maghreb	GCC	
Relevant to all goals	Demographics	Population growth rate (total)	No world average for this indicator	-19.2%	-36.4%	-21.5%	-24.4%	+25.2%	The rate of population growth in the Arab region during the period 2010-2015 showed a moderate decrease of 19.2 per cent compared to the period 1990-1995. The subregions showed similar decreases, except the GCC countries.
Goal 1: End poverty in all its forms everywhere	Income poverty	Percentage of population below $1.25 (PPP) per day[a]							The Arab region did not achieve the MDG target of halving the percentage of population below $1.25, although the value for the region (7.4 per cent) is better than world average (14.5 per cent). The regional trend is clearly unfavourable, with a 34.5 per cent increase. The trend was also unfavourable for all subregions except the Maghreb, which showed a moderately favourable trend with a 12 per cent decrease. GCC values were zero in both years.
	Income poverty	Percentage of population living below national poverty line	No world average for this indicator						The Arab regional trend for this indicator shows insignificant change. At the subregional level, the trend was moderately unfavourable for the Mashreq, while the Maghreb showed a clearly favourable decrease of 42.9 per cent. GCC values were zero in both years.
Goal 2: End hunger, achieve food security and improved nutrition, and promote sustainable agriculture	Nutritional status	Percentage of underweight children under 5 years old							The Arab region did not achieve the MDG target of halving the percentage of underweight children under 5 years old, although the value for the region (12.7 per cent) is better than the world average (14.3 per cent). The trend is moderately favourable for the region as a whole (-11.7 per cent) and the Mashreq (-27.5 per cent). It is clearly favourable for the Maghreb (-58.7 per cent) and the GCC (-62.1 per cent), both of which reached the MDG target. The LDCs do not show any trend across time.

Sustainable Development Goals	Subthemes	Indicator	Status of Arab region compared to world	Trend in Arab region	Trend in subregions				Comments
					LDCs	Mashreq	Maghreb	GCC	
Goal 2: End hunger, achieve food security and improved nutrition, and promote sustainable agriculture	Hunger	Percentage of under-nourished population							The percentage of undernourished people in the Arab region (9 per cent) is better than the world average (13 per cent). The regional trend is increasing at an insignificant (8.3 per cent) rate. Large variations were evident throughout the subregions: the Mashreq exhibited an alarmingly unfavourable trend with a 73.9 per cent increase, whereas the Maghreb showed a moderately favourable decrease of 24 per cent, and the GCC a clearly favourable trend with a decrease of 43.8 per cent. Data were insufficient to establish a trend in the LDCs.
	Food sources	Arable and permanent crop land area (cumulative total)							Arable and permanent crop land area for the Arab region (4.1 per cent) is well below the world average (10.9 per cent). Insignificant changes were recorded for the region and subregions. Arable and permanent crop area decreased from 65.2 million to 64.5 million hectares, mainly due to the difference between pre and post-secession Sudan. This also explains the moderate 11 per cent decrease in arable and permanent crop land area recorded in the LDCs.
	Food sources	Food production (average value of annual food production per capita)							The average value of annual food production per capita for the Arab region ($191.40) is well below the world average ($311). The region exhibited a moderately positive trend with an increase of 21 per cent. However, discrepancies were evident. The LDCs and Mashreq displayed moderately positive trends with increases of 20.7 per cent and 22.5 per cent respectively, and the Maghreb a more clearly favourable trend of +43 per cent. The GCC countries showed a moderate decrease of 18.5 per cent.

Sustainable Development Goals	Subthemes	Indicator	Status of Arab region compared to world	Trend in Arab region	Trend in subregions				Comments
					LDCs	Mashreq	Maghreb	GCC	
Goal 2: **End hunger, achieve food security and improved nutrition, and promote sustainable agriculture**	Food sources	Value of food imports (percentage of merchandise exports)	No world average for this indicator						The Arab region and most subregions exhibited a clearly favourable trend of decreases of the values of food imports as a percentage of merchandise exports (-42.2 per cent for the Arab region, -65.9 per cent for the LDCs, -51 per cent for Mashreq, and -43 per cent for GCC countries). The Maghreb, however, lingers behind with a small decrease of 15.5 per cent.
	Food sources	Cereal imports dependency ratio							Dependency on cereal imports (56.2 per cent) was above the world average of 50.7 per cent. The regional average increased significantly (by 33.2 per cent). The trend was upwards across the subregions: the GCC countries showed the highest increase, with 130.3 per cent, whereas the LDCs, Maghreb and Mashreq exhibited smaller increases of 34.4 per cent, 19.8 per cent and 15.8 per cent respectively.
Goal 3: **Ensure healthy lives and promote well-being for all at all ages**	Mortality	Mortality rate under 5 years old							The Arab region did not achieve the MDG target of reducing by two thirds the under-5 mortality rate, despite the progress achieved (54.3 per cent reduction). The value for the Arab region was 35.6 deaths per 1,000 live births, better than the world average of 42.5 deaths. All the subregions displayed positive trends, with the greatest progress made in GCC countries (-68.2 per cent), followed by the Mashreq (-64.7 per cent), the Maghreb (-59.6 per cent), and the LDCs (-46.1 per cent).

Sustainable Development Goals	Subthemes	Indicator	Status of Arab region compared to world	Trend in Arab region	Trend in subregions				Comments
					LDCs	Mashreq	Maghreb	GCC	
Goal 3: Ensure healthy lives and promote well-being for all at all ages	Health-care delivery	Contraceptive prevalence rate							The Arab region did not achieve the MDG target of universal access to contraception. The trend for the Arab region is moderately favourable with an increase of 22.2 per cent, however the contraceptive prevalence rate as a value (46.7 per cent) remained far below the world average (63 per cent). LDCs show the most favourable trend, with an increase of 102 per cent in use of contraceptives, followed by the Maghreb and Mashrek, with 25.9 per cent and 25.8 per cent increases respectively. The GCC countries witnessed a 20.6 per cent decrease.
	Health-care delivery	Immunization against infectious childhood diseases (one-year-old children immunized against measles)							Immunization against infectious childhood diseases in the region was at 85.8 per cent, above the world average of 84.5 per cent. The regional trend was moderately favourable, with a 10.4 per cent increase. The Maghreb and GCC countries showed moderately favourable trends, with 16 per cent and 12.4 per cent increases respectively. The LDCs showed the biggest increase in immunization, with a 34.8 per cent increase, whereas the Mashreq did not exhibit any trend.
	Nutritional status	Obesity among children							Obesity among children in the Arab region (11.3 per cent) is much worse than the world average (6.1 per cent). The Arab region and the Maghreb did not exhibit a clear trend, whereas a clearly unfavourable trend was evident in Mashreq (34.4 per cent increase) and, more flagrantly, in the GCC countries (112.9 per cent increase). However, the LDCs showed a clearly favourable trend (39.8 per cent decrease) across the same period.

Sustainable Development Goals	Subthemes	Indicator	Status of Arab region compared to world	Trend in Arab region	Trend in subregions				Comments
					LDCs	Mashreq	Maghreb	GCC	
Goal 4: Ensure inclusive and equitable quality education and promote life-long learning opportunities for all	Education level	Net enrolment rate in primary education							The Arab region did not achieve the MDG target of universal enrolment in primary education, although the regional value (91.4 per cent) is better than the world average (89 per cent). The Arab region exhibited a favourable trend (15 per cent increase), as did the LDCs (53.1 per cent increase), Maghreb (31.2 per cent increase) and GCC countries (25.4 per cent increase). The Mashreq showed no significant change.
	Education level	Gross intake into last year of primary education							The Arab region did not achieve the MDG target of 100 per cent gross intake into the final year of primary education, although the regional value (94.5 per cent) is higher than the world average (92.3 per cent). The Arab region showed a moderately positive trend with a 14.7 per cent increase, particularly in the Maghreb (42.8 per cent). For the Mashreq, no significant trend was visible, and data were not available to establish a trend in the LDCs or GCC countries.
	Literacy	Adult literacy rate							The Arab region did not achieve the MDG target of universal literacy, despite the clearly positive trend (41.4 per cent increase). The regional value of 78.1 per cent literate adults is still below the world average (85.2 per cent). The trend was clearly favourable across subregions (31.3 per cent for GCC countries, 34.5 per cent for the Mashreq, and 54 per cent for the Maghreb), except for the LDCs, where data were insufficient to establish a trend.
	Quality of education	Government expenditure on education (percentage of GDP)	No world average for this indicator						Arab Governments spent 17.6 per cent less on education, with the decreasing trend being most visible in the LDCs (31 per cent decrease), followed by the GCC countries (27.2 per cent decrease). No clear trend was visible for the Mashreq and data were insufficient to establish a trend for the Maghreb.

Sustainable Development Goals	Subthemes	Indicator	Status of Arab region compared to world	Trend in Arab region	Trend in subregions				Comments
					LDCs	Mashreq	Maghreb	GCC	
Goal 4: Ensure inclusive and equitable quality education and promote life-long learning opportunities for all	Quality of education	Pupil-teacher ratio, primary							The pupil-teacher ratio for the Arab region (20.5) is better than the world average (24.2), and the regional trend is generally improving (ratio decreasing by 23 per cent). All the subregions exhibited moderately favourable trends (LDCs -21.4 per cent, Mashreq -21.1 per cent and Maghreb -19.2 per cent), except for the GCC subregion, where the improvement was substantial (-32.6 per cent).
Goal 5: Achieve gender equality and empower all women and girls	Literacy	Adult literacy rate (female)							Female adult literacy in the Arab region (70.0 per cent) is lower than the world average (81.3 per cent). The regional value saw a clearly favourable increase of 67.5 per cent, as did the Mashreq (52.8 per cent), Maghreb (83.2 per cent), and GCC countries (52.8 per cent). Data for the LDCs were insufficient to establish a trend.
	Literacy	Adult literacy rate (male)							Male adult literacy in the Arab region (85.6 per cent) is lower than the world average (89.1 per cent). The regional trend, a 25.9 per cent increase, is moderately favourable. The Maghreb performed best with a 36.7 per cent increase, followed by the Mashreq (23.3 per cent) and GCC countries (20.5 per cent). Data were insufficient to establish a trend for the LDCs.
	Employment	Female employment to population ratio (above 15 years old)							Female employment to population ratio in the Arab region (18.6 per cent) is far below the world average (47 per cent). However, the regional trend is moderately favourable with a 20.6 per cent increase. The LDCs and the Maghreb also exhibited moderately favourable trends (19.4 per cent and 26.5 per cent increases respectively). The GCC countries made the largest improvement, with a 55.3 per cent increase. Change in the Mashreq was insignificant.

Sustainable Development Goals	Subthemes	Indicator	Status of Arab region compared to world	Trend in Arab region	Trend in subregions				Comments
					LDCs	Mashreq	Maghreb	GCC	
Goal 5: Achieve gender equality and empower all women and girls	Employment	Male employment to population ratio (above 15 years old)							The male employment to population ratio for the Arab region (67.9 per cent) is slightly below the world average (72.3 per cent). No clear trend was evident for the region or subregions.
	Political participation	Seats held by women in national parliaments (percentage)							The Arab region did not achieve the MDG target of eliminating gender disparities in the political sphere. The value for the Arab region (13.2 per cent) is lower than the world average (22.2 per cent). However, the proportion of seats held by women in national parliaments shows a clearly favourable trend for the entire region (+429 per cent) as well as for the four subregions (LDCs, +439.4 per cent; Mashreq, +127.6 per cent; Maghreb, +741.2 per cent; and GCC countries, +1,883.3 per cent).
Goal 6: Ensure availability and sustainable management of water and sanitation for all	Water	Access to an improved water source (percentage of population)							The Arab region met the MDG target of halving the population without access to an improved water source. No clear trend could be established across the region or the subregions. Only the LDCs showed a slight decline.
	Sanitation	Access to improved sanitation (percentage of population)							The Arab region met the MDG target of halving the population without access to improved sanitation, achieving a rate of 79.3 per cent. The regional trend was moderately favourable (+19.4 per cent), as it was for the Mashreq (+21.9 per cent) and Maghreb (+21.6 per cent). The progress was more evident in the LDCs, with a 35.7 per cent increase. The GCC countries, having had the highest rate in the 1990s, showed no significant change.

Sustainable Development Goals	Subthemes	Indicator	Status of Arab region compared to world	Trend in Arab region	Trend in subregions				Comments
					LDCs	Mashreq	Maghreb	GCC	
Goal 6: Ensure availability and sustainable management of water and sanitation for all	Availability of water	Annual withdrawals of ground and surface water as a percentage of available water	No world average for this indicator						Annual withdrawals for the Arab region are alarming, at over 1,200 per cent of available water, and have been high since the 1990s. The regional trend is moderately unfavourable at +12.6 per cent. The trend was unfavourable for the GCC countries, with a 74.6 per cent increase. The Mashreq and Maghreb showed no significant change, and the LDCs were not included in the analysis for lack of data.
	Water demand	Annual utilization or withdrawals of water – demand, all types	No world average for this indicator						The trend for the Arab region is moderately unfavourable, with a 29.6 per cent increase in annual withdrawals of water. The trend was unfavourable for the Mashreq (+29.5 per cent) and the Maghreb (+18.5 per cent), and clearly unfavourable for the GCC countries (+43.4 per cent). The LDCs were not included in the trend analysis for lack of data.
	Access	Urban access to an improved water source (percentage of population)							The Arab region met the MDG target of halving the population without access to an improved water source in urban areas. However, the region and subregions show no significant trend across time for this indicator.
	Access	Rural access to an improved water source (percentage of population)							The Arab region met the MDG target of halving the population without access to an improved water source in rural areas. The Arab region and the GCC subregion did not exhibit any significant trend. The LDCs exhibited a moderately unfavourable trend with a decrease of 15.8 per cent. The Mashreq and Maghreb showed moderately favourable trends, with increases of 12.2 per cent and 10.5 per cent respectively.

Sustainable Development Goals	Subthemes	Indicator	Status of Arab region compared to world	Trend in Arab region	Trend in subregions				Comments
					LDCs	Mashreq	Maghreb	GCC	
Goal 7: Ensure access to affordable, reliable, sustainable, and modern energy for all	Energy use	Share of consumption of renewable energy resources (excluding hydro-electric)							The share of consumption of renewable energy resources in the Arab region (0.2 per cent) is much worse than the world average (4.7 per cent). The region witnessed a favourable trend, as did the Mashreq and Maghreb. Values were negligible in all subregions in the 1990s, thus explaining the positive trend.
	Energy use	Energy consumption per capita							Energy consumption per capita in the Arab region (1,843 kg of oil equivalent) is slightly better than the world average (1,897.9 kg). The regional trend is clearly unfavourable, with a 70.3 per cent increase. A similar trend was apparent in all subregions save the LDCs, which showed little change.
	Access to energy	Access to electricity (percentage of population)							Access to electricity in the Arab region (86.2 per cent) is slightly better than the world average (84.6 per cent). Furthermore, a moderately favourable trend can be seen in the region, with the largest increase registered in the LDCs (+38.8 per cent).
Goal 8: Promote sustained, inclusive and sustainable economic growth, full and productive employment and decent work for all	Macro-economic performance	GDP per capita							There is a large gap between the GDP per capita for the Arab region ($4,795) and the world average ($8,055). However, the region witnessed a clearly favourable trend (+51.5 per cent), with the GCC countries registering a modest increase (24.1 per cent), compared to increases in the Mashreq, LDCs and Maghreb of 65.3 per cent, 63.7 per cent and 37.2 per cent respectively.
	Macro-economic performance	Gross capital formation (percentage of GDP)							Gross capital formation as a percentage of GDP for the Arab region (26.6 per cent) is better than the world average (22.2 per cent). A moderately favourable trend (+25.6 per cent) was observed in the region. A moderately unfavourable fall took place in the Mashreq only (-29.9 per cent). In the other subregions, significantly favourable increases occurred: LDCs (+55.9 per cent); the Maghreb (+52.5 per cent) and GCC countries (+39.7 per cent).

Sustainable Development Goals	Subthemes	Indicator	Status of Arab region compared to world	Trend in Arab region	Trend in subregions				Comments
					LDCs	Mashreq	Maghreb	GCC	
Goal 8: Promote sustained, inclusive and sustainable economic growth, full and productive employment and decent work for all	Employment	Employment to population ratio (total above 15 years old)							The employment to population ratio for the Arab region (44.6 per cent) is below the world average (59.6 per cent). No clear trend (+4.5 per cent) is seen in the region or the subregions, except in the GCC countries, which experienced an increase of +11.9 per cent.
	Employment	Youth employment to population ratio (15-24 years)							The youth employment to population ratio for the Arab region (23.7 per cent) is much worse than the world average (41.2 per cent). The regional trend is moderately unfavourable (-11 per cent). All subregions witnessed a similar decrease: LDCs (-8.1 per cent); the Mashreq (-13.7 per cent), the Maghreb (-15.2 per cent) and GCC countries (-1.8 per cent).
	Demo-graphics - population	Dependency ratio (young and old)							The dependency ratio for the Arab region (60.2 per cent) is worse than the world average (53.8 per cent). The regional average shows a clearly favourable trend (-30.8 per cent), as do the GCC countries (-51.6 per cent) and the Maghreb (-37.4 per cent). The Mashreq (-25.3 per cent) and LDCs (-20.8 per cent) show moderately favourable trends.
Goal 9: Build resilient infrastruc-ture, promote inclusive and sustain-able indus-trialization and foster innovation	Industriali-zation	Manufac-turing value added (per-centage of GDP)							The value added by manufacturing in the Arab region (12.5 per cent of GDP) is below the world average (15.8 per cent). The regional trend is moderately favourable (+12 per cent). The LDCs and the GCC countries showed favourable trends (+27.7 per cent and +33.7 per cent respectively). The Maghreb exhibited a moderately unfavourable trend (-15.7 per cent). The Mashreq did not show a clear trend.
	ICT	Internet users (percentage of population)							The number of Internet users in the Arab region (34.4 per cent) is below the world average (40.7 per cent), despite the substantial increases in the region and all subregions.

Sustainable Development Goals	Subthemes	Indicator	Status of Arab region compared to world	Trend in Arab region	Trend in subregions				Comments
					LDCs	Mashreq	Maghreb	GCC	
Goal 9: Build resilient infrastructure, promote inclusive and sustainable industrialization and foster innovation	ICT	Telephone landline subscribers (percentage of population)							The number of telephone landline subscribers in the Arab region (8.1 per cent) is below the world average (15.2 per cent), despite the significant increase in the Arab region and each of the subregions.
	ICT	Mobile cellular telephone subscribers (percentage of population							The number of mobile cellular phone subscribers in the Arab region (109 per cent) is above the world average (96.3 per cent). The average has increased significantly in the region and all subregions, reflecting a clearly favourable trend.
Goal 10: Reduce inequality within and among countries	Inequality within countries is addressed partly under gender and rural/urban differences in access to water. Inequality between Arab countries is reflected in the subregional analysis, as well as comparison to world averages, as provided throughout this snapshot.								
Goal 11: Make cities and human settlements inclusive, safe, resilient and sustainable	Disaster preparedness and response	Deaths due to disasters (cumulative total)	No world average for this indicator						Deaths due to disasters in the Arab region witnessed a clearly unfavourable increase of 275.4 per cent in the period 2006 to 2015, compared with the period 1990-1999. This is due particularly to the increase in the number of deaths in the LDCs (+518.8 per cent). In contrast, the Mashreq and Maghreb witnessed significant decreases of 89.9 per cent and 55.1 per cent respectively.
	Demographics -population	Population growth rate – rural	No world average for this indicator	-30.4%	-38.4%	-29.7%	-87.0%	+9.6%	Rural population growth for the Arab region stood at +0.2 per cent, decreasing significantly by 30.4 per cent. The largest decrease, of 87 per cent, was registered in the Maghreb, whereas the GCC countries exhibited a relatively small increase of 9.6 per cent. The trend for this indicator could not be interpreted as favourable or unfavourable.

Sustainable Development Goals	Subthemes	Indicator	Status of Arab region compared to world	Trend in Arab region	Trend in subregions				Comments
					LDCs	Mashreq	Maghreb	GCC	
Goal 11: Make cities and human settlements inclusive, safe, resilient and sustainable	Demographics - population	Percentage of urban population from total	No world average for this indicator	+14.3%	+29.9%	+6.0	+25.3%	+8.2%	Urban population as a percentage of the total in the Arab region stood at 57 per cent, increasing by 14.3 per cent. It also increased in all four subregions to varying degrees, with the Maghreb and LDCs showing higher urban population growth. The trend for this indicator could not be interpreted as favourable or unfavourable.
Goal 12: Ensure sustainable consumption and production patterns	Transportation	Passenger cars (per 1,000 people)							The number of passenger cars in the Arab region over the period 2006-2011 (70.2 per 1,000 people) fell below the world average (123.1 per 1,000 people). The regional average changed little compared to the 2000-2005 period (-8.9 per cent). In the Mashreq and Maghreb there were significant increases (+47.7 per cent and +34.6 per cent respectively), while a sharp decrease (-49.1 per cent) occurred in the GCC countries. Data for the LDCs are unavailable.
Goal 13: Take urgent action to combat climate change and its impact	Climate change - mitigation	Emissions of greenhouse gases (kg per $1 GDP, PPP)							Greenhouse gas emissions per GDP in the Arab region (0.33kg per $1 GDP) are slightly lower than the world average (0.36kg per $1 GDP). Little change has occurred in the Arab region or subregions. Data for the LDCs are lacking.
	Climate change - mitigation	Emissions of greenhouse gases (metric tons of CO_2 per capita)							Greenhouse gas emissions per capita in the Arab region (5.3 metric tons) are higher than the world average (4.9 metric tons). The regional trend is clearly unfavourable, with an increase of 54.5 per cent. A similarly clearly unfavourable trend can be observed in all subregions except the Maghreb, where the trend is moderately unfavourable.

Sustainable Development Goals	Subthemes	Indicator	Status of Arab region compared to world	Trend in Arab region	Trend in subregions				Comments
					LDCs	Mashreq	Maghreb	GCC	
Goal 14: Conserve and sustainably use the oceans, seas and marine resources for sustainable development	Coastal degradation	Percentage of total population living in coastal areas							The share of the population living in coastal areas in the Arab region (9.2 per cent) is higher than the world average (6.6 per cent). This can be viewed as unfavourable from an environmental perspective. No clear trend can be observed for the region (-3.8 per cent).
	Marine resources	Average annual fish catch (metric tons)	No world average for this indicator	+182.5%	+128.4%	+312.8%	+92.2%	+84.3%	The average annual fish catch for the Arab region (0.5 million tons per year) represents a small share of the world total (93 million tons per year). The regional average increased significantly by 182.5 per cent. The favourability of this increase cannot be established as more in-depth research about fish stock sustainability is needed.
Goal 15: Protect, restore and promote sustainable use of terrestrial ecosystems, sustainably manage forests, combat desertification, and halt and reverse land degradation and halt biodiversity loss	Ecosystem	Protected area (terrestrial and marine as a percentage of total area)[b]							Protected areas in the Arab region (9.3 per cent of total area) represent less than the world average (14 per cent). However, the Arab region witnessed a clearly favourable trend with an increase of 189.2 per cent. There was a significant increase in all subregions, especially the Mashreq (+1,871.6 per cent) and the GCC countries (+320.6 per cent).
	Forest	Vegetation cover							Vegetation cover in the Arab region (2.84 per cent) is way below the world average of 30.8 per cent. A moderately unfavourable trend is seen for the Arab region (-23.0 per cent), which is mainly due to the decrease in vegetation cover in the LDCs (-33 per cent). The other three subregions show moderate increases.

Sustainable Development Goals	Subthemes	Indicator	Status of Arab region compared to world	Trend in Arab region	Trend in subregions				Comments
					LDCs	Mashreq	Maghreb	GCC	
Goal 16: Promote peaceful and inclusive societies for sustainable develop-ment, pro-vide access to justice for all and build effective, accountable and inclu-sive institu-tions at all levels	Refugees	Refugee population by country of origin (sum total)							Refugees from the Arab region stood at 11.3 million, representing 58.1 per cent of the world total number of refugees (19.5 million). This equates to 3 per cent of the Arab population being a refugee population compared to 0.27 per cent for the world. The number of refugees from Arab countries increased alarmingly (+151.4 per cent) between 1997 and 2014 and affects mostly the Mashreq (9.5 million).
	Refugees	Refugee population by country of asylum (sum total)							The 8.5 million refugees seeking asylum in the Arab region represent 2 per cent of the population. The number increased by 142.1 per cent between 1997 and 2014, a clearly unfavourable trend. The Mashreq (+169.4 per cent) and the LCDS (+41.9 per cent) saw increases throughout this period, while the Maghreb (-31 per cent) and the GCC countries (-78.7 per cent) witnessed decreases in the number of asylum seekers.
	Violence and stability	Measure of political stability and absence of violence/ terrorism[c]	No world average for this indicator						The Arab region exhibits a clearly unfavourable trend with regard to political stability and the absence of violence/terrorism (with the index value decreasing by 66.1 per cent). All the subregions witnessed a decline to varying degrees, the worse being in the Mashreq (-89.1 per cent). In the GCC countries, Maghreb and LDCs, the decrease was 12.9 per cent, 33.7 per cent and 46 per cent respectively.
Goal 17: Strengthen the means of implemen-tation and revitalize the Global Part-nership for Sustainable Development	External financing	Net ODA received (percentage of gross national income (GNI))						!	Net ODA received in the Arab region (4.2 per cent of GNI) is above the world average (0.2 per cent of GNI). ODA decreased substantially between 1990 and 2013 for the region (-59.8 per cent). This could be perceived as favourable in terms of less dependency. However, the trend is considered here to be clearly unfavourable, as much of the region, especially the LDCs, still need ODA. Data for the GCC countries are not available.

Sustainable Development Goals	Subthemes	Indicator	Status of Arab region compared to world	Trend in Arab region	Trend in subregions				Comments
					LDCs	Mashreq	Maghreb	GCC	
Goal 17: Strengthen the means of implementation and revitalize the Global Partnership for Sustainable Development	External financing	Foreign direct investment, net inflows (percentage of GDP)							Net inflows of foreign direct investments to the Arab region (1.7 per cent of GDP) are below the world average (2.9 per cent). The average has risen significantly (+105.5 per cent) in the region and all the subregions. A clearly favourable trend can be observed in the LDCs (+372.9 per cent) and the Maghreb (+440.5 per cent).

Sources: Data have been sourced from a number of statistical databases as detailed in annex II of this report.

[a] The World Bank has updated the international poverty line to $1.90 as of October 2015 (see www.worldbank.org/en/topic/poverty/brief/global-poverty-line-faq). However, data for the Arab region are available only for the $1.25 mark.

[b] It was not possible to disaggregate marine from terrestrial protected areas.

[c] The index ranges between -2.5 (worst) to +2.5 (best).

3. Human Dignity and Well-being

Water collection point in Yemen.

"We are determined to end poverty and hunger, in all their forms and dimensions, and to ensure that all human beings can fulfil their potential in dignity and equality and in a healthy environment."

Preamble of the 2030 Agenda for Sustainable Development

3. Human Dignity and Well-being

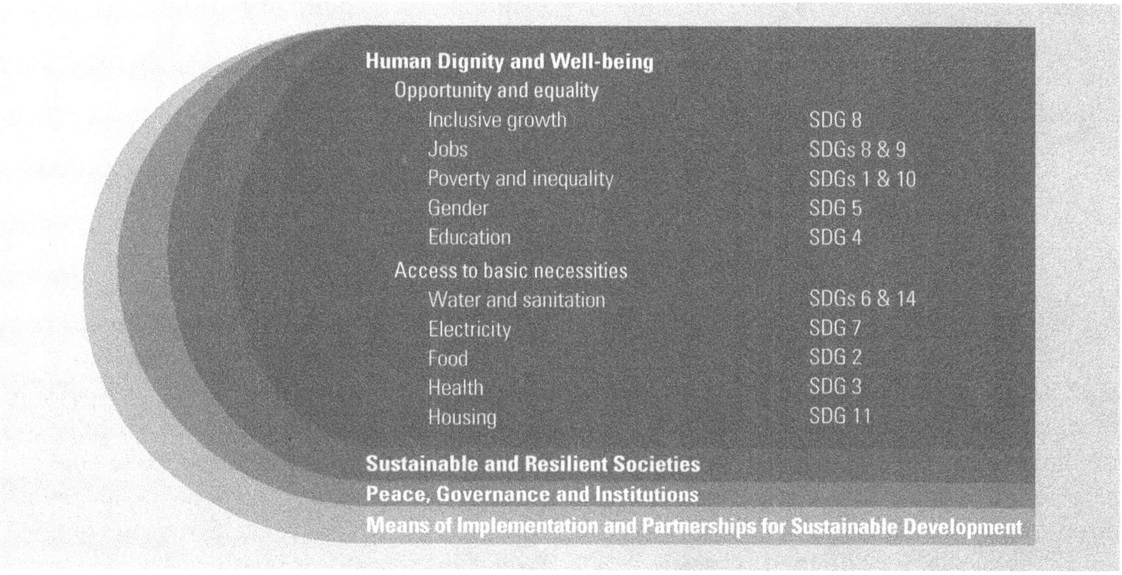

Achieving human dignity and well-being in accordance with human rights is central to sustainable development efforts. This means that economic growth should be inclusive and provide opportunities for all people to achieve their full potential through decent work, the eradication of poverty, quality education, and the reduction of income and gender inequality. In addition to opportunity and equality, human dignity and well-being also require access to the basic necessities of life, including water and sanitation, energy, food, health and housing.

Relatively high economic growth has had little positive impact on human well-being in the region. Opportunities have increased too slowly to fully employ the growing labour force, and unemployment rates are the highest in the world, especially for young people. Shortcomings in terms of the quality of education and its relevance to the needs of the labour market have exacerbated the situation. Gender gaps remain wide relative to global benchmarks. Although poverty in the region based on the international poverty line is well below the global average, inequality of opportunities and income has remained high. There is a high degree of poverty among refugees and IDPs.

Across the region, a large chunk of the population gained access to an improved water source and improved sanitation facilities between 1990 and 2015. Three of the four subregions boast almost universal access to electricity. There are, however, significant shortfalls in the LDCs in terms of access to these services. Progress on eliminating slums has been significant, again with the exception of the LDCs. Undernourishment remains a constant in the Arab region and nutritional status of children has deteriorated in the LDCs. Access to health care has improved across the region, reflected in favourable trends in child and maternal mortality rates. As communicable diseases are increasingly brought under control, non-communicable diseases are taking their place as a source of concern. Warfare and conflict are creating additional health problems in the region.

This chapter is largely based on issues briefs and expert papers prepared for the report on gender, social development, economic growth, poverty, employment, inequality, industrialization, energy, water and food.[1]

A. Opportunity and equality

1. Inclusive growth

GDP in the region has grown strongly over the past decades, however, it has declined more recently due to conflicts (figure 3.1). Although GDP growth has been relatively strong, GDP growth per capita has been considerably weaker due to increases in population (figure 3.2), highlighting that the Arab region has not been as successful as some other regions in translating growth into greater well-being for its population.

The regional average of $4,795 per capita in 2014 was well below the global average of $8,055.2 However, there is significant variation across the region, with the oil-exporting GCC countries registering close to three times the global average, while the LDCs register just 11 per cent of the global average (figure 3.3).

(a) The demographic window of opportunity

The population of the Arab region grew by 70 per cent between 1990 and 2014, from 221 million to 377 million. Although growth continues, rates have slowed since the late 1990s (figure 3.4), indicating a shift in age distribution. The decline in the ratio of children and elderly to the working age population means that the dependency ratio has decreased significantly across the region.[3] Data show that the proportion of dependents per 100 working-age people dropped by around 31 per cent between 1990 and 2015.

Figure 3.1. GDP growth rate (percentage)

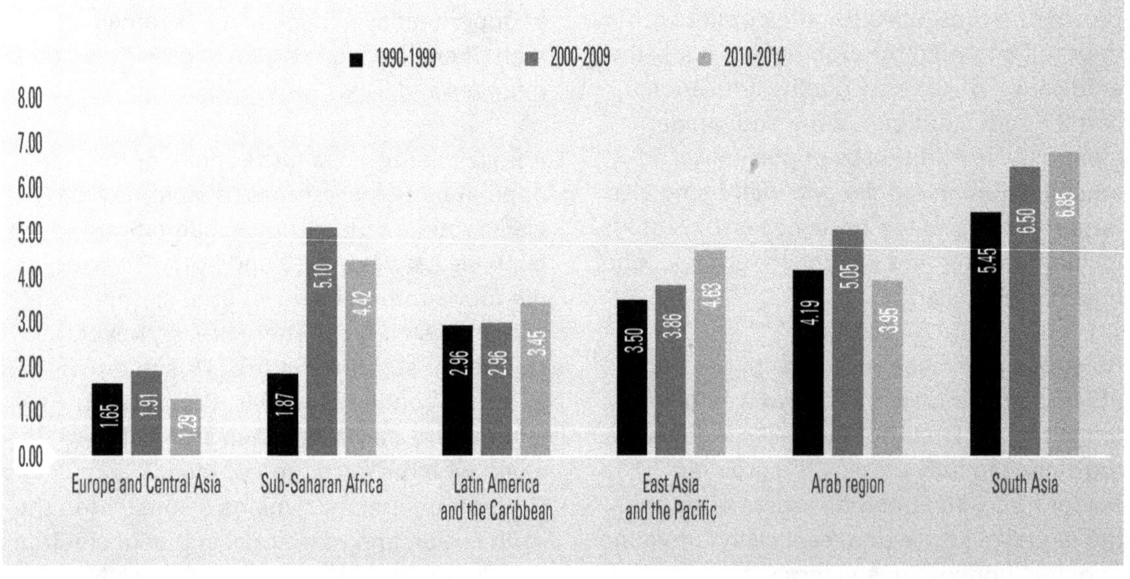

Source: Author's calculations based on the World Bank, World Development Indicators. Available from http://data.worldbank.org/products/wdi (accessed 30 August 2015).

Figure 3.2. GDP per capita growth rates (percentage)

	1990-1999	2000-2009	2010-2014
Sub-Saharan Africa	-0.85	2.37	1.67
Latin America and the Caribbean	1.21	1.65	2.30
Europe and Central Asia	1.39	1.62	0.91
Arab region	1.72	2.73	1.83
East Asia and the Pacific	2.24	3.05	3.94
South Asia	3.35	4.86	5.46

Source: Author's calculations based on World Bank, World Development Indicators (see figure 3.1).

Figure 3.3. GDP per capita (thousands of constant 2005 United States dollars)

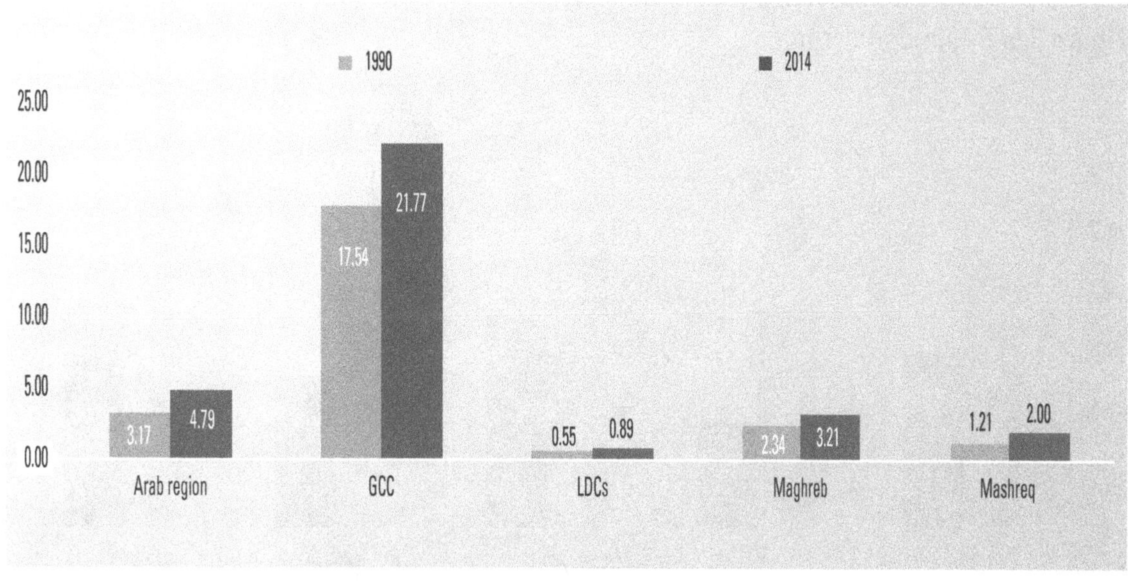

Source: Author's calculations based on World Bank, World Development Indicators.
Notes: Averages are weighted against total population. The 1990 value for Palestine is from 1994. The 2014 values for Kuwait, Palestine and the United Arab Emirates are from 2012, and the value for the Syrian Arab Republic is from 2007. Data for Somalia are missing.

The current average regional dependency ratio for Arab countries of 60.16 per cent is still above the global average of around 54 per cent in 2014.[4] Trends were particularly favourable for the GCC and Maghreb subregions, which now have ratios below the global average (figure 3.5).

The current age distribution is often considered a window of opportunity

Figure 3.4. Population growth rates

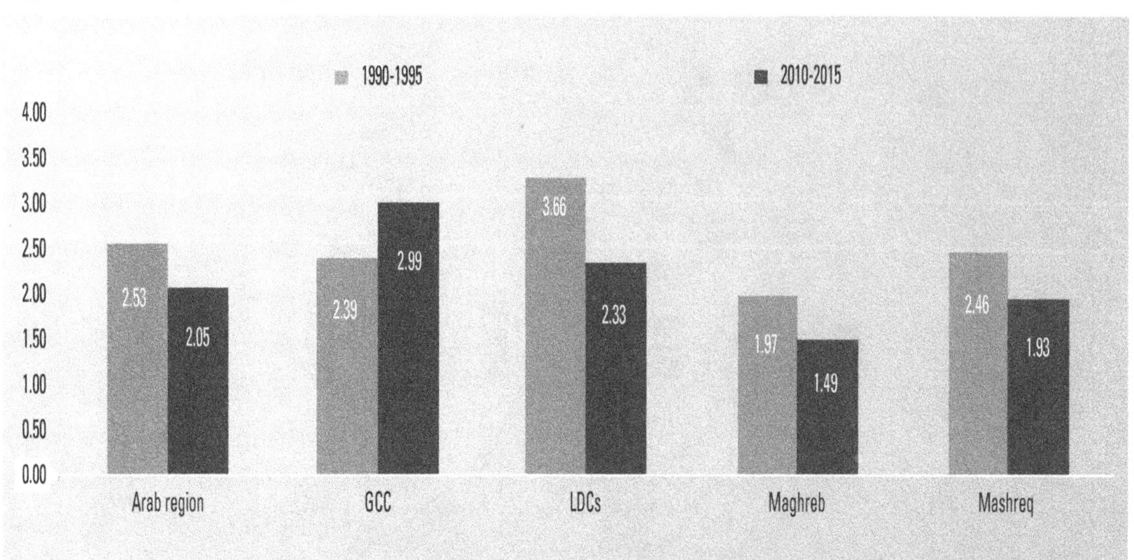

Source: Author's calculations based on data from the United Nations Department of Economic and Social Affairs (DESA), World Population Prospects: The 2015 Revision. Available from http://esa.un.org/unpd/wpp (accessed 30 August 2015).
Note: Weighted against total population.

Figure 3.5. Dependency ratio

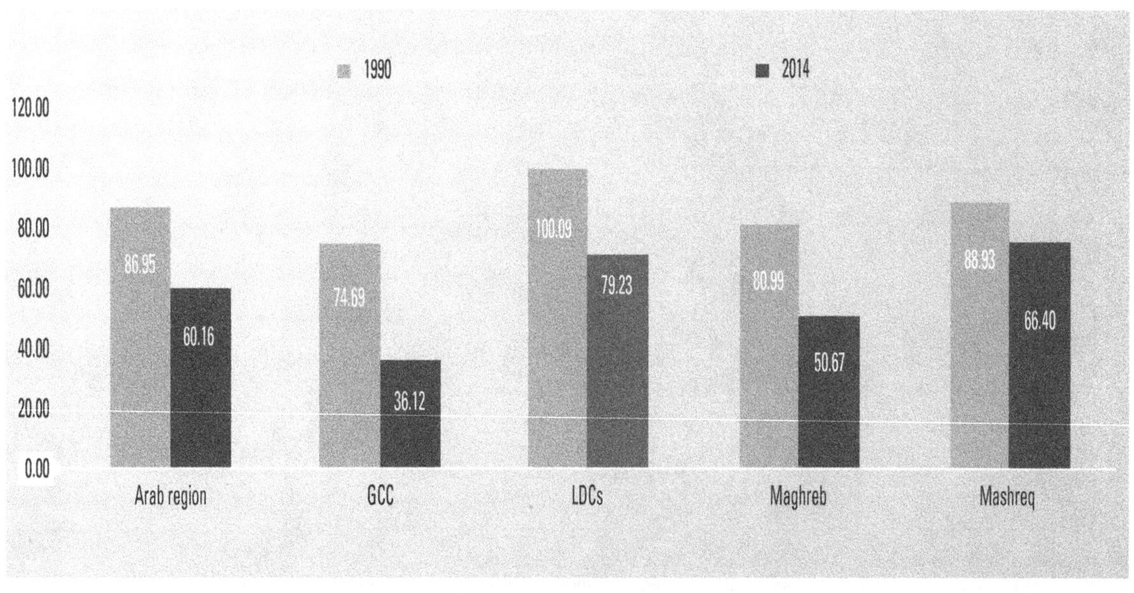

Source: Author's calculations based on data from DESA, World Population Prospects: The 2015 Revision (see figure 3.4).
Note: Weighted against population aged 15-64.

because a greater share of the population is now available to contribute to production. However, that only applies if the working age population is productively employed. The Arab countries have been less able to benefit from this opportunity than many

Figure 3.6. Economic structure of Arab countries (percentage share of sector in GDP)

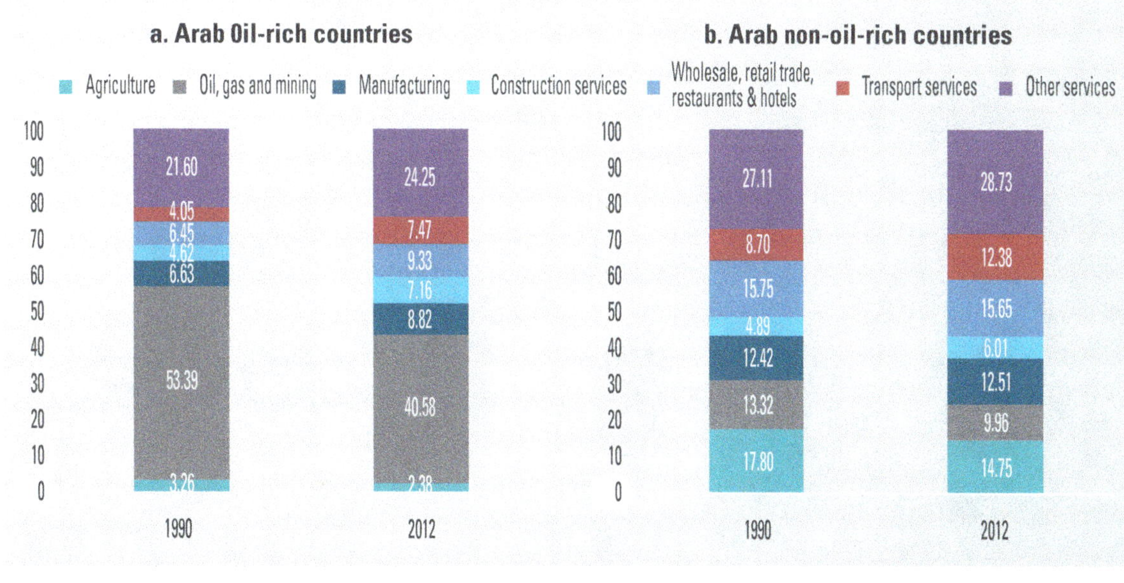

Source: Niranjan Sarangi and Khaled Abu-Ismail, "Economic growth, inequality and poverty in the Arab region", Issues Brief for the Arab Sustainable Development Report (2015). Available from http://css.escwa.org.lb/SDPD/3572/Goal1.pdf.

other regions because of low employment to population rates.

(b) Economic structure and productivity

The economic structure of the Arab countries has changed little since the 1990s. Despite some shifts, oil, gas and mining still comprise 41 per cent of GDP in the oil-rich countries and almost 10 per cent in the non-oil rich countries (figure 3.6). The emphasis on oil, gas and mining is important because these sectors generate little employment relative to other sectors. In Iraq, for example, petroleum accounts for more than half of GDP, but less than 1 per cent of employment.[5] The service sector, a high employment but low productivity sector, comprises a large and growing share of GDP. Agriculture represents a small share of GDP, but is an important source of livelihoods for many of the rural poor. Manufacturing remains a very small part of most Arab economies. Moreover, within manufacturing, there is a greater emphasis on lower technology manufacturing than would seem to be warranted by the region's generally high level of education. Indeed, only 1.5 per cent of manufactured exports in the Arab region in 2008 were considered to fit into the high-technology category, compared to a global average of 17 per cent.[6]

Higher productivity leads to increased wages, which enhances social expenditure and skill development and further productive capacity through a virtuous cycle. The region's low productivity reflects the service-focused structure of the economy. The productivity growth rate (defined as output per worker) of the Arab region over the period 1991-2010 was only 0.9 per cent, the lowest of the world's regions (figure 3.7).

Productivity can increase if the region's technological readiness and capacity to innovate are improved. According to the World Economic Forum's Global Competitiveness Index (GCI), technological readiness, defined as the agility with which an economy adopts existing technology to enhance productivity of its industries, has improved throughout the region over the past

Figure 3.7. Productivity growth rate, 1991-2010

Arab region	Sub-Saharan Africa	European Union	World	South Asia	East Asia and Pacific
0.90	1.30	1.50	2.20	4.20	4.50

Sources: ESCWA, *Survey of Economic and Social Developments in the Arab region 2012-2013* (Beirut, 2012, E/ESCWA/EDGD/2013/3); and Niranjan Sarangi and Abu-Ismail, "Economic growth, inequality and poverty in the Arab region" (see figure 3.6).

Figure 3.8. Global Competitiveness Index: Technological Readiness Score

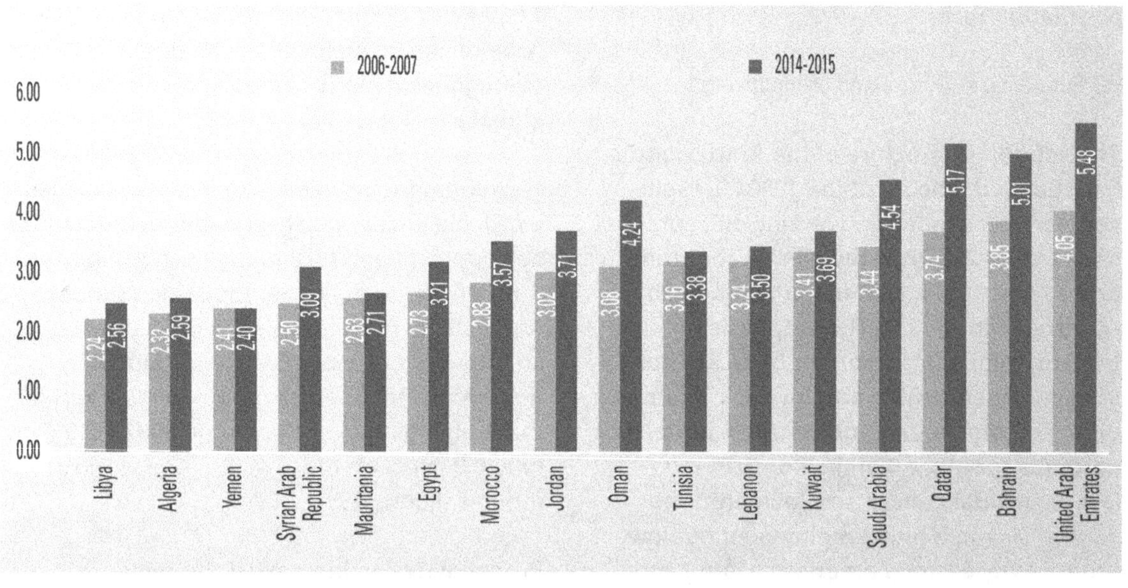

Source: Klaus Schwab and others, *The Global Competitiveness Report 2014-2015* (Geneva, World Economic Forum, 2014). Available from http://www3.weforum.org/docs/WEF_GlobalCompetitivenessReport_2014-15.pdf.
Notes: Score ranges from 1 (worse) to 7 (best). Values for some countries are not from the date indicated but from the latest available data in the source.

decade (figure 3.8). As of 2015, the United Arab Emirates is within the top quintile worldwide, and the worldwide median score is 3.7. However, capacity to innovate, as measured in the GCI by a number of research and development input and output indicators, remains low and has actually declined over the past decade in half of the countries of

Figure 3.9. Global Competitiveness Index: Innovation Score

	2006-2007	2014-2015
Yemen	1.68	2.11
Bahrain	2.55	3.32
Mauritania	2.55	2.41
Libya	2.65	1.98
Lebanon	2.65	2.75
Syrian Arab Republic	2.88	2.55
Algeria	2.96	2.60
Kuwait	2.98	2.86
Egypt	3.02	2.65
Morocco	3.08	3.11
Jordan	3.26	3.64
Qatar	3.27	4.88
United Arab Emirates	3.32	4.41
Saudi Arabia	3.44	3.80
Oman	3.67	3.29
Tunisia	3.84	3.01

Source: Schwab and others, *The Global Competitiveness Report 2014-2015* (see figure 3.8).
Notes: Score ranges from 1 (worse) to 7 (best). 2006-2007 value for Lebanon is from 2010-2011. 2006-2007 values for Libya, Oman, Saudi Arabia and the Syrian Arab Republic are from 2007-2008. 2006-2007 value for Yemen is from 2011-1012. 2014-2015 value for the Syrian Arab Republic is from 2011-2012

Figure 3.10. Gross capital formation as a percentage of GDP

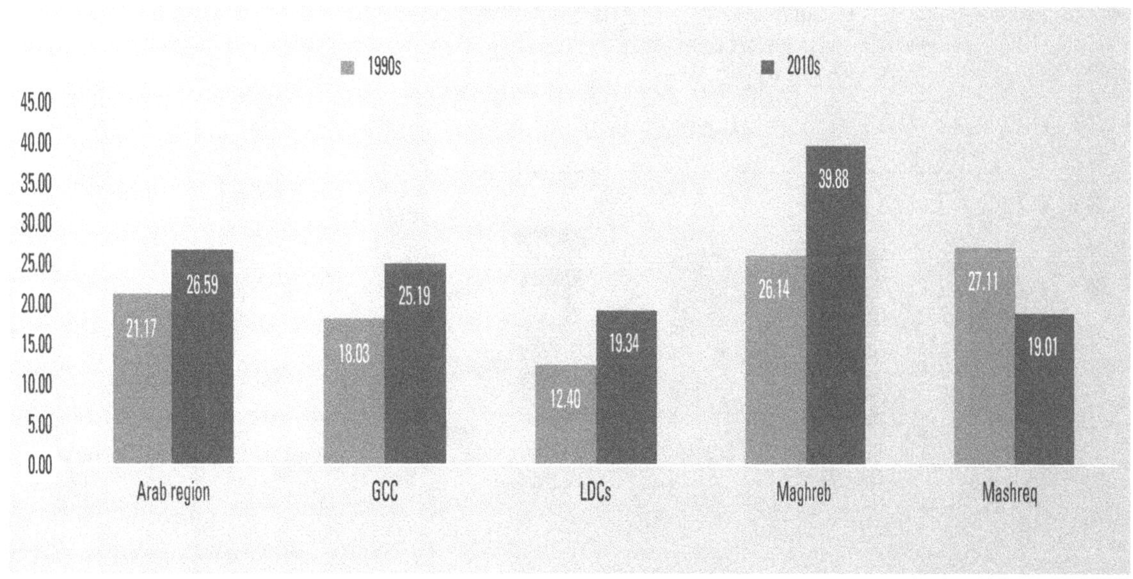

Source: Authors' calculations based on data from World Bank, World Development Indicators.
Notes: Weighted against GDP (in constant 2005 United States dollars). Values for the 2000s include a range between 2000 and 2014. 1990s values for the United Arab Emirates and Iraq are from the early 2000s. Data are missing for Somalia.

the region (figure 3.9). As of 2015, Qatar and the United Arab Emirates are within the top quintile worldwide, while Algeria, Egypt, Lebanon, Libya, Mauritania and Yemen are within the bottom quintile worldwide. The worldwide median score is 3.3.

Figure 3.11. Foreign direct investment (net inflows as a percentage of GDP)

Source: Authors' calculations based on World Bank, World Development Indicators.
Notes: Weighted against GDP (in constant 2005 United States dollars). 1990s data for Lebanon are from 2002. Data are missing for Somalia.

Figure 3.12. Percentage of adult saving by method used, 2011

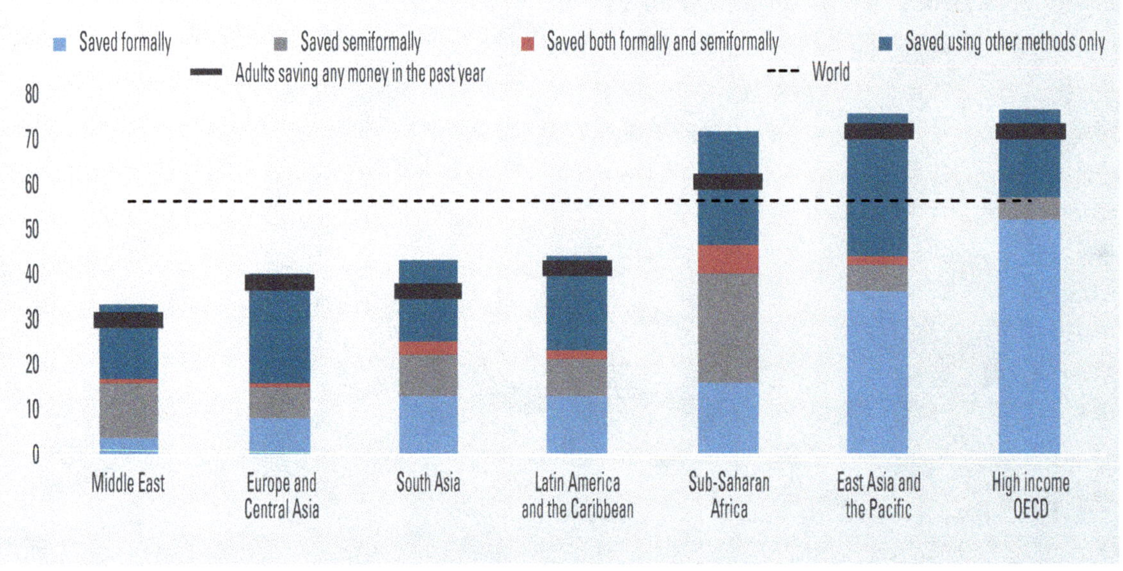

Sources: World Bank, Global Financial Inclusion (Global Findex) database, available from data.worldbank.org/data-catalog/financial_inclusion (accessed 30 August 2015); and e-mail correspondence with the World Bank.

Investment is an important driver of productivity. Fluctuations in gross capital formation (investment in fixed assets) are often seen as a reflection of future business activity, business confidence and the pattern of economic growth. Average gross capital formation has increased in the region over the past two decades by more than 25 per cent, with the 2000s value reaching 27 per cent of GDP (figure 3.10). This has been driven by considerable increases in capital investment in the LDCs (up by 56 per cent), GCC countries (up by 40 per cent) and the Maghreb (up by 53 per cent). The Maghreb achieved the highest level of capital investments (39.88 per cent of GDP). However, the Mashreq saw a drop of 30 per cent in capital formation as a percentage of GDP, reflecting recent and ongoing conflicts.

Foreign direct investment (FDI) generally brings with it new technology and new ways of organizing production. Average net FDI inflows as a percentage of GDP increased significantly across the region between 1990 and 2008, decreasing steadily since then to reach a low of 1.68 per cent, well below the global average of around 3 per cent in 2013. Increases in FDI rates were evident across all four subregions, with the LDCs registering the highest increase (figure 3.11), but rates in 2013 for the Maghreb and GCC countries were well below the global average. A more detailed analysis of FDI is presented in chapter 6.

Domestic investment is also crucial to productivity growth, particularly of small and medium enterprises. A well developed financial sector is essential for the efficient mobilization of domestic savings and allocation of credit. The Middle East[7] ranked lowest among world regions in 2011 in terms of the percentage of adults saving money by any method – and especially low in terms of formal savings (figure 3.12). This restricts investments, which come either from own savings or by borrowing from the savings of others. Adults in the region rarely make use of financial institutions.[8] Inward remittances are also important as a source for private investment (e.g. education and housing) and consumption. Egypt is the world's sixth largest recipient of remittances ($20 billion in 2014). Lebanon is in tenth place ($9 billion in 2014). The region as a whole is expected to bring in $53 billion in 2015.

2. Jobs

GDP growth improves the well-being of the population in several ways, most directly

Figure 3.13. Employment in industry (percentage of total employment)

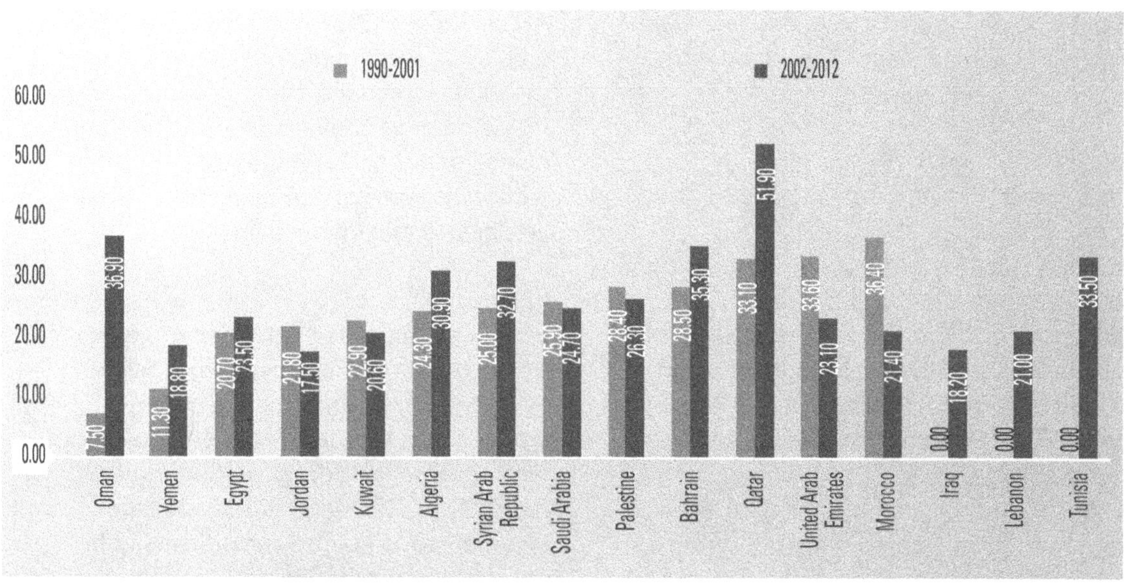

Source: World Bank, World Development Indicators.
Note: 1990-2001 are unavailable for Iraq, Lebanon and Tunisia.

Figure 3.14. Employment in agriculture (percentage of total employment)

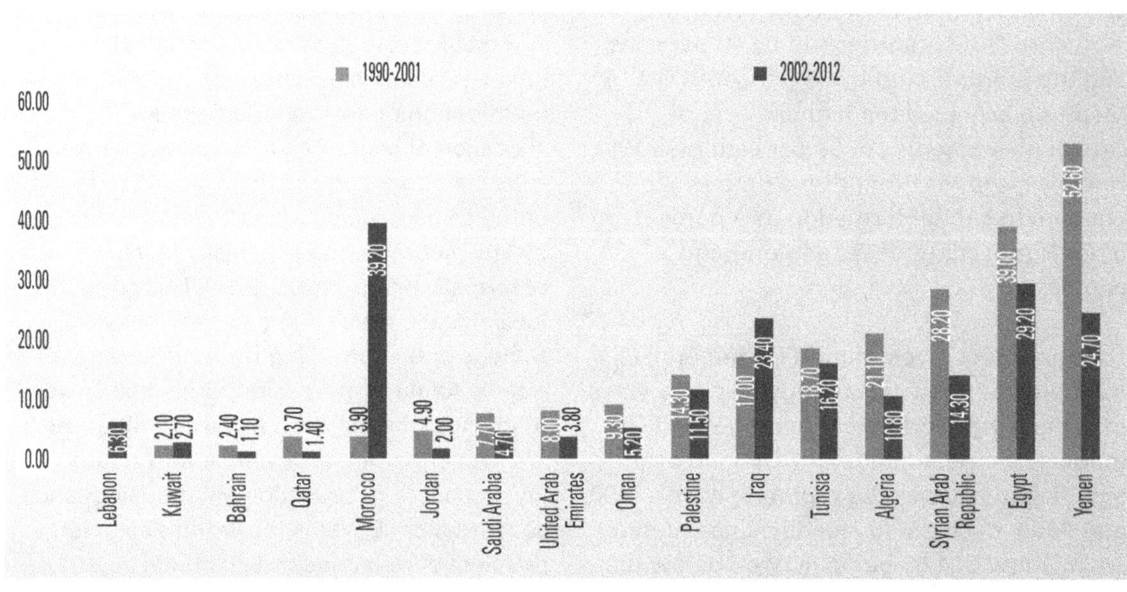

Source: World Bank, World Development Indicators.
Notes: 1990-2001 data for Iraq are from 2004, and from 2005 for Tunisia. Data are not available for Lebanon.

by increasing labour earnings, but also by increasing government revenue (for example, tax) that can be used for services (education, health, water and sanitation) and social protection transfers. This section looks at labour earnings. Social protection is addressed in the section on poverty and inequality, and other public services (such as health and education) are discussed in corresponding dedicated sections.

(a) Employment reflecting the structure of the economy

Employment in industry in the region is about the world average of 24 per cent, and lower still in non-GCC countries.[9] It has fallen in several Arab countries, including Jordan, Kuwait, Morocco, Palestine, Saudi Arabia, and the United Arab Emirates (figure 3.13).

Similarly, employment in agriculture fell significantly in a number of Arab countries, especially in Algeria, Egypt, the Syrian Arab Republic and Yemen. Morocco constitutes a notable exception: employment in agriculture rose sharply to exceed 39 per cent in the 2000s (figure 3.14).

A feature of the rentier economy and the concomitant social contract between the State and the population is the large share of service jobs in the public sector.[10] In most Arab countries, Governments are the primary employer, accounting for 14 to 40 per cent of the total workforce.[11] Bloated public sectors, including government agencies and State-owned enterprises, employ 22 per cent of Tunisians, and 33 to 35 per cent of Syrians, Jordanians and Egyptians.

In recent decades, Governments have become unable to guarantee employment, while the private sector has been insufficiently developed to absorb the expanding labour force. Morocco, however, has met with success in addressing the problem (box 3.1). Elsewhere, inadequate labour income, reduced food subsidies, and high unemployment among young graduates were among the chief causes of distress that led to the Arab uprisings.

Box 3.1. Lesson learned from civil service reform in Morocco

Civil service reform in Morocco, particularly an act on retirement reform, made it possible to deflate the bloated civil service, provided competencies frameworks for the future, and encouraged retirees to enter business. Faced with excessive centralization, lack of performance, ineffective resource allocation and a rigid civil service structure, the Government initiated, in 2004, a programme aimed at restructuring its civil service, dubbed Intilaka ("the launch"). At the beginning of the programme, 856,000 employees, or 2.3 per cent of the population (relatively low when compared with countries such as Algeria, with 4.2 per cent), made up the civil service, with a wage bill reaching 12.8 per cent of GDP in 2004. The Government aimed to encourage voluntary retirement with financial incentives and planned for almost 59,000 employees to leave service between 2005 and 2011, and 97,000 between 2012 and 2018.

Although initially success was limited, by 2005 the wage bill had dropped from 12.8 per cent to 10.6 per cent of GDP. Competencies frameworks were established and a new system of performance evaluation took into consideration quality of work, innovation, ability to achieve and productivity. As a result, the civil service was cut back, strain was taken off the budget, government effectiveness and management of human capital were improved, and former civil servants were encouraged to enter the private sector. This "positive spillover" of civil service reform, linked to the reform of public financial management, helped to achieve a smaller wage bill, provide new incentives for market entry, develop a new class of entrepreneurs, stimulate the private sector, and ultimately create new jobs and reduce unemployment. Similar models could be applied in other Arab countries, such as Egypt, Lebanon and Tunisia.

Source: اسكندر البستاني وكارل ريحان، تجربة المغرب في إصلاح الوظيفة العامة، مجلة السادسة، العدد الرابع، 2013. www.institutdesfinances.gov.lb/english/loadFile.aspx?pageid=2021&phname=PDF.

Figure 3.15. Employment to population ratio (aged 15+)

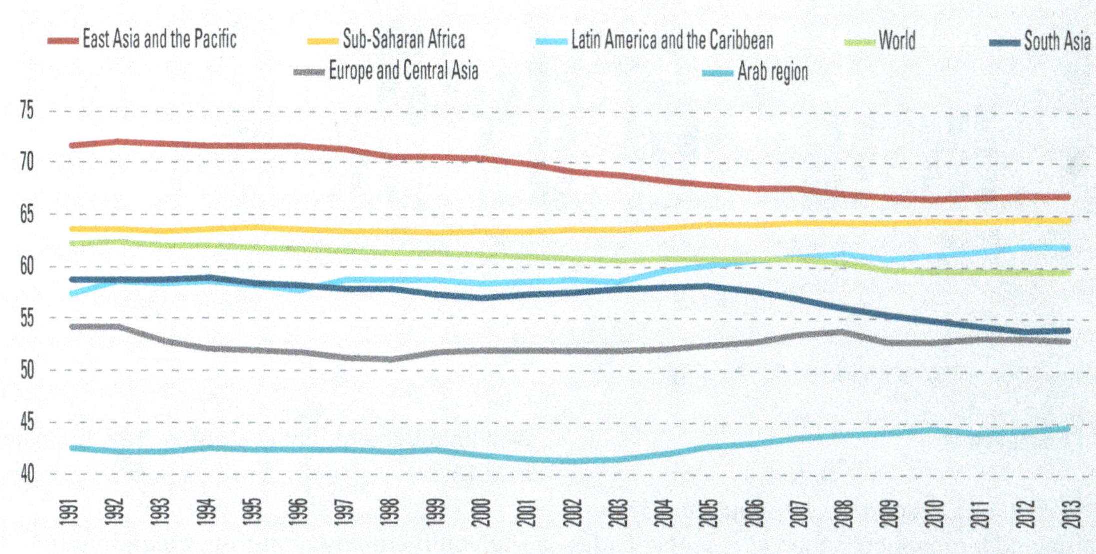

Source: World Bank, World Development Indicators.

Figure 3.16. Employment to population ratio for youth (15-24 years)

Source: Authors' calculations based on World Bank, World Development Indicators.
Note: Weighed against total population.

Figure 3.17. Unemployment rate

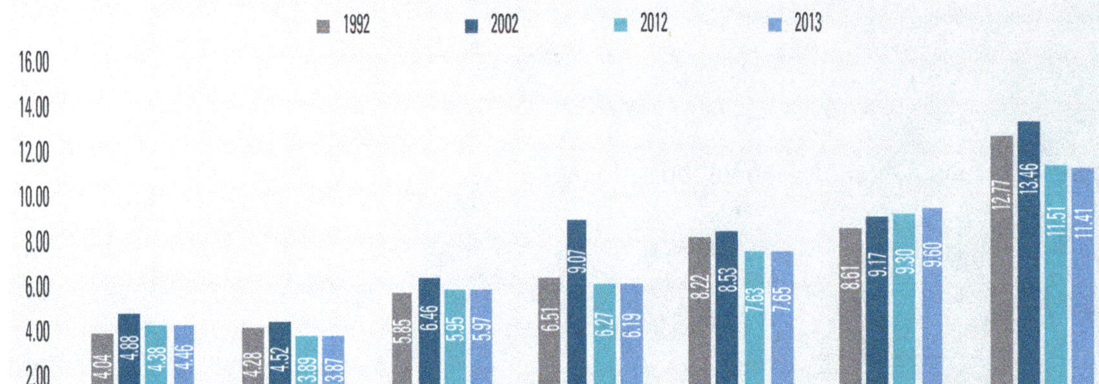

Source: World Bank, World Development Indicators.

(b) Employment

The ratio of employment to population[12] has remained largely unchanged in recent decades and is the lowest in the world (figure 3.15). The ratio for 2013 was 44.6 per cent, which falls well below the global average of 59.6 per cent in 2013.[13]

The youth employment-to-population ratio fell by nearly 11 per cent over the two decades from 26.7 in 1991 to 23.7 per cent in 2013, and

Figure 3.18. Youth unemployment rate (percentage of total labour force aged 15 to 24)

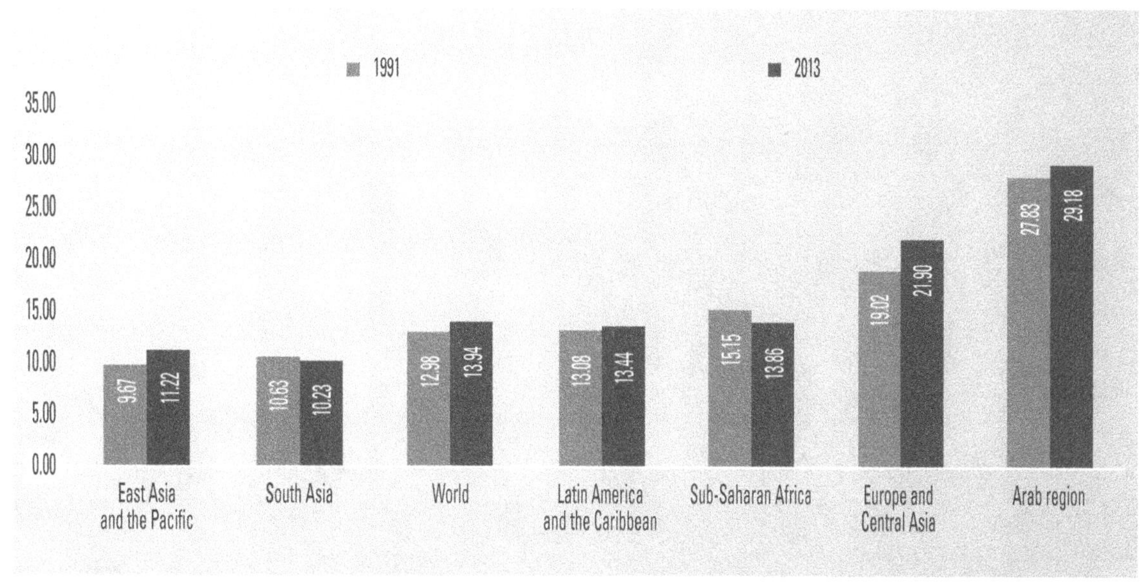

Source: World Bank, World Development Indicators, based on modelled International Labour Organization (ILO) data.

was well below the global average of 41.2 per cent in 2013. Declines are evident across all four subregions, with the Mashreq registering the lowest level in 2013, at 20 per cent (figure 3.16). Moreover, better educated youth were more likely to be unemployed than their less skilled counterparts, which highlights challenges faced by young people in making the transition from school to work and meeting the requirements of the labour market.

A large share of the labour force is unemployed, as has been the case consistently since the 1990s. In 2013, the unemployment rate for the region was 11.41 per cent, almost double the global average of 6 per cent (figure 3.17). The unemployment situation is even more challenging for women (a detailed analysis of gender issues is provided later in the chapter).

Youth unemployment in the Arab region has been alarmingly high since 1991 and by 2013 had reached around 30 per cent (figure 3.18), more than double the global average of 14 per cent.[14] In some countries, youth unemployment has structural causes that would require remedies to encourage private sector investment.

(c) Quality of jobs

The regional economy not only fails to generate sufficient employment: its structure is such that the jobs available are often poorly remunerated and insecure. Low productivity growth has meant low wage growth. Average GDP growth of 4 per cent in the 1990s and 2000s was matched by real wage growth of 1.89 per cent. In other words, the employers and capital-holders have benefitted more from economic growth than workers. In fact, the Arab region is the only one in which real wages have declined in recent years, dropping by 2.7 per cent between 2006 and 2011.[15] Labour income as a percentage of GDP declined from 30.5 per cent in 2000 to 27.6 per cent in 2010 (figure 3.19).[16]

Low productivity growth and limited employment gains have led to an expansion of the informal sector, generally made up of lowly paid, low quality and low productivity jobs. People employed in the formal sector in the

Figure 3.19. Labour income as a percentage of GDP

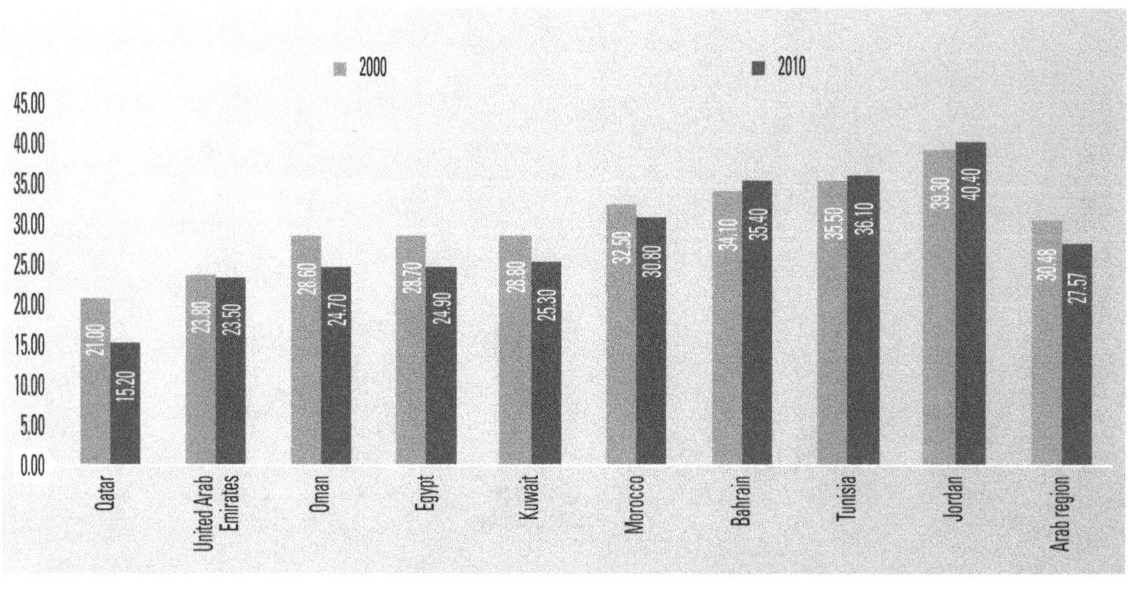

Source: Authors' calculations based on ILO, ILOSTAT database. Available from www.ilo.org/ilostat (accessed 30 August 2015).
Notes: The regional average is population weighted. 2000 data for the United Arab Emirates are from 2001. 2010 data for Bahrain, Egypt, Jordan and Tunisia are from 2009. 2010 data for Morocco and Qatar are from 2008.

region represent only 19 per cent of the working age population (compared to 27 per cent in Latin America and 40 per cent in Eastern Europe).[17] The share of vulnerable employment (own-account and contributing family workers) in total employment has remained fairly stable over the past two decades.

(d) Economic migration

High unemployment and low wages have led to widespread migration. Large numbers of workers in many Arab countries, frustrated by the lack of opportunities at home, have sought employment in GCC countries or left the region. Others, rejecting available low wage and insecure jobs, continue to seek preferable employment (often in the public sector) or leave the labour force.

Jobs refused by nationals in the region's wealthier countries are generally filled by immigrants from poorer Arab countries (such as Egypt, the Sudan and Yemen) or from outside the region (for example, from South Asia, the Philippines or Indonesia). Thirty-eight per cent of immigrants entering the Arab region originate in other Arab countries (figure 3.20).

A large number of Arab emigrants (particularly from the Mashreq, Yemen and the Sudan) move to GCC countries, in particular the United Arab Emirates and Saudi Arabia (figure 3.21). In 2010, the Jordanian Ministry of Labour estimated that 350,000 Jordanians worked abroad, mostly in GCC countries and largely in the private sector. Similarly, around 70 per cent of emigrants registered with the Secretariat of Sudanese Working Abroad in 2010 were working in Saudi Arabia. However, labour migrants go to other countries as well, depending on factors such as bilateral links and skill levels. For example, while most Egyptian migrants go to GCC countries, they are also present in significant numbers in Jordan and Libya, and some opt for irregular or regular emigration to Europe. Mauritanian migrants are often found in other West African countries, given their proximity and close links.

Figure 3.20. Main countries of origin for immigrants to the Arab region, 2013

0.95; 3%
1.80; 6%
2.92; 10%
3.16; 10%
6.85; 22%
3.23; 11%
11.40; 38%
Indonesia
Philipines
Pakistan
Bangladesh
India
Rest of the world
Arab countries

Source: Authors' calculations based on United Nations, Department of Economic and Social Affairs (DESA), Trends in International Migrant Stock: Migrants by Destination and Origin (United Nations database, POP/DB/MIG/Stock/Rev.2013, accessed 30 August 2015).
Note: The numbers of immigrants are expressed in millions and percentages.

Figure 3.21. Inflows to Arab countries from other Arab countries (thousands)

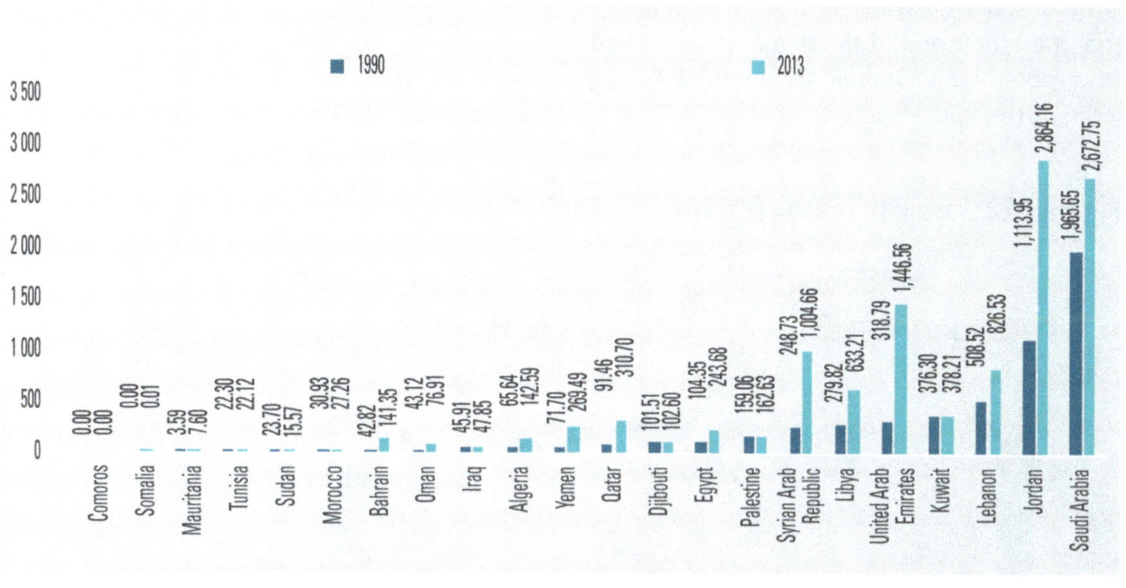

Source: United Nations, DESA, Trends in International Migrant Stock: Migrants by Destination and Origin (see figure 3.20).
Note: Figures for Jordan and Lebanon include Palestinians living in those countries (exceeding 2 million and 500,000 respectively in 2013).

Migrants in the Arab region include people of all ages from a variety of social and economic backgrounds. Their experiences, vulnerabilities and needs differ. Women migrants make up an important proportion of migrants in and from the region, although their numbers remain well below the global average.[18]

Regulation of the labour market and the flow of migrant labour should be consistent with the human rights of workers. The kafala (sponsorship) system ties migrant workers legally to their employers rather than to the State, opening the door to abuses. The treatment and conditions of migrant domestic workers in the region, most of whom are women who receive no protection under national labour laws, has been strongly criticized, including by the human rights bodies of the United Nations. They suffer from insufficient remuneration, deprivation of freedom of movement, the withholding of passports and lack of legal recourse.[19]

3. Poverty and inequality

The above-mentioned social contract, whereby the State provides employment and subsidies in exchange for political acquiescence, has until recently helped to keep poverty and consumption inequality in the region low by global standards.[20] However, the growing incapacity of States to maintain their end of the bargain has stoked frustration, which helped to fuel the 2011 Arab uprisings.

(a) Social protection

Social protection in the Arab region has focused on subsidies rather than targeted programmes, including cash transfers. General subsidies, including for fuels and food, account for more than 10 per cent of GDP and at least 20 per cent of total expenditure in the region. Fossil fuel subsidies, in particular, cost GCC countries more than $200 billion in 2011, around 9 per cent of GDP. Mashreq countries spent $146 billion, or 11 per cent of GDP, in the same year (figure3.22). In per capita terms, GCC countries spent the most, with Governments providing subsidies of around $4,400 per capita in 2011. The LDCs spent the least on fuel subsidies in absolute and relative terms. Total expenditure on fossil fuel subsidies in Arab countries reached over $423 billion, or $1,180 per capita, in 2011.

These subsidies put an unsustainable strain on national budgets. Moreover, they are generally not targeted and mostly benefit the non-poor. In the case of fuel subsidies, the wealthiest quintile benefits far more

Figure 3.22. Fossil fuel subsidies, 2011

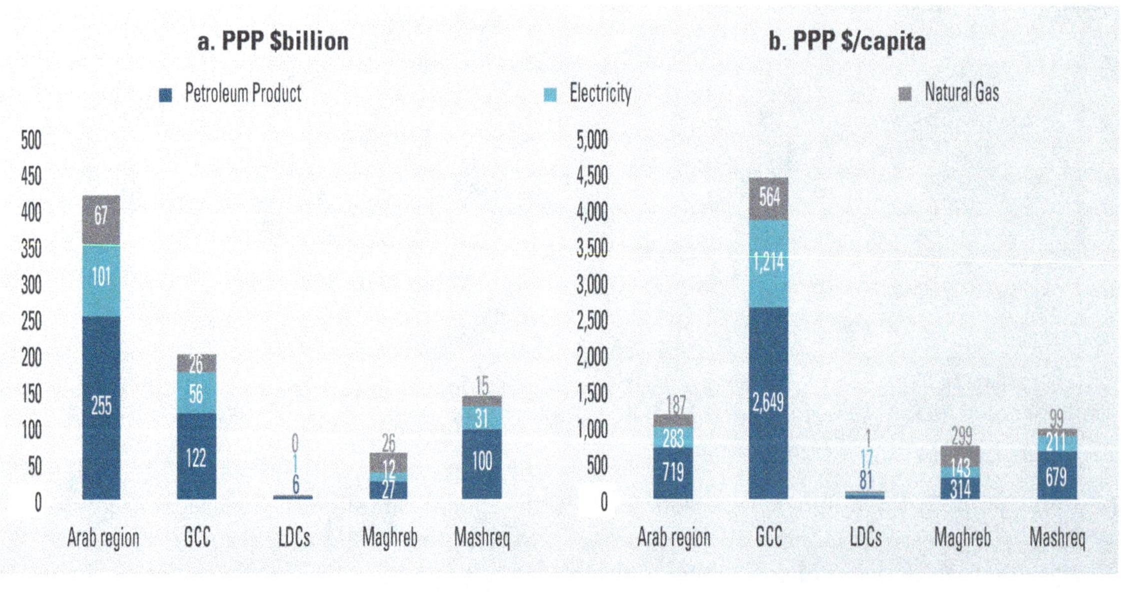

Source: Sherif Arif and Fadi Doumani, "A strategic investment framework for green economy in Arab countries from an energy perspective", document prepared for ESCWA (2015).

Figure 3.23. Allocation of fuel subsidies by quintile

Percentage of fuel subsidy benefits

	Poorest Quintile	Q2	Q3	Q4	Richest Quintile
Jordan 2010	3.00	9.50	15.00	22.00	51.00
Egypt 2009	7.00	9.50	10.50	14.00	62.00
Yemen 2005	9.00	12.00	16.00	21.00	42.00

Source: World Bank, "Predictions, perceptions and economic reality", *MENA Quarterly Economic Brief,* Issue No. 3 (Washington, D.C., July 2014).

Figure 3.24. Social insurance coverage, latest available year between 2004 and 2012 (percentage of population)

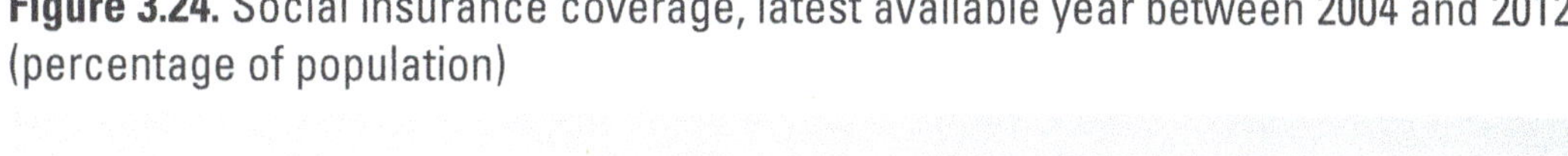

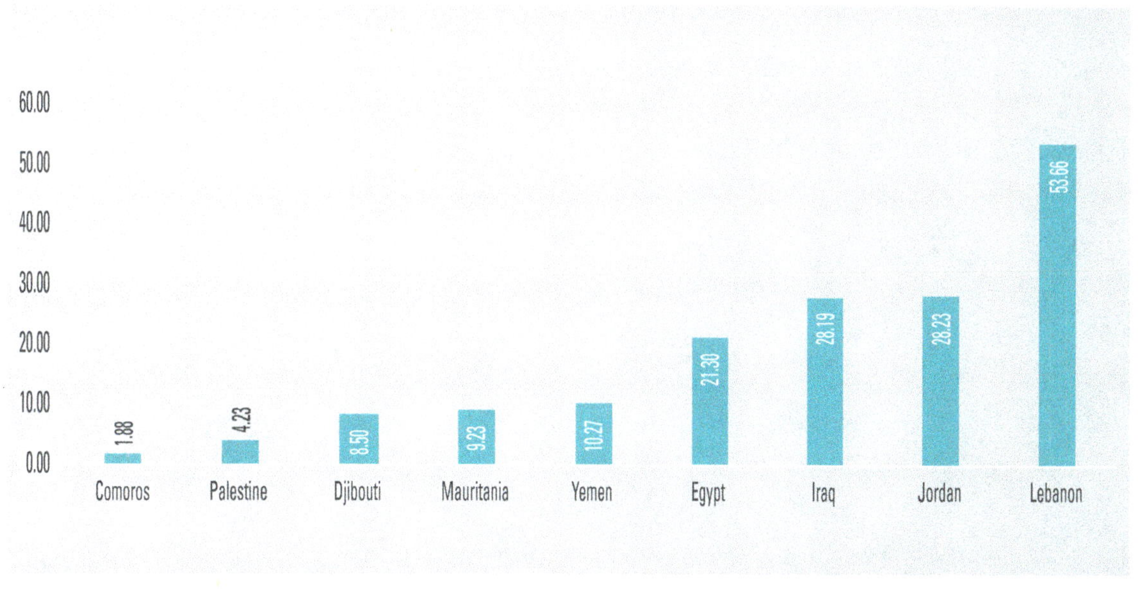

Source: World Bank, World Development Indicators.

than any other (figure 3.23). There have been some efforts to rationalize subsidies in Egypt, Jordan and Tunisia, but the matter of reform remains contentious and largely unresolved.

Targeted social protection programmes remain minimal, generally limited to employees of the public sector and major companies. Such programmes are potentially very efficient and fair but they require a high degree of administrative capacity and are not suitable for all countries. The coverage of social insurance programmes (contributory programmes to minimize the impact of adverse shocks), except in the case Lebanon, is low (figure 3.24).

Provision of old-age pension and unemployment benefits is the second lowest in the world in the Arab region, after sub-Saharan Africa. Old-age pension coverage in countries of the Middle East

Figure 3.25. Old age pension coverage, latest available year (percentage of population)

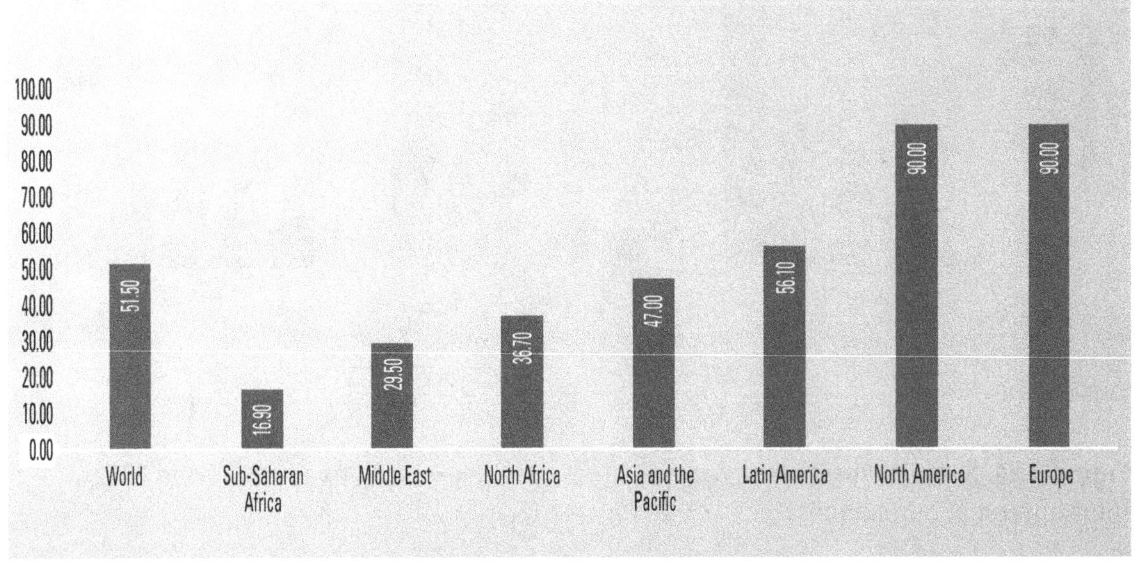

Source: ILO, *World Social Protection Report 2014/15: Building Economic Recovery, Inclusive Development and Social Justice* (Geneva, 2014).

Figure 3.26. Unemployment benefits coverage, latest available year (percentage of population)

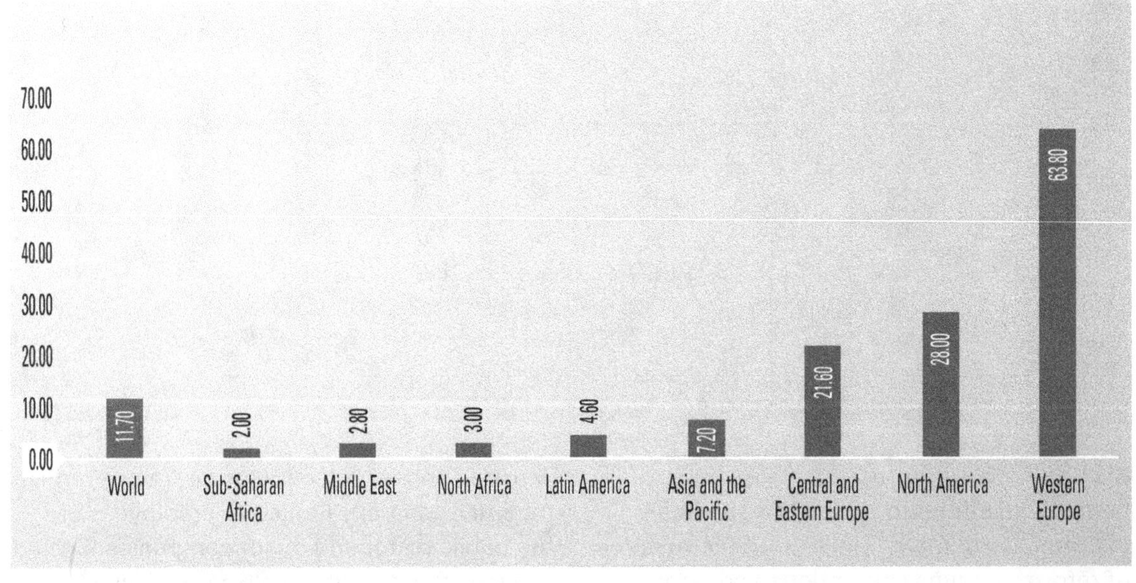

Source: ILO, *World Social Protection Report 2014/15.*

(29.5 per cent) and North Africa (36.7 per cent) is well below the global average of 51.5 per cent. The situation is worse for the coverage of unemployment benefits, which stands at just 3 per cent throughout the Arab region - a quarter of the global average of 11.7 per cent (figures 3.25 and 3.26).

(b) Poverty

Poverty as measured by the international poverty line has increased in recent years, notably in countries affected by conflict. Overall, average poverty rates in the Arab region increased by more than a third over the past two decades (based on the international poverty line of $1.25 per day), reaching 7.4 per cent in 2012. The regional trend was driven mainly by a significant increase in the LDCs and a moderate increase in the Mashreq (figure 3.27).

Poverty rates are higher when measured in terms of nationally accepted standards of living (figure 3.28). Moreover, armed conflict and instability in the region have driven those levels higher still in some countries in recent years, especially in Egypt, the Syrian Arab Republic and Yemen. Rural poverty is especially high in the LDCs, and significantly higher than in urban areas in Mashreq and Maghreb countries, including Egypt, Iraq and Morocco. Only in Palestine is rural poverty, based on the national poverty line, lower than that in urban areas (figure 3.29).

(c) Inequality

If the concept of poverty focuses on absolute levels of well-being, inequality measures relative well-being. Indicators of inequality include the Gini Index,[21] quintiles and analysis that also utilizes national accounts data. In terms of the Gini Index, inequality is relatively moderate in the Arab region and has changed little over the past two decades. Gini Index estimates in the 2000s for the Arab region (around 34.3) compare favourably with

Figure 3.27. Poverty rate based on the international poverty line (percentage of population below $1.25 PPP per day)

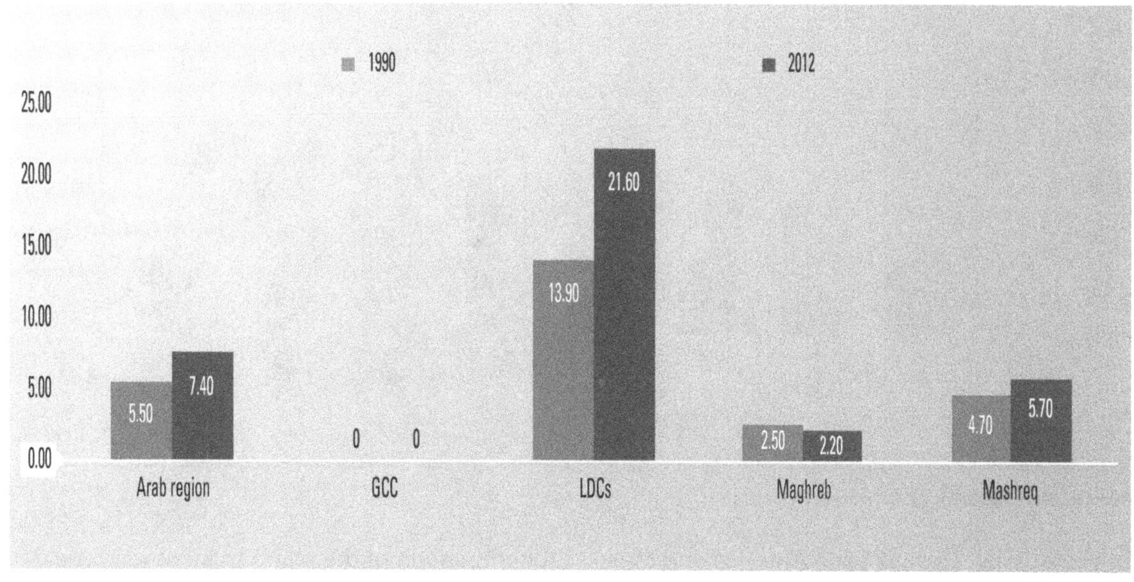

Source: United Nations and League of Arab States, *Arab Millennium Development Goals Report: Facing Challenges and Looking Beyond 2015* (Beirut, 2013, E/ESCWA/EDGD/2013/1); World Bank, World Development Indicators; and ESCWA estimates.
Notes: Values are weighted averages. GCC values are insignificant.

Figure 3.28. Percentage of population below national poverty lines

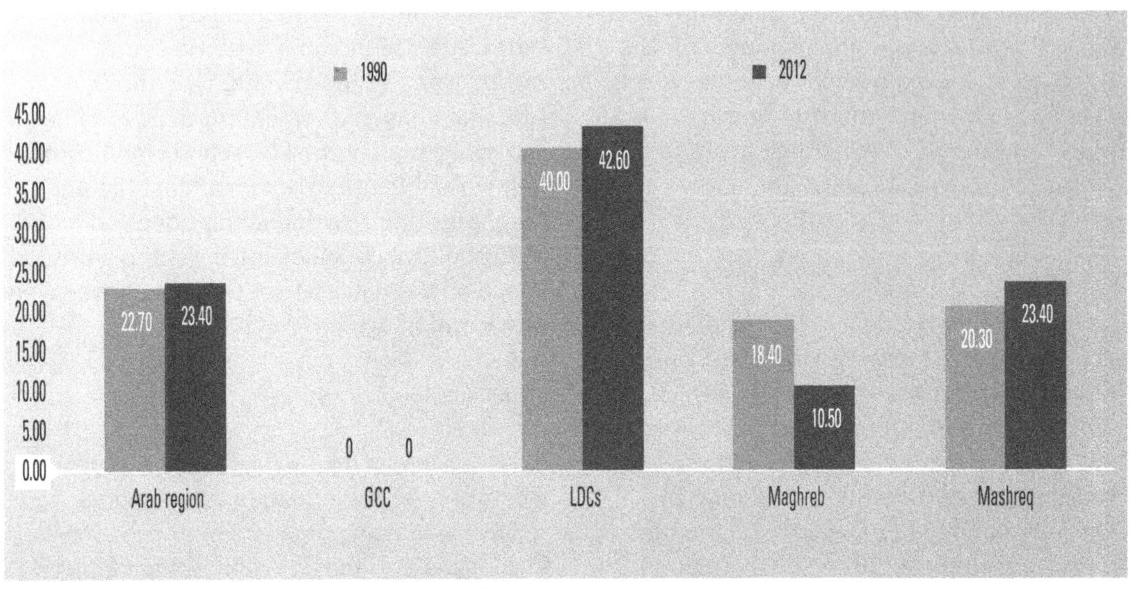

Source: United Nations and League of Arab States, *Arab Millennium Development Goals Report*; World Bank, World Development Indicators; and ESCWA estimates.
Notes: Values are weighted averages by population size. GCC values are insignificant.

Figure 3.29. Rural versus urban poverty rate, latest available year between 1998 and 2012 (based on national poverty lines)

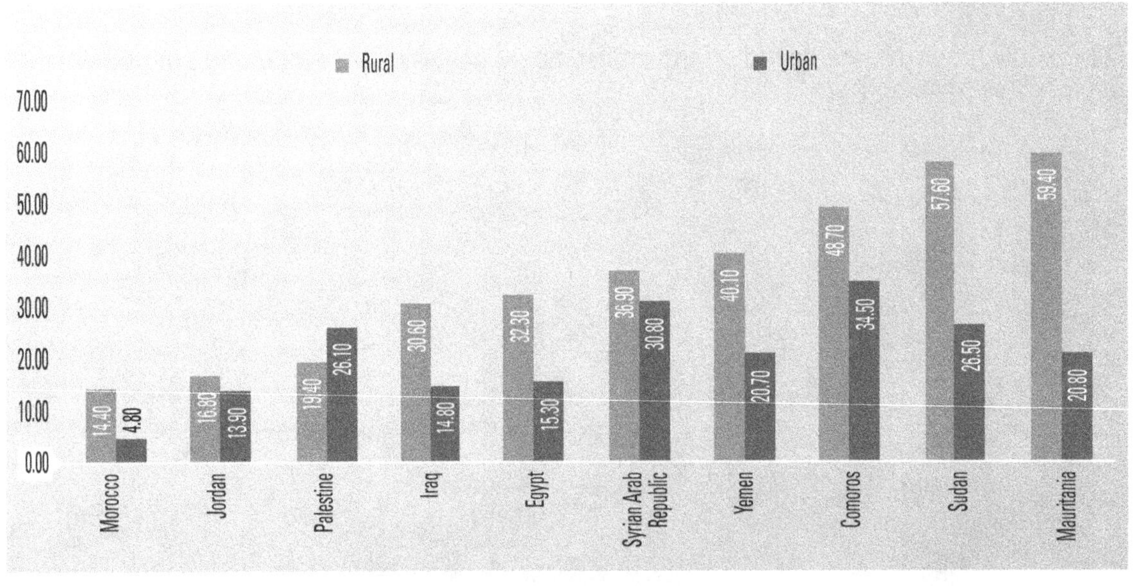

Source: World Bank, World Development Indicators.

other regions, such as Latin America and the Caribbean (51.8), sub-Saharan Africa (44.7), Europe and Central Asia (35.8), South Asia (32.4), and East Asia and the Pacific (34.2).[22]

A comparison of the share in income in the highest and lowest quintiles[23] shows a mixed trend in the Arab region between the 1990s and 2000s. In figure 3.30, higher values indicate a more unequal distribution of income or consumption, with Morocco and Yemen showing a slight negative trend since the 1990s, while Egypt, Jordan, Mauritania and Tunisia show positive trends.

Although the ratio of income of the highest to lowest quintiles using World Development Indicators data shows a trend of improvement in equality, other studies using different methodologies and data have found high and worsening inequality. Using a combination of national accounts and household survey data to re-estimate the mean consumption of the rich, ESCWA found that in 2011, the average per capita expenditure of the rich in Egypt was over 16 times higher than that of the poor, and 7 times higher than that of the middle class.[24] Another recent study suggests that in the period up to 2030, economic growth paths are likely to be associated with higher inequality and a shrinking middle class in Arab countries.[25]

Inequality of consumption is a useful summary measure, but does not fully reflect inequality in terms of other aspects of well-being, many of which (including education, health care, water and sanitation) are addressed in dedicated sections of this report. Before turning to them, however, we present analysis of inequality in several composite measures.

The Inequality-Adjusted Human Development Index (IHDI) attempts to account for inequality across income, health and education. It is based on the Human Development Index (HDI), but discounts the index for inequalities: the IHDI will be equal to the HDI when there is no inequality, but falls below the HDI as inequality rises (figure 3.31). The discount due to inequality averaged 24 per cent in the region in 2013, which is comparable to the global average. In all Arab countries analysed, the discount due to inequality is largely driven by inequality in education, and to a lesser extent by income and health inequality.

4. Gender

Nearly all Arab States have ratified the Convention on the Elimination of all Forms of Discrimination against Women and have

Figure 3.30. Ratio of income of highest quintile to income of lowest quintile

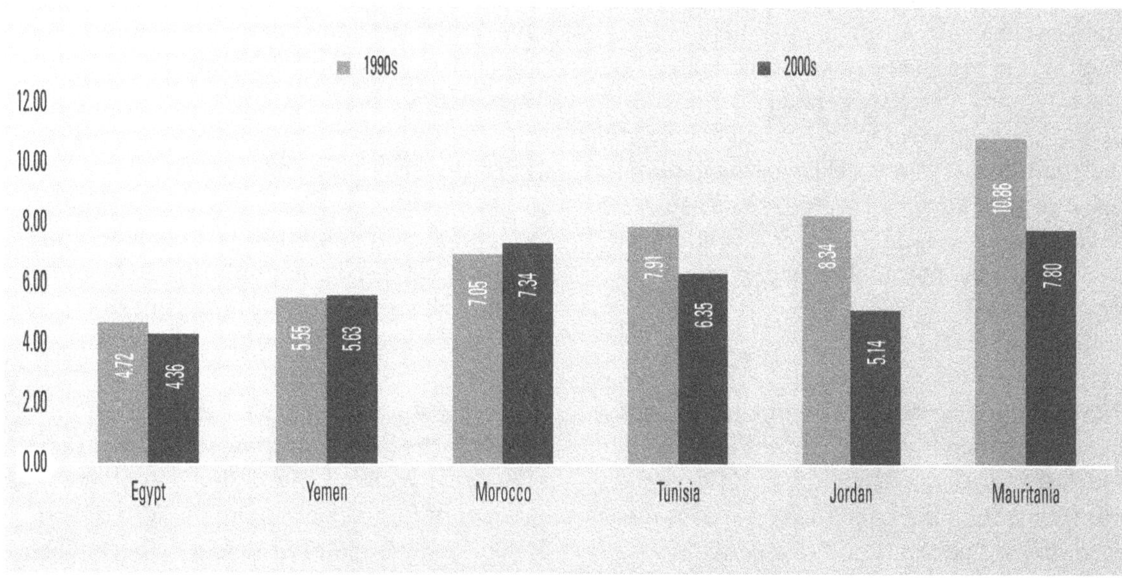

Source: World Bank, World Development Indicators.

Figure 3.31. Human Development Index and Inequality-adjusted Human Development Index, 2013

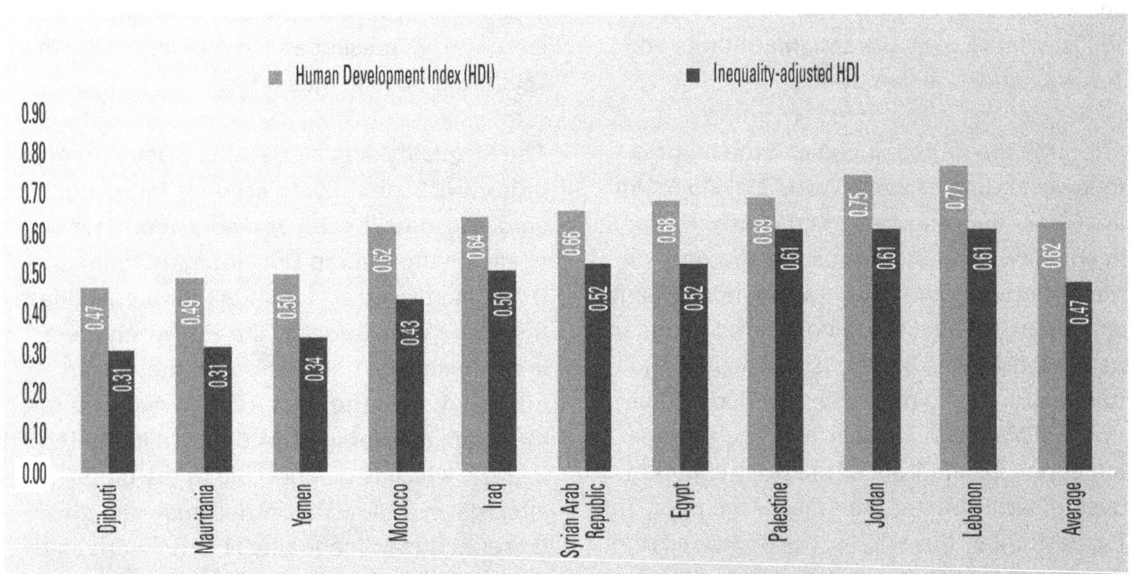

Source: United Nations Development Programme (UNDP), "Table 3: Inequality-adjusted Human Development Index", Human Development Reports database. Available from http://hdr.undp.org/en/content/table-3-inequality-adjusted-human-development-index (accessed 30 August 2015).
Note: The average is a simple average of values of chosen countries.

engaged actively with its reporting mechanisms. However, most entered reservations and noted that its provisions would be implemented insofar as they did not contradict the sharia, which is interpreted differently across the world.[26] Reservations mostly pertain to personal status issues such as marriage, inheritance, divorce and the acquisition of nationality. Consequently, there are serious repercussions on the ability of women to participate fully in the economic and political life of their countries. Gender gaps have narrowed considerably in several key areas, but the region continues to rank poorly by international standards.

(a) Political participation

The average number of parliamentary seats held by women in Arab countries increased fourfold between the 1990s and 2014, from 2.5 per cent to 13.2 per cent. The world average rose from 13 per cent to 22 per cent (figure 3.32). The sharp increase in the Maghreb subregion contributed significantly to the regional improvement. There are significant variations from one country to another, especially between countries that opted for affirmative action, such as quotas or reserved seats (Algeria,[27] Djibouti, Iraq, Jordan, Saudi Arabia, Somalia and Tunisia) and those that have not (Kuwait and Qatar). The percentage of seats held by women actually fell in Egypt, Oman and Yemen.

(b) Female employment and education

Moderate improvements were seen in female employment-to-population ratios, which increased by more than 20 per cent over the two decades in the region as a whole, with increases in all subregions except for the Mashreq, where levels stagnated at the lowest in the region at only 14 per cent (figure 3.33). Nevertheless, the regional average of 19 per cent of females employed is well below the global average of around 47 per cent in 2013. Many working women are in vulnerable employment. In fact, the ratio of women

Figure 3.32. Percentage of parliamentary seats held by women

	1990s	2014
Arab region	2.50	13.20
GCC	0.40	7.93
LDCs	2.45	13.22
Maghreb	2.85	23.98
Mashreq	4.78	10.88

Source: Authors' calculations based on World Bank, World Development Indicators.
Notes: Regional and subregional averages are simple unweighted averages. Data are unavailable for Palestine. 1990 data for Bahrain and Saudi Arabia are actually from 2003, for Libya from 2005, and for Qatar from 2006. 2014 data for Egypt are from 2012.

Figure 3.33. Employment-to-population ratio for females aged 15+ years

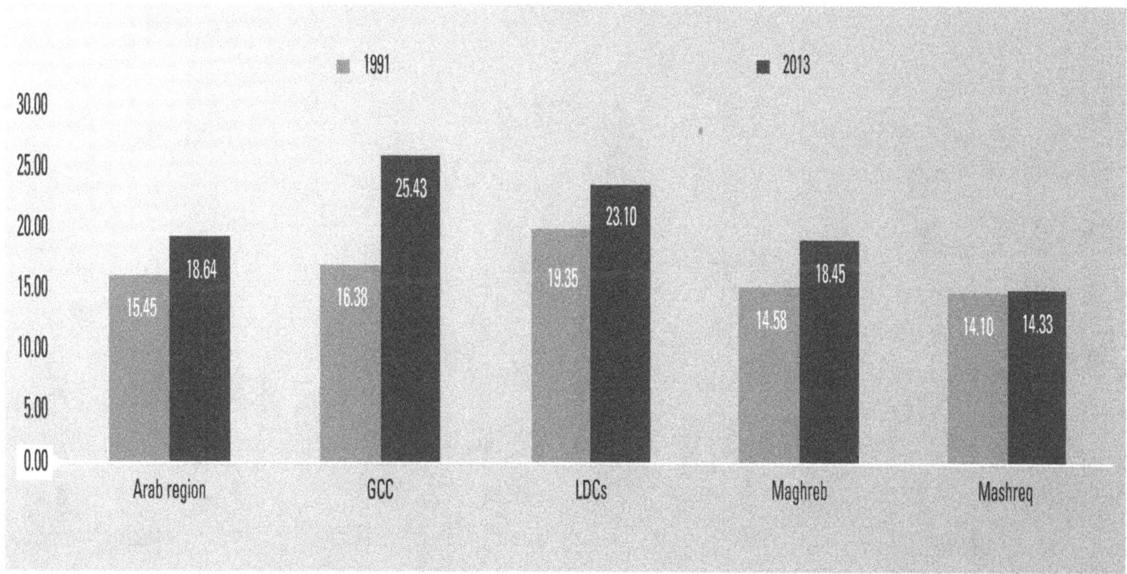

Source: Authors' calculations based on World Bank, World Development Indicators.
Notes: Weighted against total population. Data are missing for Djibouti.

compared to men in vulnerable employment has risen over the last two decades. In 2010, the female-to-male ratio of 177 was higher than in all other developing regions.[28]

Analysis of the gender distribution of national wealth similarly demonstrates women's limited economic participation, as well as lower earnings. In 2013, the mean female-to-male ratio

Figure 3.34. Female-to-male ratio in GNI per capita, 2013

Country/region	Ratio
Jordan	0.15
Iraq	0.18
Palestine	0.19
Syrian Arab Republic	0.20
Egypt	0.26
Lebanon	0.29
Mashreq	0.22
Algeria	0.17
Tunisia	0.29
Morocco	0.30
Libya	0.33
Maghreb	0.28
Saudi Arabia	0.21
Oman	0.31
Qatar	0.32
United Arab Emirates	0.33
Kuwait	0.38
Bahrain	0.67
GCC	0.34
Yemen	0.29
Mauritania	0.30
Sudan	0.33
Comoros	0.36
Djibouti	0.44
LDCs	0.34
Arab region	0.30
South Asia	0.30
Europe and Central Asia	0.41
Latin America and the Caribbean	0.48
East Asia and the Pacific	0.65
Sub-Saharan Africa	0.65
World	0.49

Source: UNDP, "Table 5: Gender-related development index", Human Development Reports database. Available from http://hdr.undp.org/en/content/table-5-gender-related-development-index-gdi (accessed 30 August 2015).
Note: Subregional averages are simple averages of the values of respective countries.

Figure 3.35. Male and female unemployment rates, 1991 and 2013

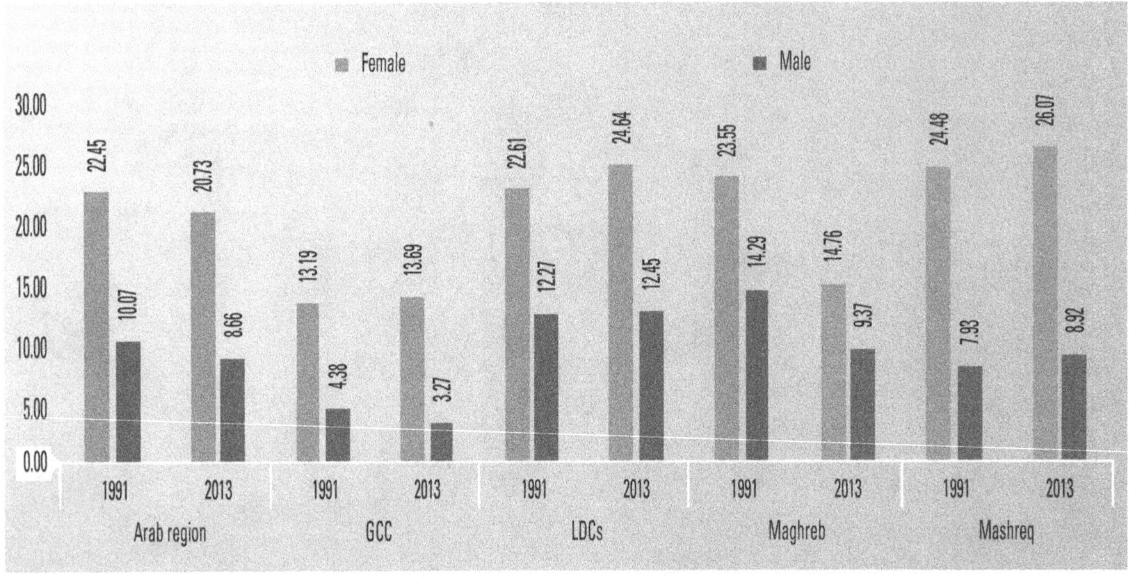

Source: ILO, Global Employment Trends 2014: supporting data sets. Available from www.ilo.org/global/research/global-reports/global-employment-trends/2014/WCMS_234879/lang--en/index.htm (accessed 30 August 2015).
Note: Data for LDCs are preliminary estimates.

of gross national income (GNI) per capita for the region stood at 0.3, the lowest in the world (figure 3.34). There are considerable variations across subregions and countries, with the ratio standing at 0.67 in Bahrain, and not exceeding 0.2 in Algeria, Iraq, Jordan or Palestine.

Figure 3.36. Statutory duration of maternity leave, 2013 (percentage)

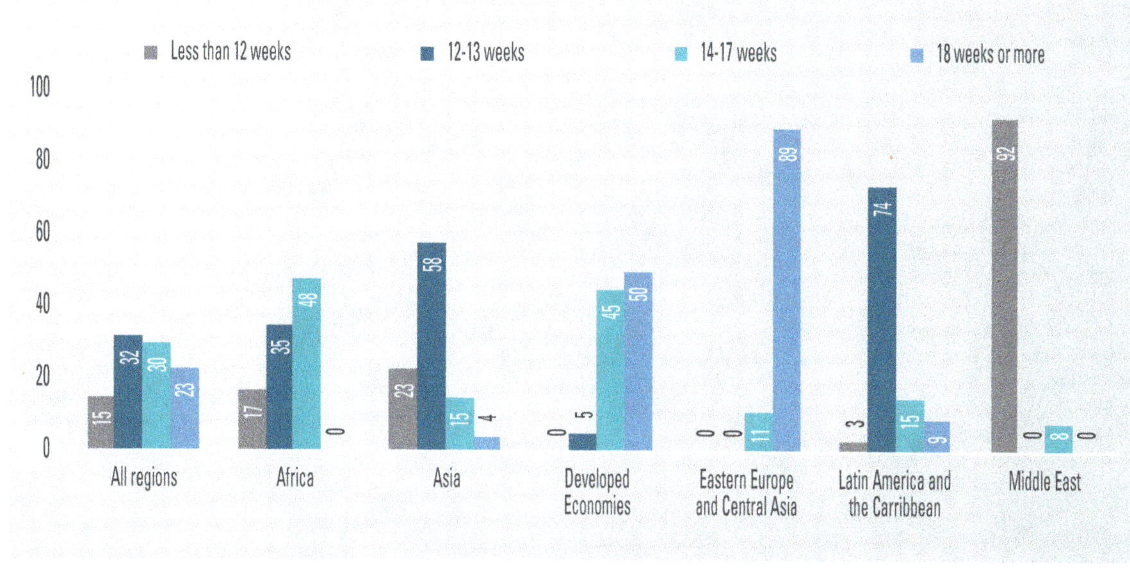

Source: ILO, Working Conditions Laws database. Available from www.ilo.org/travdatabase (accessed 30 August 2015).
Note: Percentages of countries within a region may not add up to 100 per cent due to rounding.

Unemployment rates among women in the region are high (figure 3.35), especially in the case of young women, around 48 per cent of whom could not find work in 2013. That was more than three times the global average of 15.7 per cent.[29]

Continued high gender gaps in employment are generally attributed to traditional (sometimes perceived as religious) roles of women and gender-biased economic policies. In addition to the scarcity of social services (such as affordable child and elderly care programmes and culturally appropriate transportation), maternity leave policies make it difficult for women to remain in the workforce. Of 12 Arab States examined in one study, only the Syrian Arab Republic, with 17 weeks of leave, meets the 14-week minimum established under the Maternity Protection Convention, 2000 (No. 183) of the International Labour Organization (ILO).[30] The remainder all provide fewer than 12 weeks, and the regional average of 9.2 weeks is the world's lowest (figure 3.36). Morocco is the only Arab State to have ratified the Convention. Whereas in most regions maternity leave is paid through social security, in the Middle East it is mainly employers who pay, which makes female workers less attractive to them.

Whatever their cause, the continued gender gaps are particularly striking considering that women in the Arab region are relatively well educated, compared to men and in absolute terms (figure 3.37). Indeed, more women than men receive tertiary education in the Maghreb and GCC countries.

(c) Gender violence

Gender violence and abuse take many forms, data are not always available for all countries and some cases go unreported. Conflict and displacement exacerbate the incidence of gender violence.[31] We highlight the issues of female genital mutilation and beating in what follows.

Female genital mutilation/cutting remains widespread in Djibouti, Egypt, Somalia and the Sudan (figure 3.38). Domestic violence is also widespread in the region (figure

Figure 3.37. Female-to-male ratio of enrolment in tertiary education

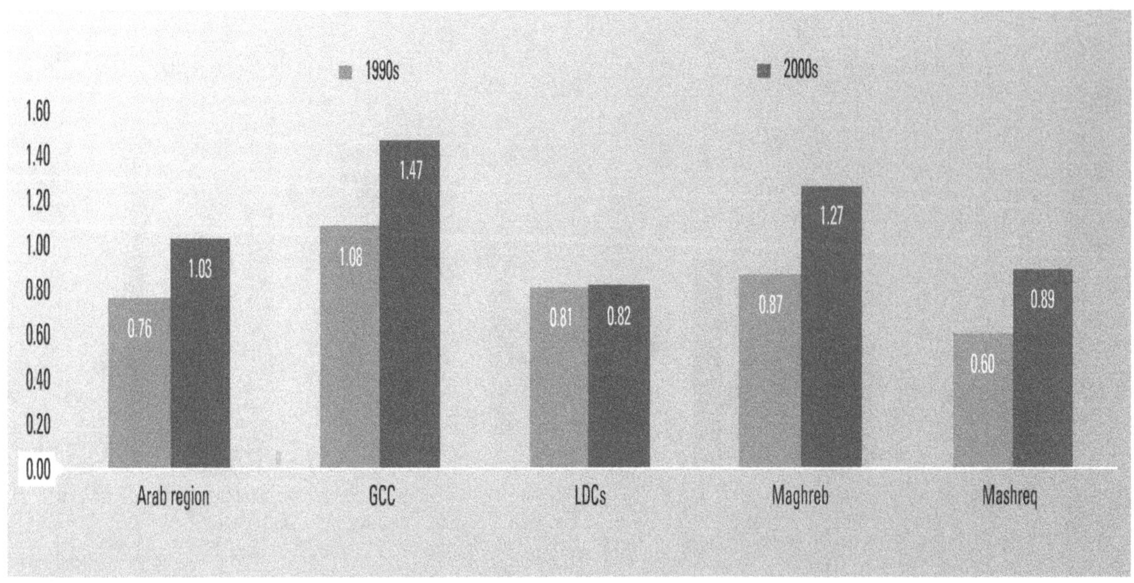

Sources: Authors' calculations based on the United Nations, Millennium Development Goals Indicators database, available from http://mdgs.un.org/unsd/mdg/Data.aspx (accessed 30 August 2015); and United Nations Educational, Scientific and Cultural Organization (UNESCO), UNESCO Institute for Statistics (UIS) database, available from http://data.uis.unesco.org/Index.aspx?DataSetCode=EDULIT_DS# (accessed 30 August 2015).
Note: Data are missing for Somalia and the United Arab Emirates.

Figure 3.38. Prevalence of female genital mutilation/cutting (percentage)

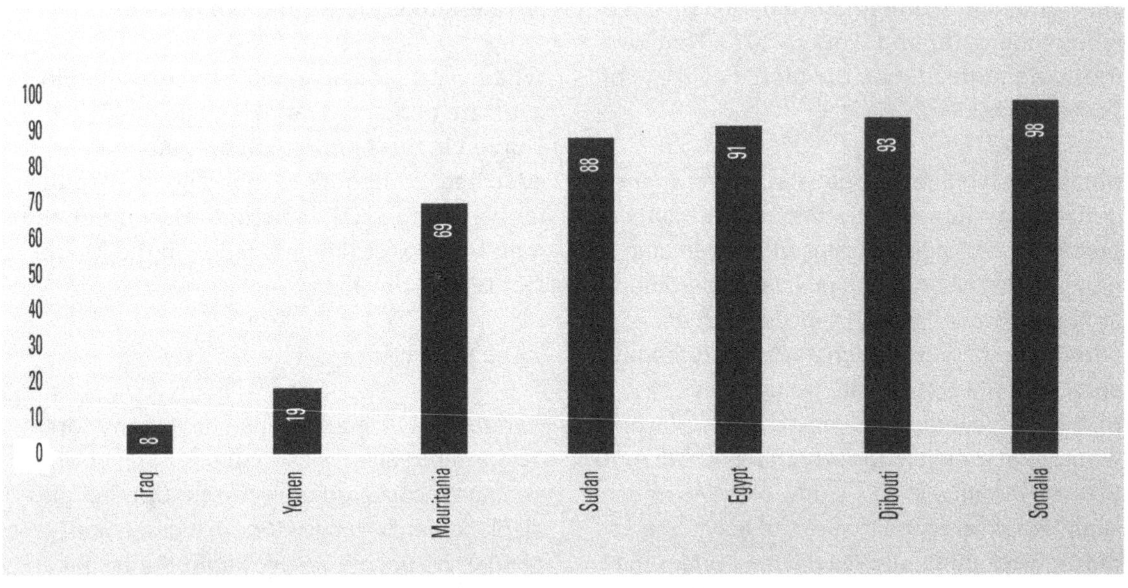

Sources: Based on data from USAID, Demographic and Health Surveys database, available from http://dhsprogram.com (accessed 30 August 2015); United Nations Children's Fund (UNICEF), Multiple Indicator Cluster Survey database, available from http://mics.unicef.org (accessed 30 August 2015); and national sources.

3.39). Many girls and women consider that a husband is justified in beating his wife. The rate is as high as 76 per cent in Somalia and 70 per cent in Jordan, compared to 32 per cent worldwide and 52 per cent in the LDCs.

Figure 3.39. Percentage of women (15–49 years old) who consider it legitimate for a husband to beat his wife

Lebanon	Tunisia	Mauritania	Comoros	Egypt	Sudan	Iraq	Morocco	Algeria	Jordan	Somalia
10	30	38	39	39	47	51	64	68	70	76

Source: Based on data from USAID, Demographic and Health Surveys database; UNICEF, Multiple Indicator Cluster Survey database; and national sources (see figure 3.38).

Figure 3.40. Adult literacy rates

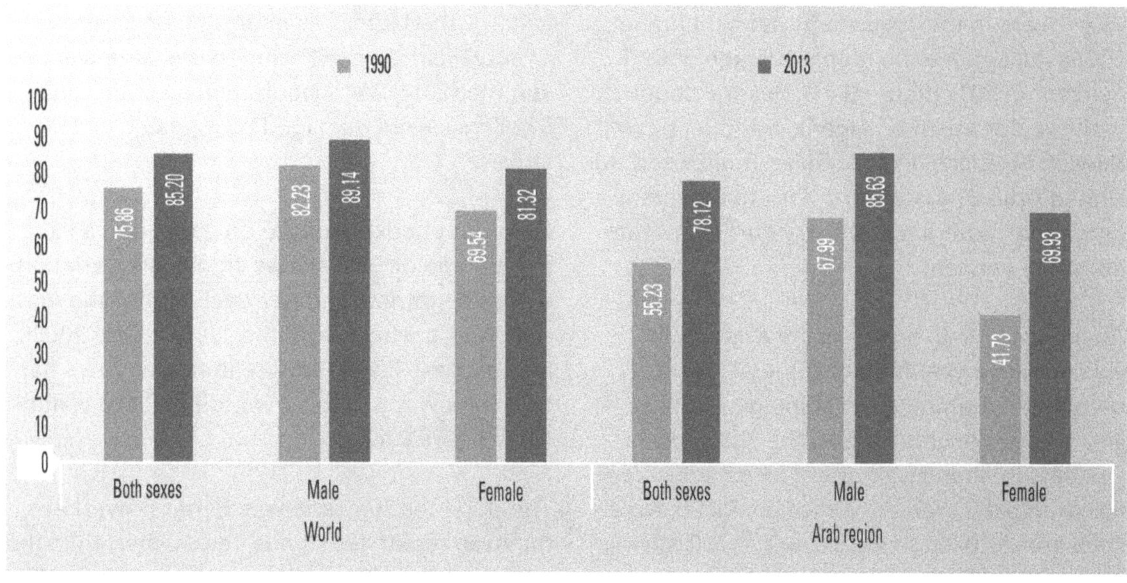

Source: UNESCO, UIS database (see figure 3.37).

5. Education

Adult literacy rates in the Arab region increased from 55 per cent in 1990 to 78 per cent in 2013, remaining below the global average of 85 per cent (figure 3.40). Female literacy improved dramatically by 67 per cent over the past two decades, reaching an average of nearly 70 per cent in 2013, still below the global average of 81 per cent.[32]

Figure 3.41. Net enrolment in primary education (percentage)

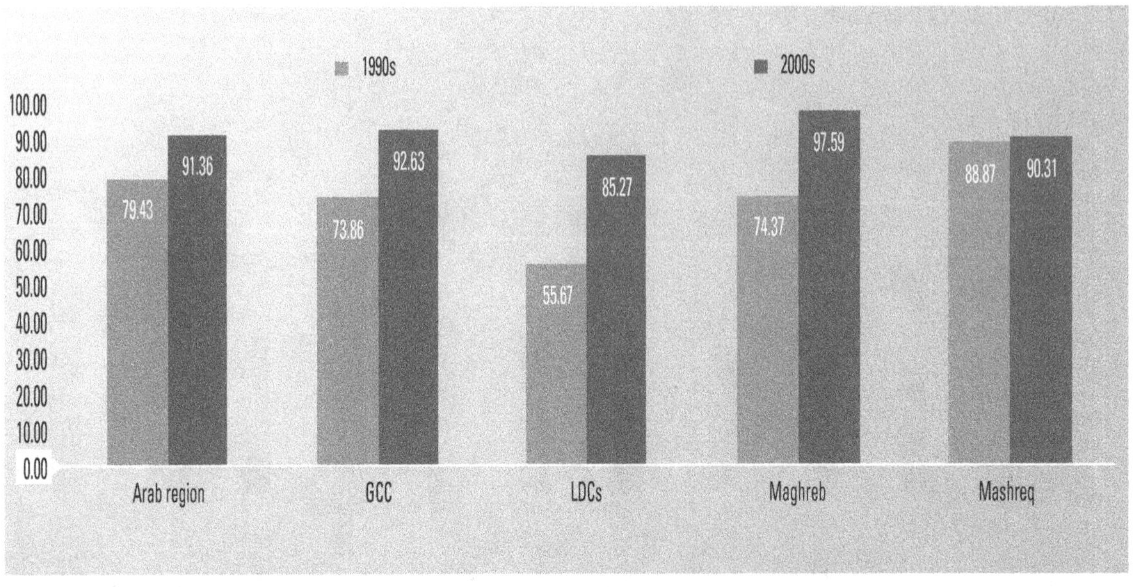

Source: Authors' calculations based on data from UNESCO, UIS database.
Notes: Values are weighted against population of the official age for primary education (both sexes). Data are missing for Libya, Saudi Arabia, Somalia and the Sudan. 2000 Bahrain data are actually from 1999 (latest available).

Primary school net enrolment rates rose from 79 per cent in the 1990s to 91 per cent in the 2000s, just above the global average of 89.1 per cent in 2011 (figure 3.41). Several countries in the region, such as Algeria, Bahrain, Egypt, Kuwait, Morocco, Oman, Qatar, Tunisia and the United Arab Emirates, are close to universal enrolment, with a net primary enrolment rate above 95 per cent.[33]

Attendance rates, however, are a cause for concern in several Arab countries. Conflict, occupation, bombings, checkpoints, curfews and school closures hamper the ability of students to attend school and focus on learning. For example, in Yemen, armed conflict between 2009 and 2010 led to the closure of 700 schools for five months.[34] In 2011, 73 Yemeni students who participated in protests for political change lost their lives, and 139 students were injured. Education in Iraq, a regional leader in education before the early 1990s, has been devastated by factors such as school closures and the loss of teachers. Palestinian schools and universities are consistently targeted by air strikes, attacked by Israeli settlers and, in some cases, used by Israeli armed forces as interrogation centres or surveillance posts.[35] During the Gaza war in summer 2014, 244 schools, 6 universities and 5 colleges were damaged by repeated Israeli strikes.[36]

Government expenditure on education as a percentage of GDP shows significant variation across countries, and has declined for the Arab region as a whole from the 1990s to the 2000s. In most cases, expenditure in recent years has been below the global average of 5 per cent of GDP (figure 3.42).

The pupil-teacher ratio was better (lower) in the Arab region (20 pupils per teacher) than the world average (24 pupils per teacher) in 2013[37] and has improved in most countries over the past decades, with the exceptions of Morocco and Yemen (figure 3.43).

Although the Arab region generally performs well in terms of quantity of education, there are major concerns about quality. Arab

Figure 3.42. Government expenditure on education (percentage of GDP)

	1990s	2000s
Arab region	5.45	4.49
GCC	6.13	4.46
LDCs	4.52	3.12
Maghreb	-	-
Mashreq	3.62	3.79

Source: Authors' calculations based on data from World Bank, World Development Indicators.
Notes: Figures are weighted against GDP in constant 2005 United States dollars. 1990s data are from the early 2000s for some countries. Data are missing for Iraq, Jordan, Palestine, Somalia and the United Arab Emirates. Data for the Maghreb subregion are insufficient to establish a trend.

Figure 3.43. Pupil-teacher ratio

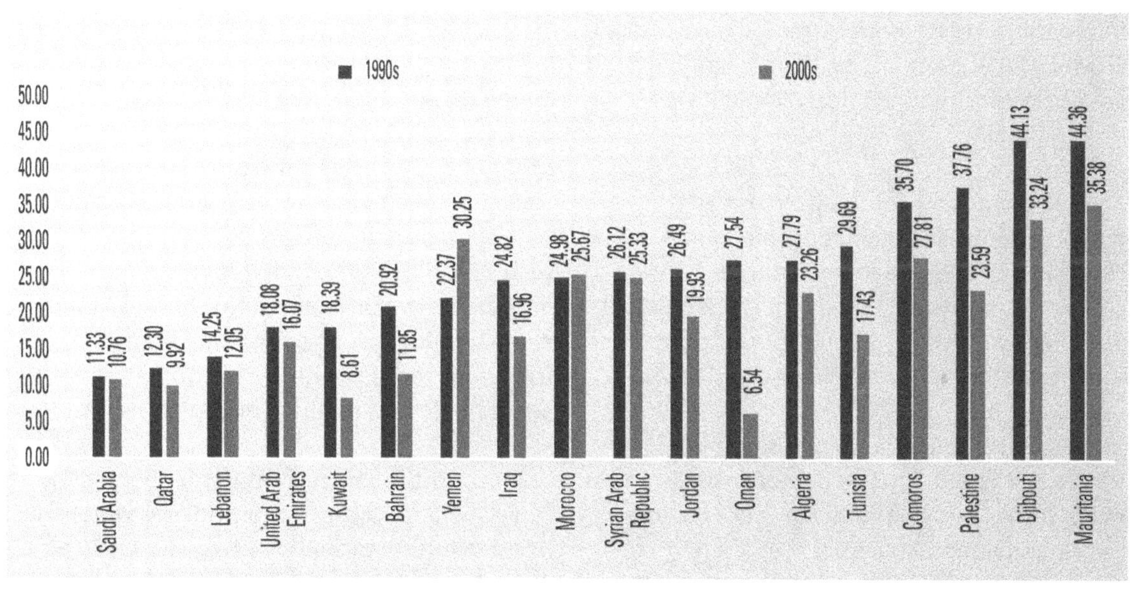

Source: World Bank, World Development Indicators.
Notes: Somalia and the Sudan have only one data point and Libya has none, so they could not be featured in this figure. 1990s data for Saudi Arabia are from the early 2000s.

countries fall far below international averages and benchmarks. Algeria, Egypt, Libya and Yemen have been ranked in one study in the bottom decile in that respect, with Yemen second last and Algeria and Libya ranked at 131 and 132.[38] According to the Trends in

Figure 3.44. Percentage of primary and secondary students not meeting basic numeracy standards

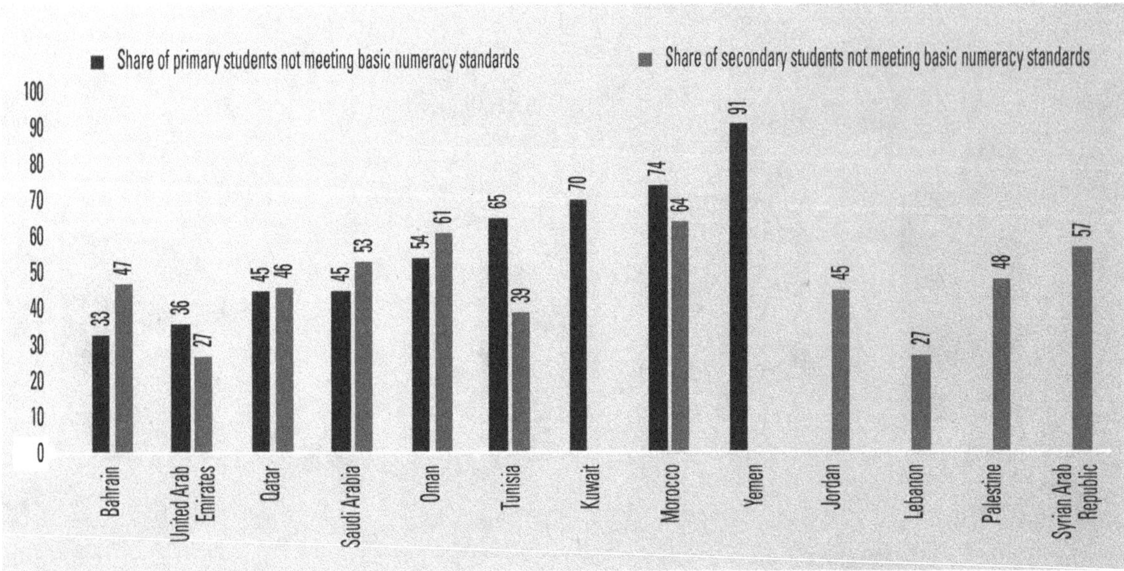

Source: Liesbet Steer and others, *Arab Youth: Missing Educational Foundations for a Productive Life?* (Washington, D.C., Center for Universal Education at Brookings, February 2014). Available from www.brookings.edu/~/media/research/files/interactives/2014/arab-world-learning-barometer/arabworld_learningbarometer_en.pdf.

International Mathematics and Science Study (TIMSS) 2011, none of the 14 participating Arab countries reached the international level (figure 3.44).

The problem is still more acute in rural areas, especially in secondary education. A recent study showed that in 6 out of 11 Arab countries, the proportion of young people not learning was at least 10 percentage points higher in rural than in urban areas.[39]

Poor quality education means that many young Arabs are unprepared for work. A recent study found that two thirds of them believed that their education did not prepare them for the job market.[40] The lack of information or assistance provided to students on the nature and availability of jobs, and how to find them, exacerbates youth unemployment. Teaching methods and textbooks in the region often fail to foster critical thinking and rely heavily on "highly didactic, teacher-directed" learning at all levels of education.[41]

B. Access to basic necessities

1. Water and sanitation

Most Arab States suffer from extreme freshwater scarcity, which is exacerbated by population growth and urbanization. Access issues at the individual level are addressed in this section. The broader sustainability issues are examined in the following chapter within the context of sustainable and resilient societies.

The proportion of the population across the region with access to safe drinking water improved only marginally between 1990 and 2014 (figure 3.45), rising from 82 per cent to 84 per cent, still below the global average of 91 per cent (as of 2015).[42] Although progress was made in most of the region, access to safe drinking water did not keep pace with population growth in the LDCs. Moreover, this indicator fails to tell the complete story: many of those with access to improved water

Figure 3.45. Percentage of the population with access to an improved water source

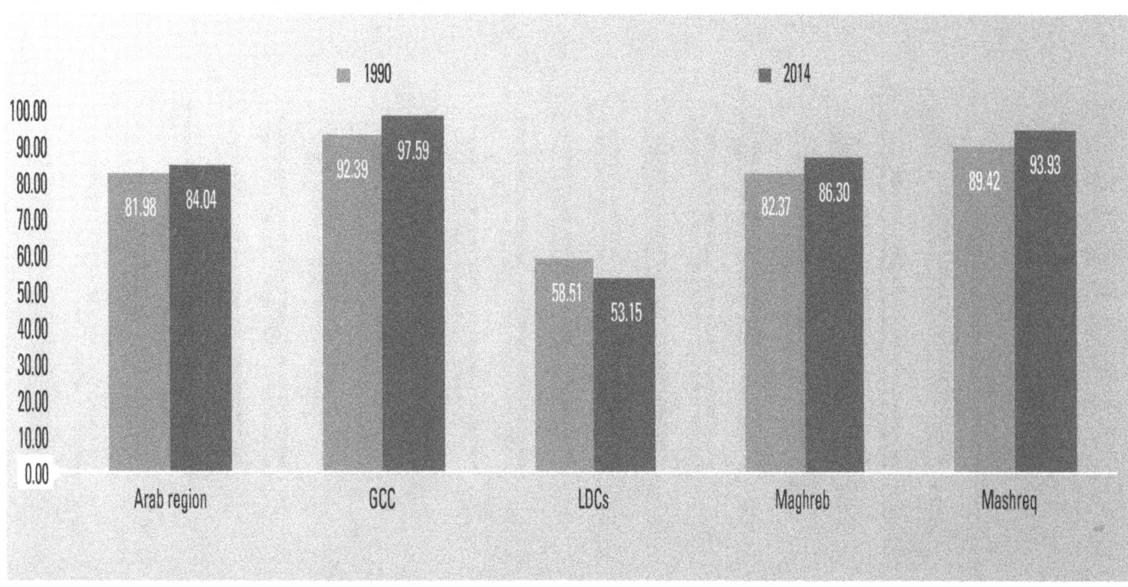

Source: Authors' calculations based on World Health Organization (WHO) and UNICEF, *Progress on Sanitation and Drinking Water: 2015 Update and MDG Assessment* (Geneva, 2015). Available from www.wssinfo.org/fileadmin/user_upload/resources/JMP-Update-report-2015_English.pdf.
Notes: Values are weighted against total population. 1990 data are from 1994 for Lebanon, 1992 for Qatar and 1993 for Somalia. 2014 data are from 2001 for Libya, 2011 for Somalia and 2012 for Yemen.

Figure 3.46. Percentage of the rural population with access to an improved water source

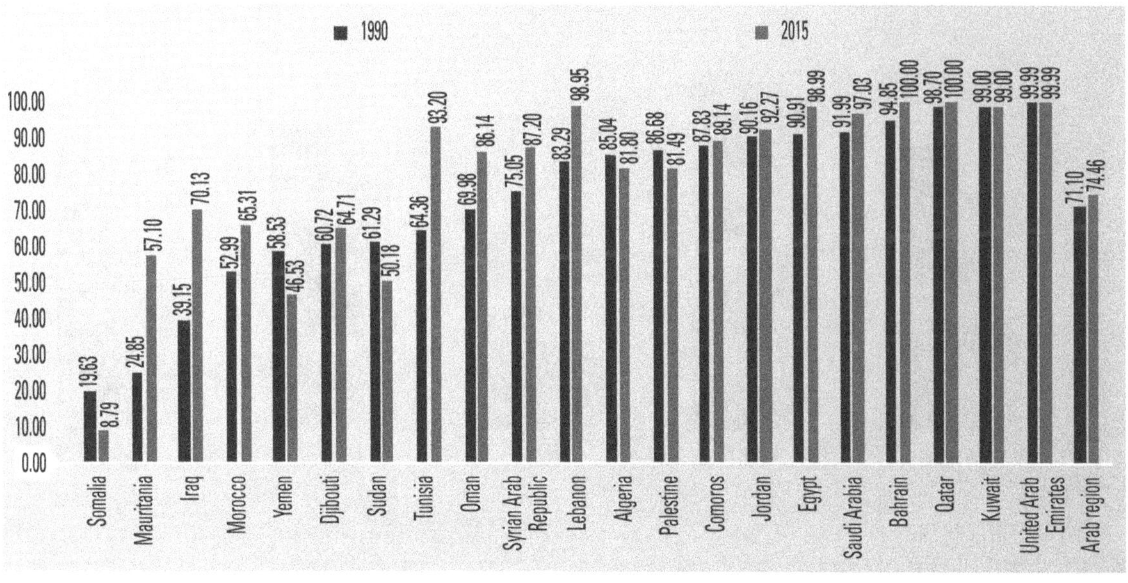

Source: Authors' calculations based on WHO and UNICEF, *Progress on Sanitation and Drinking Water.*
Notes: Average for the Arab region is weighted against total rural population. 1990 data for Lebanon are from 1994, for Palestine from 1991, for Qatar from 1992, and for Somalia from 1993. 2015 data for Libya are from 2001, for Somalia from 2011, for the Sudan from 2014 and for Yemen from 2012.

sources receive the service only intermittently and the water received may not be suitable for drinking.

The percentage of the rural population of the Arab region with access to improved water sources, above the world average

Figure 3.47. Percentage of the urban population with access to an improved water source

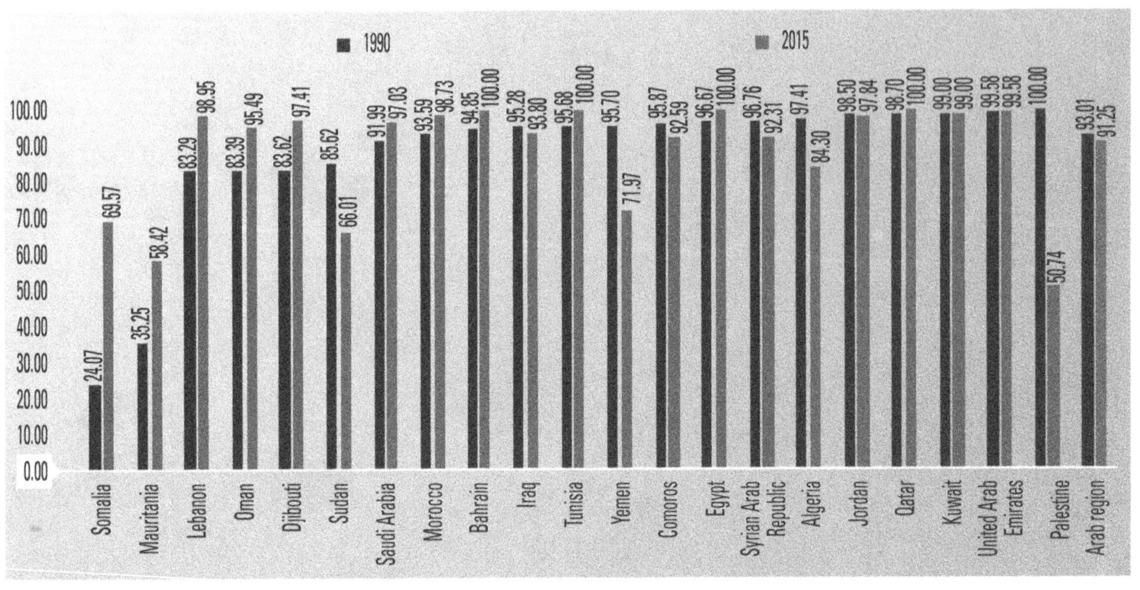

Source: Authors' calculations based on WHO and UNICEF, *Progress on Sanitation and Drinking Water.*
Notes: The Arab region average is weighted against total urban population. 1990 data for Lebanon are from 1994, for Qatar from 1992, and for Somalia from 1993. 2015 data for Libya are from 2001, for Somalia from 2011, for the Sudan from 2014, and for Yemen from 2012.

Figure 3.48. Percentage of the population with access to improved sanitation facilities

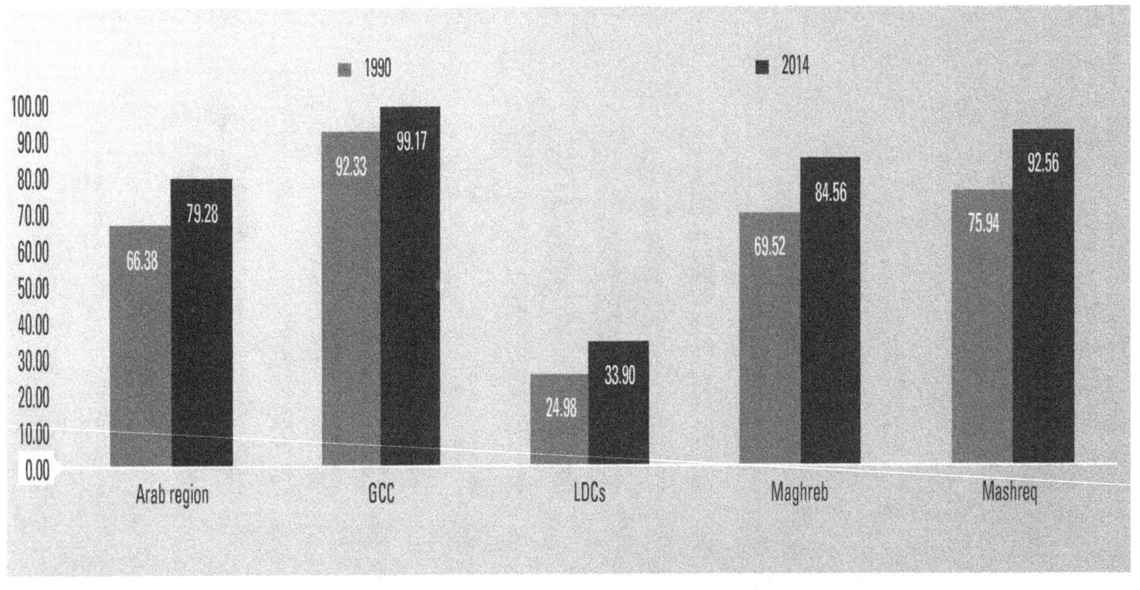

Source: Authors' calculations based on WHO and UNICEF, *Progress on Sanitation and Drinking Water.*
Notes: Values are weighted against total population. 1990 data are from 1991 for Iraq and Palestine, from 1998 for Lebanon, and from 1993 for Somalia. 2014 data for Somalia are from 2011, and for Yemen from 2012.

in 1990, is now lower.[43] The percentage of the rural population with access to improved water sources fell in 5 of the 22 Arab countries, namely Algeria, Palestine, Somalia, the Sudan and Yemen (figure 3.46). The percentage of the urban population with access to improved water sources is higher than in rural areas, but it slipped slightly

Figure 3.49. Percentage of the rural and urban populations with access to sanitation, 2015

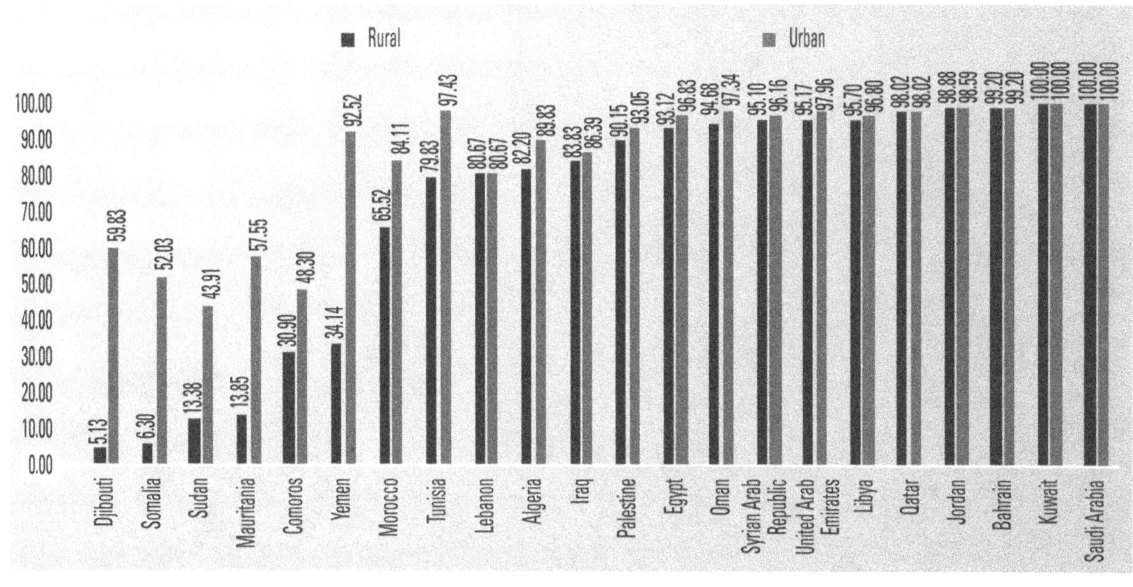

Source: WHO and UNICEF, *Progress on Sanitation and Drinking Water.*
Note: Data for Somalia are from 2011, for the Sudan from 2014 and for Yemen from 2012 (both urban and rural).

between 1990 and 2015 and is below the world average.[44] The percentage of the urban population with access to an improved water source fell in 8 of the 22 Arab countries: namely Algeria, the Comoros, Iraq, Jordan, Palestine, the Sudan, the Syrian Arab Republic and Yemen (figure 3.47).

Access to water is complicated by conflict and occupation. Palestine is practically deprived of its water resources. After the 1967 war, Israel declared that all West Bank water resources belonged to it and placed them under the control of the army. Israel illegally exploits almost 85 per cent of West Bank water resources and continues to prevent the Arab population from drilling wells.[45] In Gaza, more than 96 per cent of water resources did not meet WHO health standards regarding nitrate concentrations in 2013 and 2014.[46]

Between 1990 and 2014, access to improved sanitation facilities rose across the Arab region, reaching 79 per cent of the population (figure 3.48), well above the global average of 68 per cent (as of 2015).[47] However, nearly 66 million people in the Arab region do not have such access.[48]

The disparity between urban and rural areas is greater for access to improved sanitation facilities than in the case of access to an improved water source. The greatest disparities can be observed in the LDCs, Morocco and Tunisia (figure 3.49).

2. Electricity

Access to electricity is comprehensive across the GCC, Mashreq and Maghreb subregions; more than 97 per cent of the population had access to electricity in 2012 (figure 3.50). The LDC average of only 38 per cent brings the Arab regional average to around 86 per cent. The Arab region average compares favourably with the global average of 84.6 per cent in 2012.[49] There are still pockets of inadequate access in rural areas. In the Sudan, for instance, the access rate to electricity in rural areas was 18 per cent in 2012, compared with 62 per cent in urban areas.[50] Intermittent access is a problem

Figure 3.50. Percentage of population with access to electricity

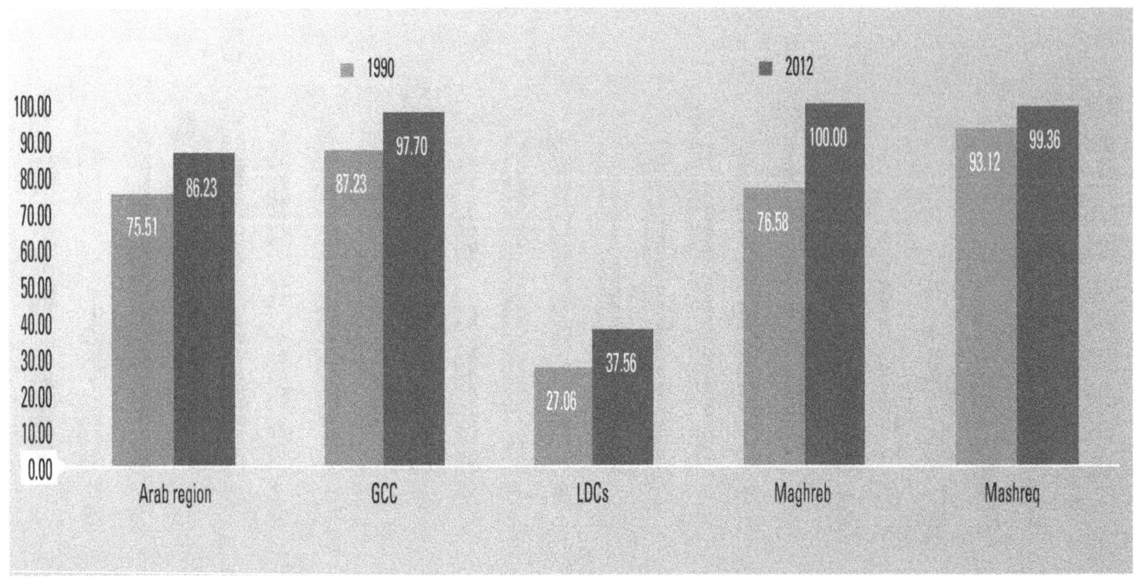

Source: Authors' calculations based on World Bank, World Development Indicators.
Note: Values are weighted against total population.

masked by high access figures (for example in Lebanon).[51]

3. Food

Food security encompasses issues of availability, accessibility and utilization that can be measured in many ways. In this section, only indicators of hunger and malnutrition are analysed. Other aspects of food security are addressed in chapter 4.

Hunger and malnutrition in Arab countries arise from problems relating to the affordability of food. In the past 20 years, there has been a major increase in food availability in the region, primarily due to imports. Based on the daily energy supply and the energy supply adequacy measures, the region is well above the developing country and global averages. The Arab region's daily energy supply was 3,045 kilocalories per capita per day in 2010, well-above the 2,720 kilocalories per capita per day for developing countries and 2,840 kilocalories per capita per day globally. These regional averages, however, are not representative of the reality in some countries and mask high disparities between subregions.

Fourteen Arab countries (Algeria, Bahrain, Egypt, Jordan, Kuwait, Lebanon, Libya, Mauritania, Morocco, Oman, Qatar, Saudi Arabia, Tunisia and the United Arab Emirates) achieved the MDG hunger target of halving the prevalence of hunger (proportion of hungry people in the total population) by 2015. Kuwait and Oman also achieved the more stringent World Food Summit target of halving the absolute number of hungry people.[52] However, the region as a whole has witnessed a significant setback in the fight against hunger due to conflicts, protracted crises and the rising number of refugees (box 3.2). It is the only region that has seen both an increase in the prevalence of hunger and a doubling in the number of hungry people since the early 1990s.

Stunting among children under the age of 5 stands at 22.4 per cent, of medium severity by WHO standards,[53] and below the global

Box 3.2. Poverty and vulnerability among Syrian refugees living outside camps in Jordan

Two out of three Syrian refugees living outside camps in Jordan live below the absolute national poverty line of $96/person/month. This is the chief finding of a survey conducted by the Office of the United Nations High Commissioner for Refugees (UNHCR) between January and June 2014 of nearly 42,000 registered Syrian refugee households. Households headed by women, representing around one third of the sample, are worse off still. With outgoings equivalent to 1.6 times their income, families attempt to cope in ways that increase their vulnerability by the day and affect children the most. Around half of the surveyed households live in unsanitary make-shift housing and reported cutting their food intake, and 43 per cent skimped on food quality. Around half the children in the surveyed families were taken out of school.

Source: Frances Voon and others, *Living in the Shadows: Jordan Home Visits Report 2014* (UNHCR, 2014).

Figure 3.51. Underweight children (percentage of children aged under 5)

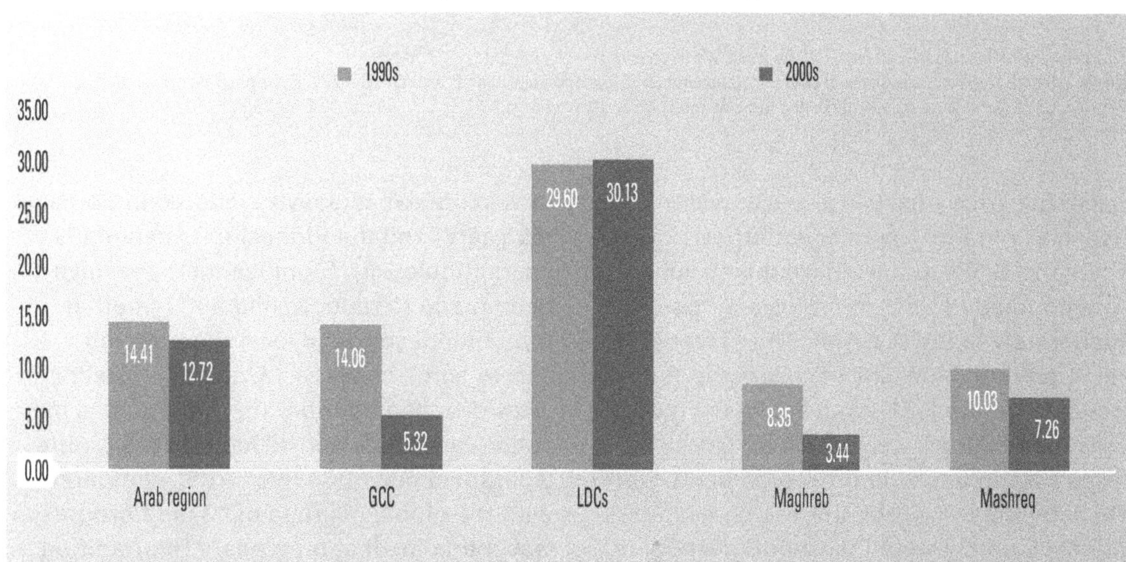

Source: Authors' calculations based on World Bank, World Development Indicators.
Notes: Values are weighted against total under-5 population (both sexes). 1990s data for Somalia are from 2000. Data are missing for Bahrain, Qatar and the United Arab Emirates.

average of 24.5 in 2013.[54] Variations exist between subregions, with the Mashreq registering 20.4 per cent, the Maghreb 15 per cent, GCC countries 8 per cent and the LDCs a very high 43.4 per cent.

Since the 1990s, the percentage of underweight children in the region has decreased to reach 13 per cent, with significant improvements in the GCC, Maghreb and Mashreq subregions (figure 3.51). The regional average is held back by the growing percentage (around 30 per cent) of underweight children in the LDCs, double the global average of 14.3 per cent in 2014.[55] This is accompanied by the persistence of micronutrient deficiencies in vitamins and minerals, with one third of the population being anaemic.

Figure 3.52. Child obesity (percentage of children aged under 5)

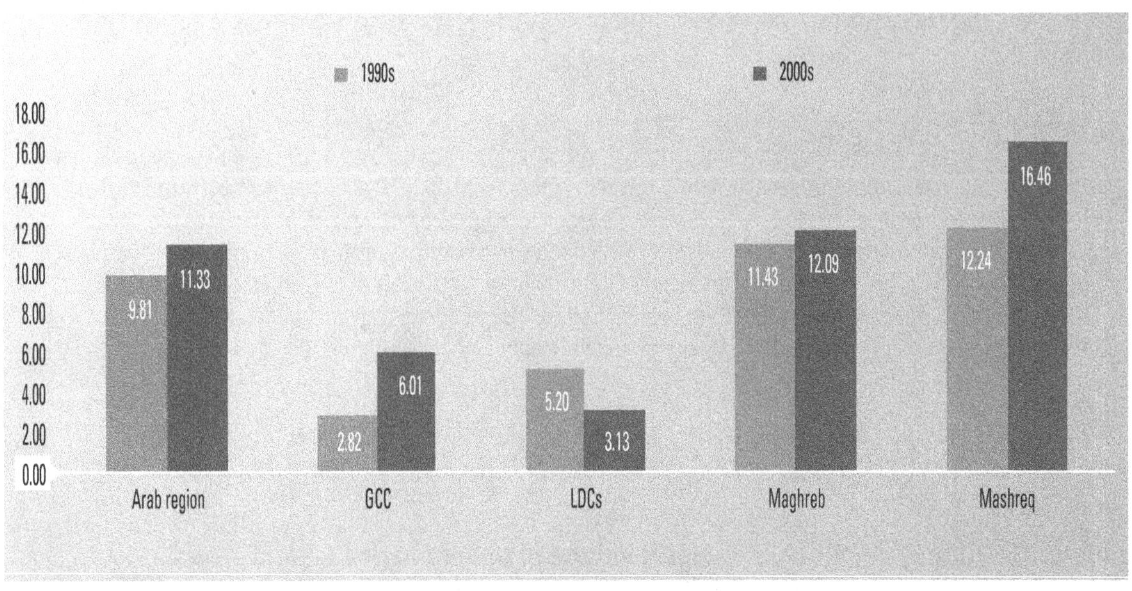

Source: Authors' calculations based on World Bank, World Development Indicators.
Notes: Weighted based on estimates of child population from DESA, World Population Prospects: The 2015 Revision. Data are missing for Bahrain, Libya, Qatar, Somalia and the United Arab Emirates. 1990s data are from 2002 for Djibouti and 2000 for Iraq.

Excessive food intake is also a concern, especially in the wealthier countries. From the 1990s to the 2000s, the obesity rate doubled in GCC countries and rose moderately in the Mashreq. The average regional rate of obesity in children is 11.3 per cent (figure 3.52), well above the global average of 6.1 per cent in 2014.[56] Obesity rates among adults in the region are more than double the world rate, standing at 23.6 per cent, compared to the world average of 11.7 per cent. Variations among countries are large, with women consistently experiencing higher levels of obesity than men. Obesity rates for women are over 50 per cent in Egypt, Jordan, Kuwait and the United Arab Emirates.[57]

4. Health

Life expectancy at birth in the Arab region has increased significantly from 65 years in 1990 to 70 years in 2013, close to the global average of 71 years.[58] However, there are wide variations between countries, with the lowest life expectancy registered in Somalia (55 years) and the highest in Lebanon (79 years) (table 3.1). Significant strides have been made to reduce child and maternal mortality despite the turmoil sweeping across some countries. Under-5 mortality rates dropped by more than half across the Arab region between 1990 and 2015 (figure 3.53) to 36 per 1,000 live births, compared with the global average of 43, and progress was made in all subregions.[59] The tradition of strong family and social support in the region is believed to have contributed to this success.[60]

The disease profile of the region is now similar to that of the United States and countries in Western Europe. Since the 1990s, premature death and disability caused by communicable diseases (except HIV/AIDS), nutritional deficiencies and complications related to childbirth and early childhood has declined dramatically.[61] Non-communicable diseases now represent the major health challenge for the region.[62] Since 1990, heart

Table 3.1. Life expectancy at birth

Country	Both sexes		Male		Female	
	1990-1995	2010-2015	1990-1995	2010-2015	1990-1995	2010-2015
Algeria	67.21	74.42	65.63	72.14	68.83	76.84
Bahrain	72.87	76.37	71.98	75.58	74.06	77.42
Comoros	57.82	62.83	56.27	61.20	59.40	64.50
Djibouti	57.02	61.62	55.42	60.04	58.67	63.24
Egypt	65.45	70.84	63.08	68.71	67.87	73.05
Iraq	67.39	69.19	64.34	66.99	70.64	71.44
Jordan	70.43	73.79	69.09	72.21	71.91	75.52
Kuwait	72.44	74.27	71.68	73.34	73.57	75.56
Lebanon	71.05	78.85	69.62	77.14	72.54	80.87
Libya	69.35	71.45	67.81	68.79	71.17	74.41
Mauritania	58.89	62.78	57.50	61.29	60.23	64.25
Morocco	65.98	73.61	64.26	72.60	67.66	74.62
Oman	68.52	76.41	66.74	74.66	70.65	78.85
Palestine	68.85	72.65	67.33	70.74	70.39	74.66
Qatar	75.25	77.94	74.48	77.10	76.59	79.68
Saudi Arabia	69.97	74.09	68.31	72.82	72.09	75.47
Somalia	44.99	54.88	43.49	53.28	46.53	56.51
Sudan	56.00	63.08	54.46	61.60	57.59	64.60
Syrian Arab Republic	70.77	69.54	69.51	63.98	72.11	76.26
Tunisia	70.30	74.60	68.12	72.30	72.71	77.04
United Arab Emirates	72.18	76.69	71.27	76.02	73.64	78.23
Yemen	58.61	63.51	57.05	62.18	60.02	64.88

Source: DESA, World Population Prospects: The 2015 Revision.

Figure 3.53. Under-5 mortality rate (per 1,000 live births)

	1990	2015
Arab region	77.96	35.60
GCC	39.69	12.62
LDCs	134.53	72.43
Maghreb	60.13	24.26
Mashreq	68.83	24.28

Source: Authors' calculations based on United Nations, Millennium Development Goals Indicators database (see figure 3.37).
Note: Values are weighted against estimates of total under-5 population (both sexes) from DESA, World Population Prospects: The 2015 Revision.

Figure 3.54. Contraceptive prevalence (percentage of women aged 15-49)

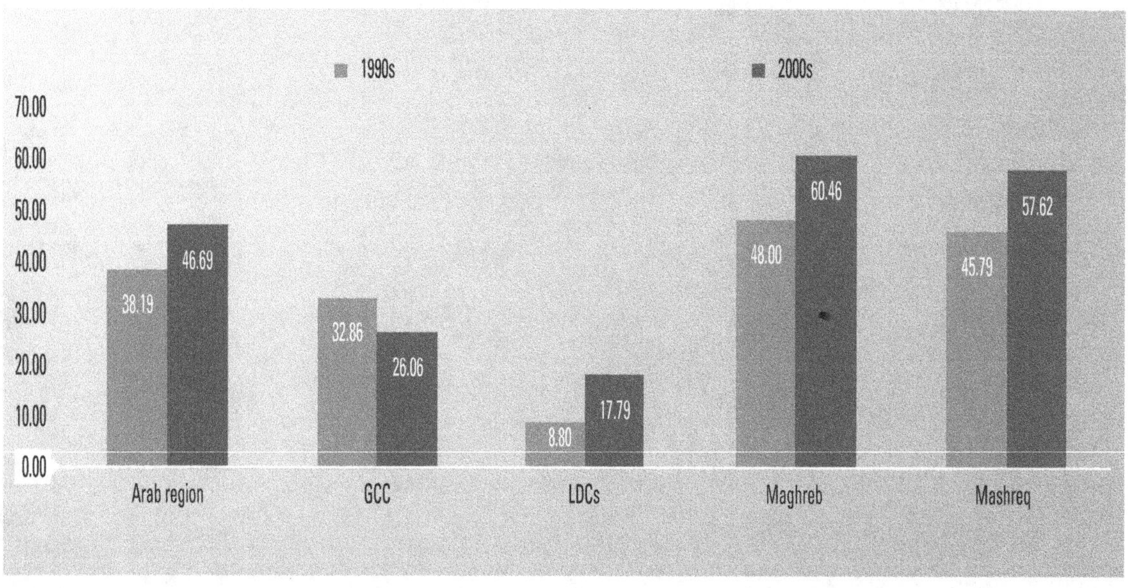

Source: Authors' calculations based on United Nations, Millennium Development Goals Indicators.
Notes: Values are weighted against estimates of the number of women aged 15-49 who are married, taken from DESA (see www.un.org/en/development/desa/population/theme/marriage-unions/marriage_estimates.shtml). 2000s data for Kuwait are from 1999. Data are missing for Bahrain, Qatar and the United Arab Emirates.

disease has overtaken lower-respiratory infections as a leading cause of premature death in Arab countries.[63] Smoking continues to be a major cause of morbidity and mortality. In terms of disability-adjusted life years, non-communicable diseases such as heart disease, musculoskeletal disorders, diabetes and cirrhosis have increased since

Figure 3.55. Slum prevalence, 2014 (percentage of urban population living in slums)

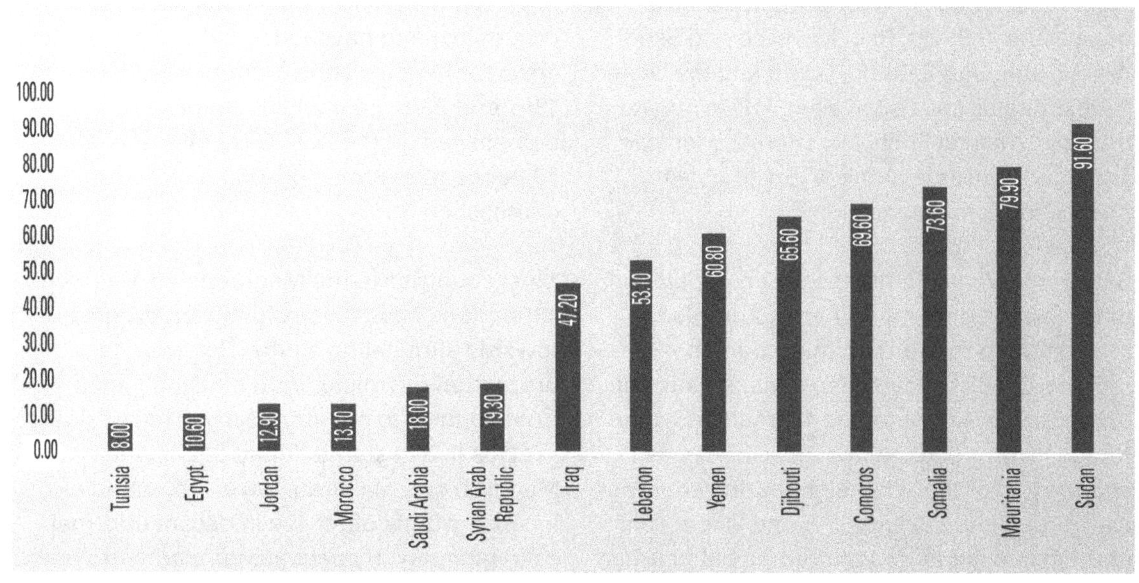

Source: Based on data from United Nations, Millennium Development Goals Indicators.
Note: Data for Lebanon and Saudi Arabia are from 2005.

1990. The incidence of HIV/AIDS has also risen substantially. Mental health problems are increasingly prevalent, especially among women and girls.[64]

In the Arab region, more than two thirds of births are attended by skilled health personnel, with an increase from 54 per cent in the 1990s to 69 per cent in 2010.[65] This compares favourably with the global average of 67.3 per cent in 2010.[66] However, the LDCs lag behind, with only around 34 per cent of births attended by skilled health personnel, below the 45 per cent average for sub-Saharan Africa. Pregnant women receiving prenatal care in the region averaged 81.1 per cent in 2009, slightly below the global average of 82.5 per cent.[67]

Contraceptive prevalence rates are increasing across all subregions except for the GCC countries, with nearly half of married women now using contraceptives (figure 3.54). The average rate across the Arab region is 46 per cent, well below the global average of 63.5 per cent.[68] Overall, contraceptive use rates are highest in the Maghreb (62 per cent) and lowest in the LDCs (15 per cent). Use of contraceptives declined by 22 per cent in GCC countries over the last two decades. Adolescent birth rates also declined from 54 to 42 per 1,000 women over the same period.[69]

The impact of conflict and instability on health is a growing source of concern in the Arab region. It is estimated that, for every person killed in conflict, three are left with a permanent disability. Although direct harm in terms of disability-adjusted life years is comparatively limited,[70] the impact of conflict on health extends well beyond direct harm. Conflict causes trauma, depression and anxiety and, in countries such as Iraq, prolonged warfare has even shortened life expectancy.[71] Conflict disrupts health services and makes medicines harder to obtain.

5. Housing

The housing shortfall has been estimated at more than 3.5 million homes across the Arab region, where land and construction costs are high. The shortage of affordable housing is most acute in Egypt, Iraq, Morocco and Saudi Arabia, although Bahrain, Oman and the United Arab Emirates are also affected.[72] The immature mortgage market limits opportunities for low- and middle-income homebuyers to obtain finance for home ownership.[73]

Between 1970 and 2010, the urban population of the Arab region more than quadrupled. In addition to rural-urban migration, the region's conflicts have been a major cause of urbanization. An estimated 4.1 million Syrian refugees have fled their country in the past few years, most of them to neighbouring countries like Jordan and Lebanon.[74] Some 80 per cent of them live not in refugee camps but in urban areas, increasing demand for housing and straining infrastructure and public services.[75] In Palestine, house demolitions are a regular occurrence and have led to a dramatic shelter crisis for families and communities. Between 1967 and 2010, over 24,800 homes were demolished. In the 2014 Gaza offensive alone, 13 per cent of homes (20,000 units) were demolished.[76]

Most countries in the Maghreb and Mashreq subregions have made significant progress towards eliminating slums. However, the proportion of substandard housing varies from country to country. Many urban residents in LDCs live in slums (figure 3.55). In the Maghreb and Mashreq, lower- and middle-income groups often live in decent informal settlements with adequate infrastructure but lacking land title.[77]

4. Sustainable and Resilient Societies

Marshlands of Mesopotamia (Al-Ahwar) in southern Iraq.

> "We are determined to protect the planet from degradation, including through sustainable consumption and production, sustainably managing its natural resources and taking urgent action on climate change, so that it can support the needs of the present and future generations."
>
> *Preamble of the 2030 Agenda for Sustainable Development*

4. Sustainable and Resilient Societies

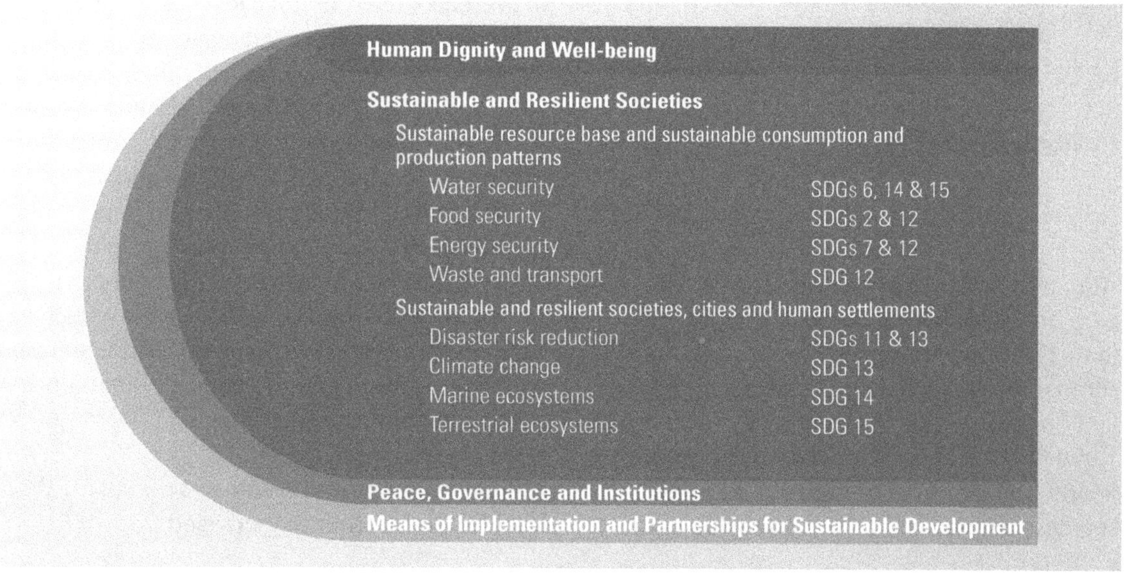

Laying the foundations for human dignity and well-being will require making societies sustainable and resilient. Sustainable societies will ensure that the natural resource base upon which human well-being depends is maintained in the long-term. That means providing an ongoing source of water, energy and food security; keeping the environment healthy and promoting sustainable consumption and production patterns. Resilient societies will address risks to their people, assets and infrastructure arising from natural disasters, pollution, natural resource depletion and climate change, and conserve marine and terrestrial ecosystems to achieve a healthy and productive environment.

Such goals pose a particular challenge in the Arab region, where water scarcity is a defining characteristic; food production is limited by numerous constraints; water and energy consumption are increasing at unsustainable rates; marine and terrestrial ecosystems are facing significant pressures; population is increasing, notably in urban areas, which now host more than half of the total population of the region; and dependence on desalination is high in several countries. Extreme weather events in the region, especially droughts, storms and floods, have become more frequent and intense in the past several decades, and have taken an increasing toll on people and infrastructure. The impact of climate change is already being felt, and the region is likely to experience rising temperatures and a growing variability in precipitation.

On the bright side, efforts have been made to preserve biodiversity in Arab countries, through the expansion of protected areas and measures to reduce emissions; several countries have prepared public statements of their Intended Nationally Determined Contributions. Nevertheless, the increase in per capita greenhouse gas emissions and of the economy's carbon intensity remain a worrying trend.

This chapter is largely based on issues briefs prepared for this report covering the topics of energy, water, food, climate change, industrialization, cities, disaster risk reduction, sustainable consumption and production, marine resources and terrestrial ecosystems.[1]

A. Sustainable resource base, consumption and production patterns

1. Water security

(a) Natural water scarcity and increased use

Arab countries account for more than 5 per cent of the world's population, but less than 1 per cent of its freshwater resources.[2] Almost three quarters of the Arab population live under the freshwater scarcity level of 1,000 cubic metres per capita per year, and nearly half live in conditions of extreme scarcity, with access to less than 500 cubic metres.[3] Rainfall is low and variable, evaporation rates are high and droughts are frequent. Countries in the region, classified as arid and semi-arid, cover 10 per cent of the world's surface area but receive only 2.1 per cent of its average annual precipitation.[4]

In Morocco, the drought cycle has accelerated from one year in every five-year period in the 1990s to one every two years, with droughts in 2012 and 2014. Extended drought in northeast Syria from 2006 to 2009 drove an estimated one million people out of their homes and farms to seek refuge in cities, and thereby reportedly contributed to the popular uprisings in that country.[5]The Horn of Africa is experiencing one of the worst droughts in decades, which in Somalia has caused widespread resource-based conflicts between communities, population migration and recurrent famine.

Annual withdrawal of water as a cumulative total for Arab countries increased from 166

Figure 4.1. Annual water withdrawals (cumulative, billion cubic metres per year)

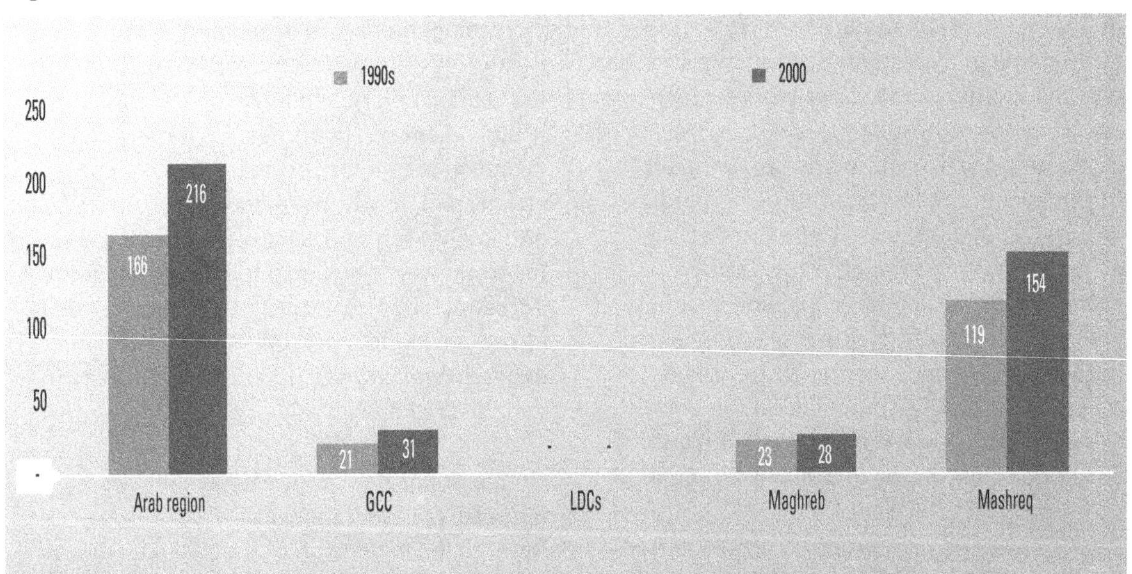

Source: Authors' calculations based on data from the Food and Agriculture Organization of the United Nations (FAO), AQUASTAT. Available from http://www.fao.org/nr/water/aquastat/main/index.stm (accessed 30 August 2015).

Notes: Data reflect the annual quantity of water withdrawn for agricultural, industrial and municipal purposes. Renewable freshwater resources and potential over-abstraction of renewable groundwater or withdrawal of fossil groundwater and potential use of desalinated water or treated wastewater are included. In-stream uses, which are characterized by a very low net consumption rate, are not included. Data for the LDC subregion are insufficient to establish a trend.

billion cubic metres per year in the 1990s to 216 billion cubic metres in the 2000s, an increase of 30 per cent (figure 4.1). The fastest rate of growth was observed in the GCC countries (around 50 per cent).

Although, as seen in the previous chapter, the demand for drinking water and sanitation in the region has grown significantly since 1990 and is likely to continue to do so, agriculture remains the biggest consumer of water. As figure 4.2 shows, agriculture accounts for 84 per cent of water use, compared to a world average of 70 per cent, and water is often used inefficiently.

Renewable (ground and surface) water is being withdrawn at an alarming rate,[6] averaging well over 1,000 per cent of available water, and increasing by nearly 13 per cent in the 2000s compared to the 1990s (figure 4.3). Reasons for this include: population growth; industrial diversification; poor maintenance of distribution networks, with high prevalence of leakage; and subsidized water pricing that does not reflect real cost (and therefore does not encourage efficiency). Using groundwater resources

Figure 4.2. Water use by sector (percentage of total water use)

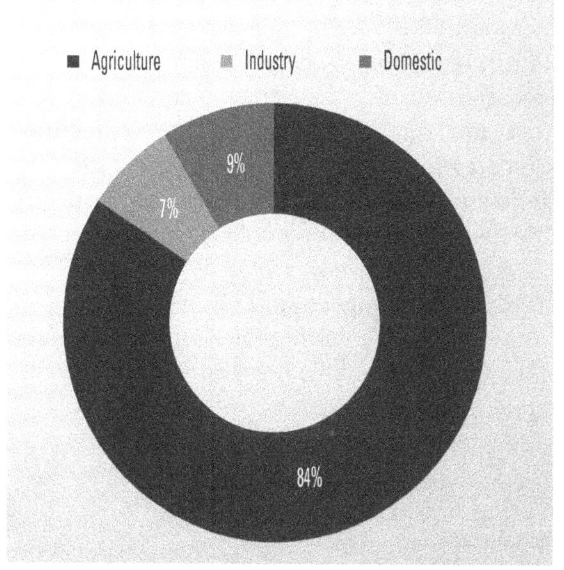

Source: Authors' calculations based on data from FAO, AQUASTAT (see figure 4.1).
Notes: All data points between 1998 and 2015 for each Arab country were used to provide a simple average for that country. The average for the region for each sector is calculated as the sum of the averages of water use by each country in that sector. The percentage of water consumed in each sector across the region is the cumulative sum of water use in the sector, divided by the total water use in the 22 countries of the Arab region.

Figure 4.3. Withdrawal of renewable water resources (percentage of available water)

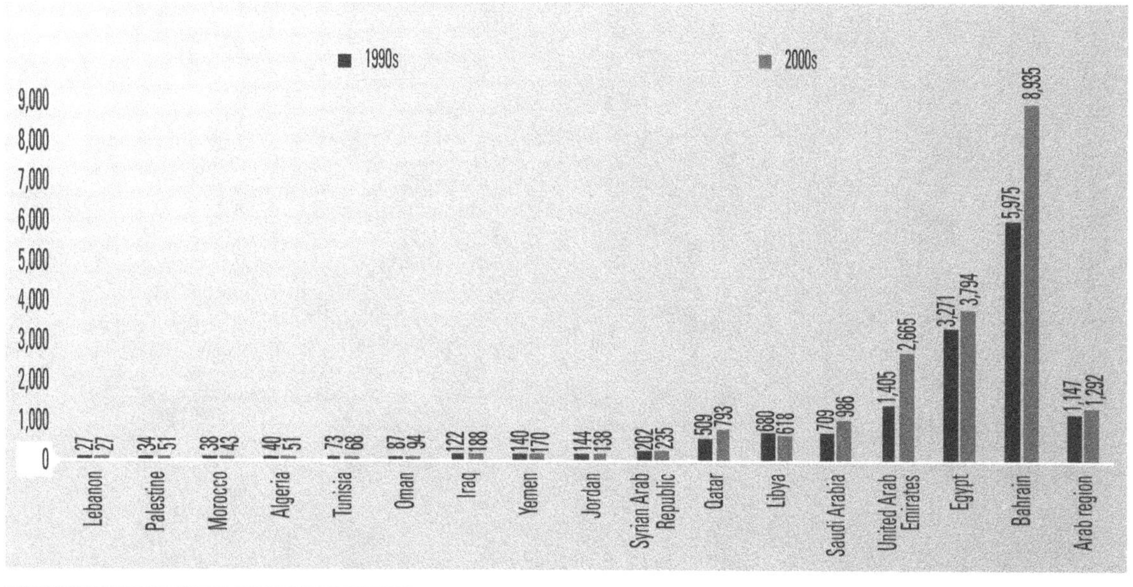

Sources: FAO, AQUASTAT and World Bank, World Development Indicators.
Note: The Arab region value is a weighted average against the represented countries' populations.

beyond their natural replenishment rates has resulted in rapid depletion of aquifer reserves in a number of countries and salinization and deterioration in water quality due to seawater intrusion.[7] Groundwater resources in most Arab countries are also threatened by pollution from agricultural, industrial and domestic activities. The growing shortages have increased the frequency of water supply interruptions, to the degree that intermittent supply patterns have become the norm in many countries.[8] The Arab Strategy for Water Security in the Arab Region to Meet the Challenges and Future Needs for Sustainable Development 2010-2030, and its associated action plan, are key policy documents adopted by the Arab Ministerial Water Council of the League of Arab States in 2011 and 2014 respectively.

Rapid population growth over the past decades has caused a dramatic 39 per cent reduction in per capita renewable water resources, from an average of 1,232 in 1992 to an alarming 751 in 2014, below the water scarcity line of 1,000 cubic metres per person per year (figure 4.4). The world average of 7,525 cubic metres per person per year in 2014 was 10 times more. By 2025, the figure is projected to fall below 500 cubic metres.[9]

In 2014, 18 of the 22 Arab countries fell below the water scarcity line of 1,000 cubic metres per person per year,[10] and 13 are among the world's 19 most water-scarce nations.[11] Per capita water availability in nine countries is already below 200 cubic metres, less than half the amount designated as absolute water scarcity.[12] Thus, around 40 per cent of the Arab population live in conditions of absolute water scarcity, having less than 500 cubic metres per person per year in 2014.[13]

The situation is exacerbated by the fact that more than half of total renewable water resources in the Arab region (about 174 billion cubic metres a year of a total of 315 billion cubic metres) originates from outside the region (water dependency ratio of 55 per cent),[14] with two thirds crossing at least one international border. Water security in the Arab region

Figure 4.4. Annual per capita renewable water resources (cubic metres)

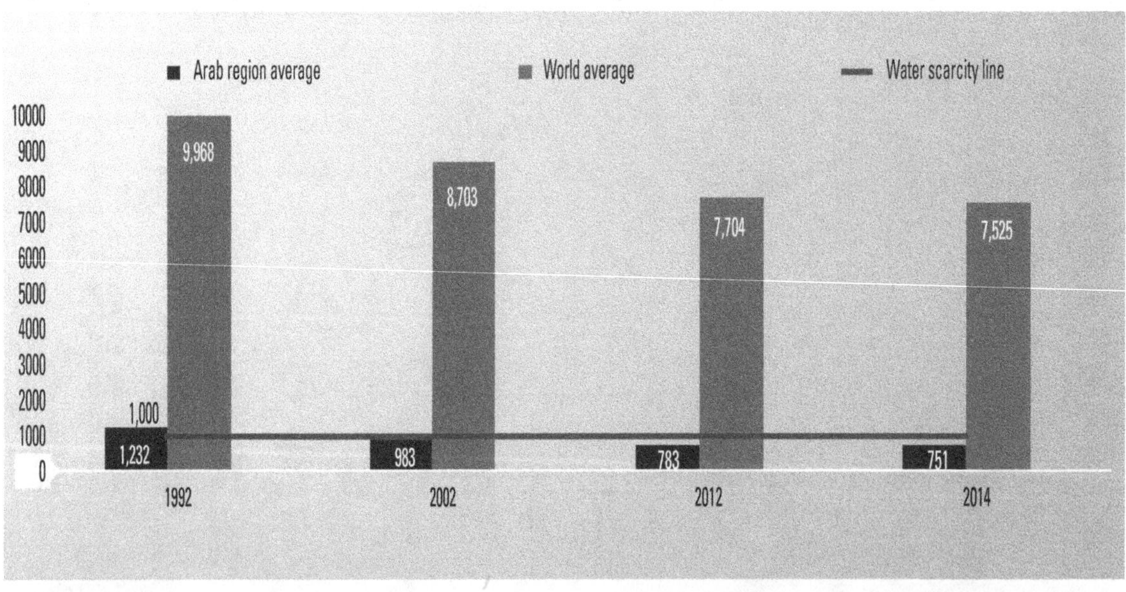

Source: Authors' calculations based on FAO, AQUASTAT and DESA, World Population Prospects.
Note: Regional values are divisions of total renewable water resources of all 22 Arab countries by the total population for corresponding years. The same methodology is applied to world averages.

thus has a political dimension as it is largely dependent on the effective management of transboundary water resources, between Arab States and between Arab and non-Arab States. Almost every Arab country depends for its water supply on rivers or aquifers shared with neighbouring countries.[15] These include major rivers such as the Nile, Senegal, Tigris and Euphrates. Many smaller rivers are also shared between Arab countries, including the Medjerda and Orontes. However, most of the region's freshwater is from groundwater resources. Most large aquifer systems in the Arab region cross at least one international border, with many shared among Arab countries. Most of these aquifers contain non-renewable groundwater resources and lie deep below the Sahara Desert and the Arabian Peninsula.

The fact that several water basins are shared with Israel further hampers constructive dialogue on shared water resources. The Jordan River basin, for instance, is shared by five riparian countries (Israel, Jordan, Lebanon, Palestine and the Syrian Arab Republic) and control over its water adds to existing regional tensions. The impact of power asymmetry is clear: Israel is the largest user of water from the Jordan River basin, and the only user of water from Lake Tiberias.

(b) Water desalination and wastewater reuse

To meet future increases in domestic demand for water, Arab Governments will either have to divert about 11 billion cubic metres per year from the agricultural sector to meet growing demand, reduce demand or resort to non-conventional water sources, such as desalination and treated wastewater reuse.[16] Although desalinated water contributes only 1.8 per cent of the total supply of water in Arab countries, it accounts for nearly all the water supply in many cities, particularly in the Gulf.[17] It is estimated that desalinated water will account for 8.5 per cent of the region's total water supply by 2025. This is consistent with global trends; the capacity of desalination plants increased by nearly 60 per cent between 2008 and 2013.[18]

The increased capacity will be concentrated largely in the hyper-arid GCC countries, where

Figure 4.5. Desalination capacity of the top five countries worldwide, 2013 (million cubic metres per day)

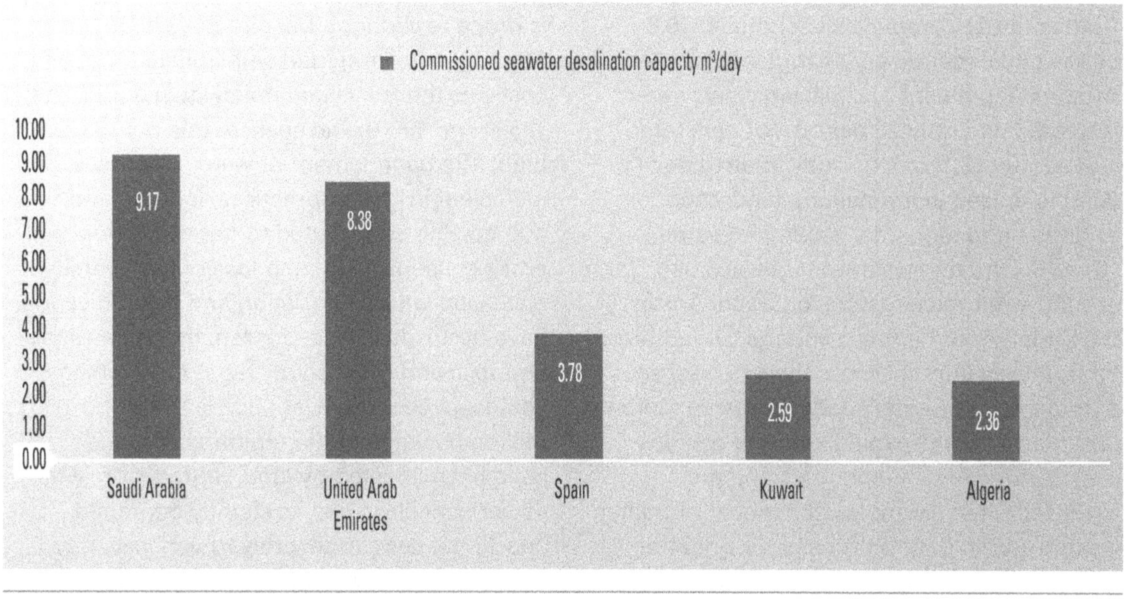

Source: Data from the International Desalination Association. Available from http://idadesal.org (accessed 30 August 2015).

desalination is the only viable option for supplying water to cities and industry. More than 55 per cent of the water supplied to cities in the GCC comes from desalinated water, used directly or blended with groundwater, and this share is expected to rise as groundwater resources shrink.[19] The GCC countries host nearly half of the global desalination production capacity. Four of the top five countries in terms of desalination capacity are from the Arab region: Algeria, Kuwait, Saudi Arabia and the United Arab Emirates (figure 4.5).

The cost of desalination is falling, but can still be as much as $1.50 per delivered cubic metre ($4 in extreme cases) for Governments, in contrast to the subsidized price of 4 cents per cubic metre at which water is sold in some Arab countries. Desalination raises energy security concerns and energy consumption creates a larger carbon footprint, although in GCC countries it takes place mostly in thermal-powered co-generation stations that produce both water and electric power, thereby improving energy efficiency and cost effectiveness.[20] Countries around the Arabian Gulf are also increasingly concerned about the threat to marine life and ecosystems posed by water discharged from thermal desalination plants.[21]

Arab countries produce an estimated 10.8 billion cubic metres per year of wastewater. Around 60 per cent of collected wastewater is treated and only 20 per cent of generated wastewater (2.17 billion cubic metres per year) is reused in agriculture, landscape irrigation and industrial cooling. In some countries, treated wastewater is also used for groundwater recharge. Egypt, Saudi Arabia, the Syrian Arab Republic and the United Arab Emirates account for more than 75 per cent of total reused wastewater in the Arab region. Irrigation for landscaping and golf courses is increasing in GCC countries and the Maghreb.[22] For example, 28 per cent of treated wastewater in Bahrain is used for irrigation. Concerted efforts, supported by regional and international organizations, will be needed to overcome economic, institutional, health and environmental obstacles in order to increase the volume of treated water that is reused.

2. Food security

The previous chapter highlighted challenges facing a number of Arab countries in fighting hunger and malnutrition. This section addresses food availability.

The issue of food security is intimately tied to the issues of water scarcity, arid climate and population growth. The region relies heavily on food imports, with dependency on cereal imports reaching 56.2 per cent compared to the world average of 57.6 per cent. Although the value of annual food production per capita for the Arab region ($191.4) is well below the world average of $311, local agriculture will remain important to protect countries of the region against international price volatility.[23] Domestic agriculture is also an important means of livelihood for the rural poor, many of whom are women. Increased efficiency and reduced waste along the entire food chain can maximize the region's scarce resources.

Nearly 90 per cent of the region lies within arid, semi-arid and dry subhumid areas, and is prone to drought. Despite the evident water scarcity, achieving food self-sufficiency at any cost was the prevailing policy goal during the 1960s and 1970s. The costs of this policy were high. Mismanagement of water resources, inefficient irrigation practices, logging and overgrazing contributed to desertification, soil erosion, salinization, and loss of biodiversity. Increased land degradation and desertification have occurred in Iraq, Jordan, the Syrian Arab Republic and most countries in the Arabian Peninsula over the past decade.[24] Around 15.3 million hectares of the region's crop lands have been affected by land degradation, with 42 per cent classified as slightly degraded and 12 per cent as severely to very severely degraded.[25] Rangelands and forests have also suffered, which is affecting livestock and

Box 4.1. National gene banks, genetic resources conservation and sustainable use: Tunisia

Aware of the magnitude of the problem of genetic resources erosion, Tunisia has ratified the United Nations Convention on Biodiversity, Framework Convention on Climate Change and Convention to Combat Desertification. It was also among the first signatories to the International Treaty on Plant Genetic Resources for Food and Agriculture. The inauguration of the Tunisian National Gene Bank (www.bng.nat.tn) in November 2007 was an important step towards the conservation and evaluation of plant, animal and micro-organism biodiversity. It has stocked more than 200,000 accessions since its creation and played a key role in coordinating operators in the area and promoting conservation activities and sustainable use of genetic resources at the national, regional and international levels.

Political commitment and clear legislation are needed to sustain a national gene bank. A key to success for the Tunisian Gene Bank was networking with all stakeholders (research institutions, universities, development agencies, farmers and non-governmental organizations) within the framework of nine thematic groups. They were all involved in the bank's programme planning and implementation and benefited from capacity-building activities.

However, the failure by some international agencies to work with the bank and their continued work with individuals or parties outside its network somewhat undermined the bank's mandate.

Source: M. Djemali and S. Bedhiaf, "Setting-up a cryobank in a developing country: lessons to be learned", in *Proceedings of the Ninth World Congress on Genetics Applied to Livestock Production*, German Society for Animal Science, eds. (2010).

Figure 4.6. Total arable and permanent crop land area (million hectares)

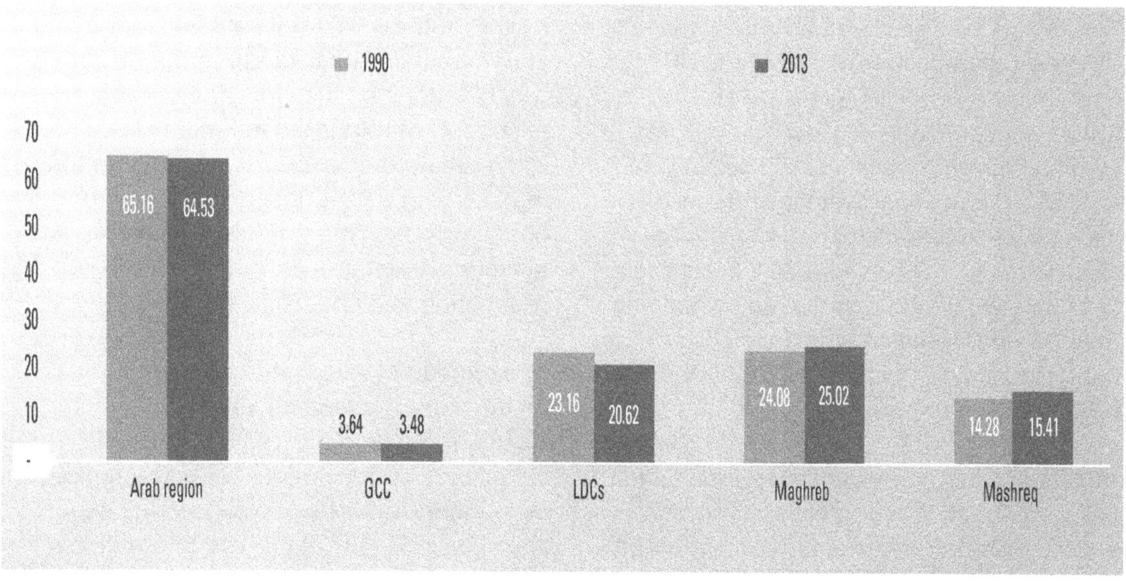

Source: Authors' calculations based on FAO, FAOSTAT.
Note: The 1990 value for the Sudan is based on the sum of the 2011 values for the Sudan and South Sudan (2,760,000 hectares). The arable land and permanent crop value for 2013 was taken directly from FAOSTAT.

biodiversity, and increasing the potential for landslides. Biodiversity loss has reduced the productivity of ecosystems, jeopardizing the basis for sustainable livelihoods. However, efforts are being made to establish national gene banks (box 4.1).

Figure 4.7. Average arable and permanent crop land area (million hectares)

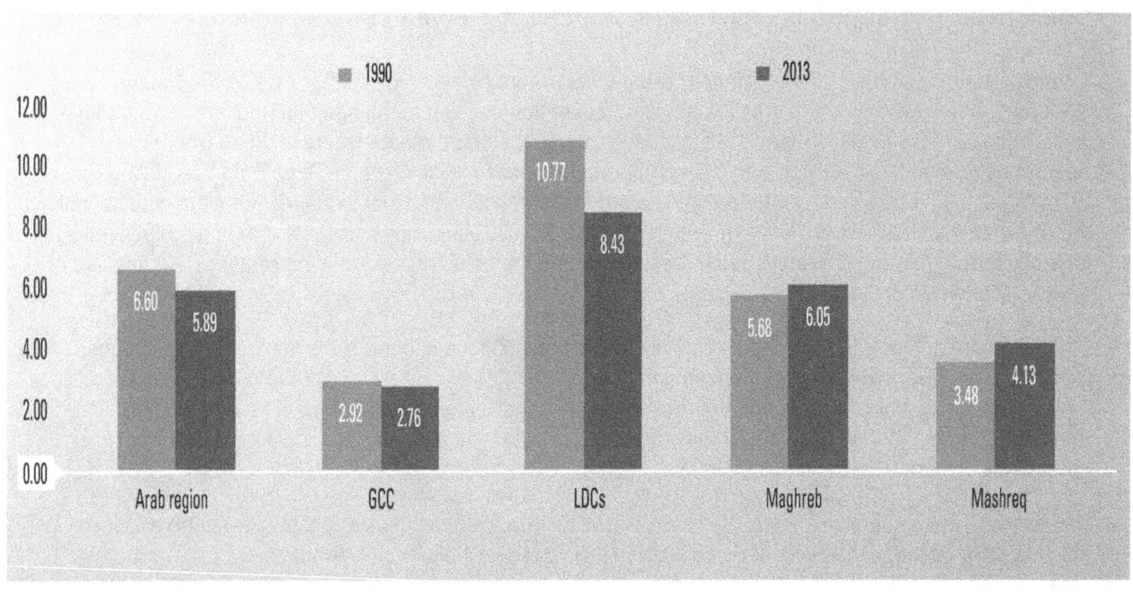

Source: Authors' calculations based on FAO, FAOSTAT.
Notes: Values are weighted averages against land area. The 1990 value for the Sudan is based on the sum of the 2011 values for the Sudan and South Sudan (2,760,000 hectares). The arable land and permanent crop value for 2013 was taken directly from FAOSTAT. For other countries, arable land and permanent crop value for 2013 was taken directly from the Central Intelligence Agency (CIA), The World Factbook. Available from https://www.cia.gov/library/publications/the-world-factbook (accessed 30 August 2015).

Total arable land and cropped area in the region decreased slightly between 1990 and 2013 to 64.53 million hectares (figures 4.6 and 4.7), or 4.1 per cent of total land area. That was less than half the global average of 10.9 per cent in 2013.[26] The regional average is around 0.17 hectares of arable land per person, which is close to the global average of 0.2 hectares in 2013.[27] Values vary across the region, ranging from 0.01 (Palestine and the United Arab Emirates) and 0.04 (Egypt) to 0.29 (Libya) and 0.36 (the Sudan).[28]

Demand for new cropland faces competition from continued urbanization and the expansion of infrastructure. Another threat may come from a new rush for land as highlighted in box 4.2.

Agricultural productivity of cereals in the Arab region increased by 38 per cent between 1990 and 2013 (figure 4.8), registering a slightly higher rate of increase relative to the world (34 per cent) over the same period.[29] However, the Arab regional yield for 2013 of approximately 1,950 kilogram per hectare was half the global yield of 3,851 kilogram per hectare. Livestock production increased from 23.4 million tons in 1961 to 144 million tons in 2012, with an average annual growth rate of 9.9 per cent. This is double the worldwide average annual growth rate for livestock production (4.48 per cent).[30]

The scarcity of water places natural limits on developing domestic food production. As the population has grown, food self-sufficiency has declined and food imports have increased. Reliance on imports exposes Arab countries to volatility in international food prices, as they found during the 2007-2008 global food crisis. The escalating food import bill ($30 billion in 2008 for main food commodities) has caused large trade deficits and strained public budgets where subsidies are provided.[31] It is estimated that the food import bill for the region will reach nearly $100 billion by 2030.[32]

Box 4.2. International food prices and the new rush for land: Responding to future needs

Although agricultural land area worldwide has been increasing by 1.8 to 4 million hectares per year, international prices reached unprecedented levels in 2008, due to grain production shortages and increased cargo costs. Countries dependent on grain imports were alarmed. In response, the Arab Organization for Agricultural Development has focused increasingly on the potential for grain production in East African countries, particularly the Sudan, abundant in land and water.

GCC investment in those countries (and some Asian countries) is booming. According to an Oxfam report, up to 227 million hectares were sold or leased between 2001 and 2011, with the bulk of the acquisitions occurring in the latter years of that period. A 2010 World Bank report found that investors expressed interest in around 56 million hectares of land in 2009 alone, with about two thirds of investments taking place in sub-Saharan Africa. The Global Land Project estimated that between 51 and 63 million hectares of land were either part of finalized land deals or under negotiation in 27 African countries in 2009. However, not all the land has been converted to farmland and many of the deals have had undesirable effects.

Source: UNEP, *21 Issues for the 21st Century: Results of the UNEP Foresight Process on Emerging Environmental Issues* (Nairobi, 2012).

Figure 4.8. Cereal yield (kilograms per hectare)

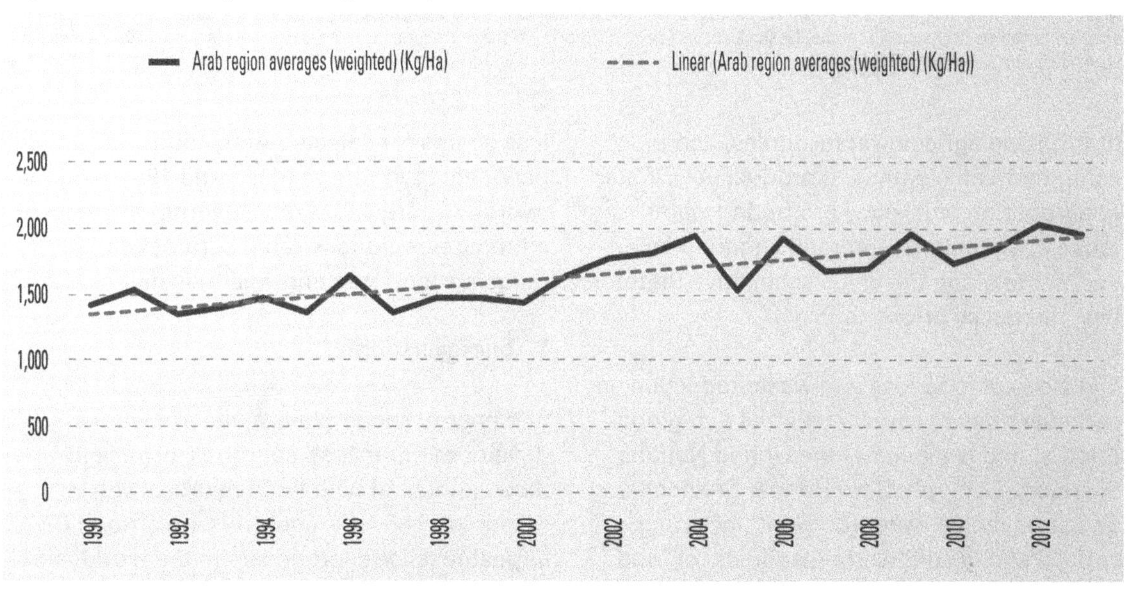

Source: Authors' calculations based on FAO, FAOSTAT.
Note: For the years 1990 to 1994, values for Palestine were copied from 1994 in order to ensure homogenous weighting across time for the region.

On average, 37 per cent of the region's population was engaged in agriculture in 2006, down from 48 per cent in the 1990s.[33] Although agriculture's average contribution to GDP in 2005 was a low 12.5 per cent (ranging from 0.3 per cent in Kuwait and Qatar to 34 per cent in the Sudan),[34] many of the poorest people in rural areas continue to rely on agriculture for their livelihood.

The chances of maximizing food self-sufficiency and supporting the region's farmers depend on reversing the trend of degradation

Figure 4.9. Food loss, 2015

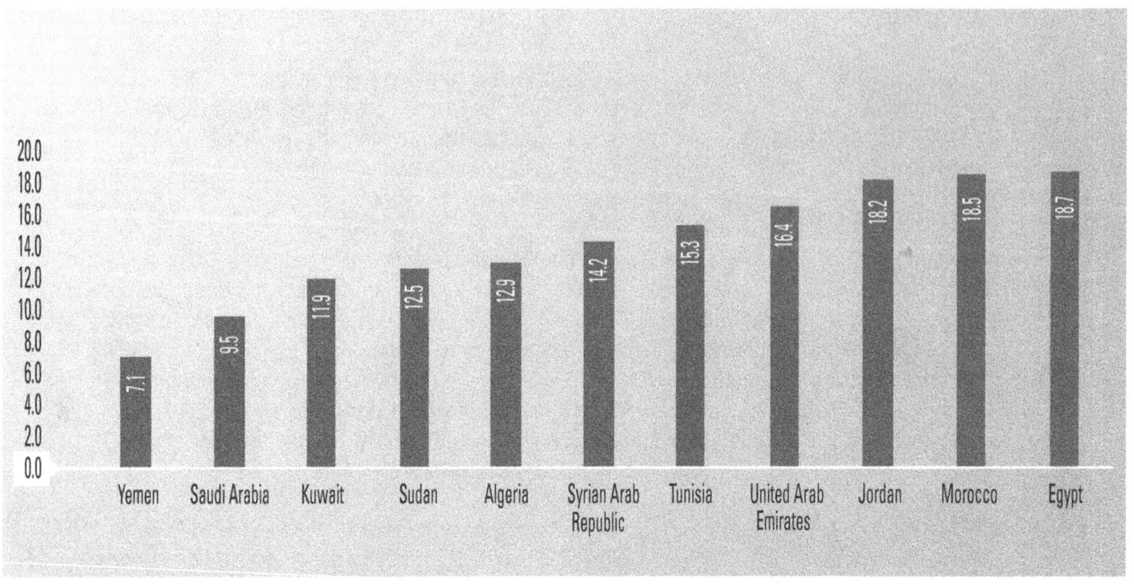

Source: The Economist Intelligence Unit, Global Food Security Index. Available from http://foodsecurityindex.eiu.com/Index/Overview (accessed 30 August 2015).
Note: "Food loss" as defined here is a measure of post-harvest and pre-consumer food loss as a ratio of the total domestic supply (production, net imports and stock changes) of crops, livestock and fish commodities. The higher the score, the more loss occurs (a score of 0 indicates the lowest loss and a score of 100 the highest).

of available agricultural resources, and in using them efficiently and productively. Water and irrigation efficiency, promoting water reuse in agriculture and reducing food loss and waste along the value chain have therefore become policy priorities.[35]

The issue of food loss and waste reduction, in particular, has become a regional and global priority, and is a pillar of the United Nations Secretary-General's Zero Hunger Challenge. The annual blue water footprint (including surface and groundwater resources) of food losses and waste in the North Africa/Western Asia/Central Asia region has been estimated at 40 billion cubic metres, or 90 cubic metres per capita, which represents 17 per cent of the global figure, despite having only 7 per cent of world's population.[36] Roughly 44 per cent of food losses and waste occur during handling, processing and distribution, while waste at the consumption stage is estimated to be 34 per cent, of which most is generated in urban areas.[37] Post-harvest and pre-consumer food loss scores for selected Arab countries ranged between 7.1 in Yemen (best) and 18.7 in Egypt (worst) (figure 4.9). Arab Governments have adopted a regional strategic framework for reducing food loss and waste by half by 2024.[38]

3. Energy security

The energy sector plays a vital role in the development of Arab countries, especially those endowed with large hydrocarbon resources. The GCC countries are among the largest fossil fuel producers in the world, and the Arab region as a whole accounted for 16 per cent of world gas production in 2013 (behind the United States and the Russian Federation).[39]

Domestic consumption of energy resources has risen faster than production in the Arab countries: the ratio of consumption of oil and gas compared to production rose from 23 per cent in 1990 to 35 per cent in 2013 (figure 4.10).

Figure 4.10. Primary energy production and consumption (billion tons of oil equivalent)

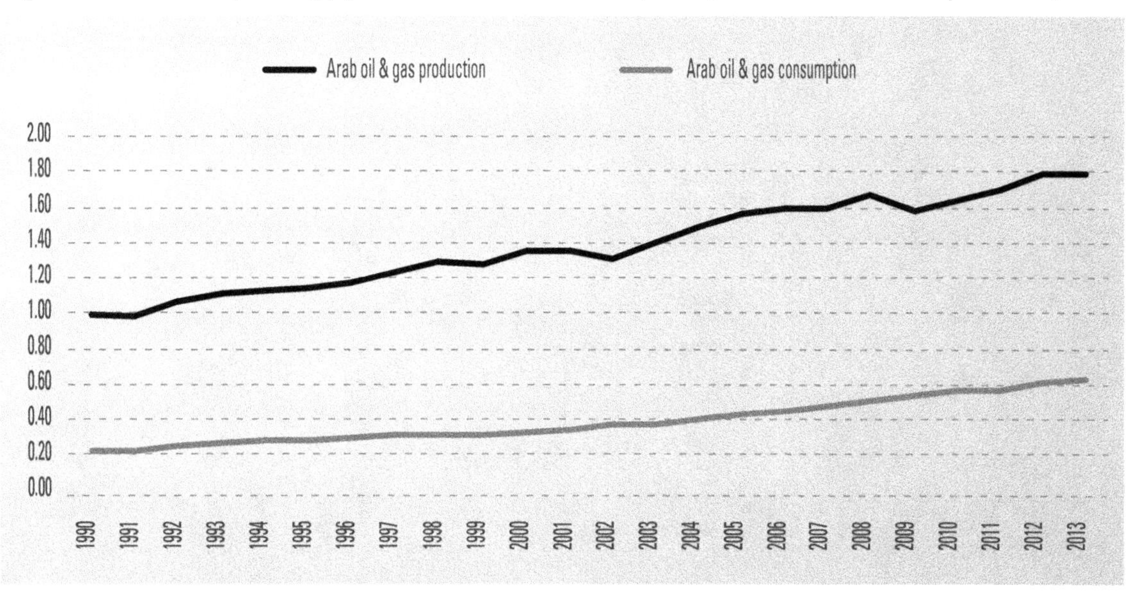

Source: Authors' calculations based on International Energy Agency (IEA), World Energy Statistics and Balances. Available from http://www.oecd-ilibrary.org/energy/data/iea-world-energy-statistics-and-balances_enestats-data-en (accessed 30 August 2015).
Note: Values are missing for the Comoros, Djibouti, Mauritania, Palestine and Somalia.

Regional per capita energy consumption stood at 1,843 kilogram of oil equivalent (kgoe) in 2012, slightly below the global average of 1,898 kgoe.[40] However, while consumption in the LDCs, Maghreb (except Libya) and Mashreq was well below the global average in 2012, in GCC countries it was much higher - as much as 10 times the global average in Qatar (figure 4.11).

More than 35 per cent of total primary energy is consumed in electricity generation (96 per cent of which comes from oil and gas) due to changing consumption and production patterns, according to the Arab Union of Electricity. Between 1971 and 2011, electricity consumption grew at an average of 9.2 per cent, far outpacing population growth of 2.6 per cent or GDP growth of 3.4 per cent over the same period. While economic growth has multiplied by a factor of 5 during that period, electricity and energy consumption have multiplied by factors of 35 and 12 respectively (figure 4.12).

The amount of energy the Arab countries use to generate $1,000 of GDP (in constant 2005 United States dollars) increased by 23 per cent from 0.34 to 0.42 tons of oil equivalent between 1990 and 2011 (figure 4.13),[41] in contrast to all other regions, where energy intensity is decreasing. The global average energy intensity was 0.25 tons of oil equivalent per $1,000 in 2011, down from 0.29 tons in 1990.[42] The global average reflects improved energy efficiency and an increasingly service-focused economy in China, the Russian Federation, India, the European Union and the United States.[43]

The high consumption rates of oil and gas in parts of the Arab region are largely attributable to widespread energy subsidies. Six of the world's 10 largest energy subsidizers are in the Arab region. It is widely believed that energy subsidies primarily benefit the rich,[44] as discussed in chapter 3.

Despite the region's rich endowment in renewable energy resources, the share

Figure 4.11. Energy consumption per capita, 2012 (kilogram of oil equivalent)

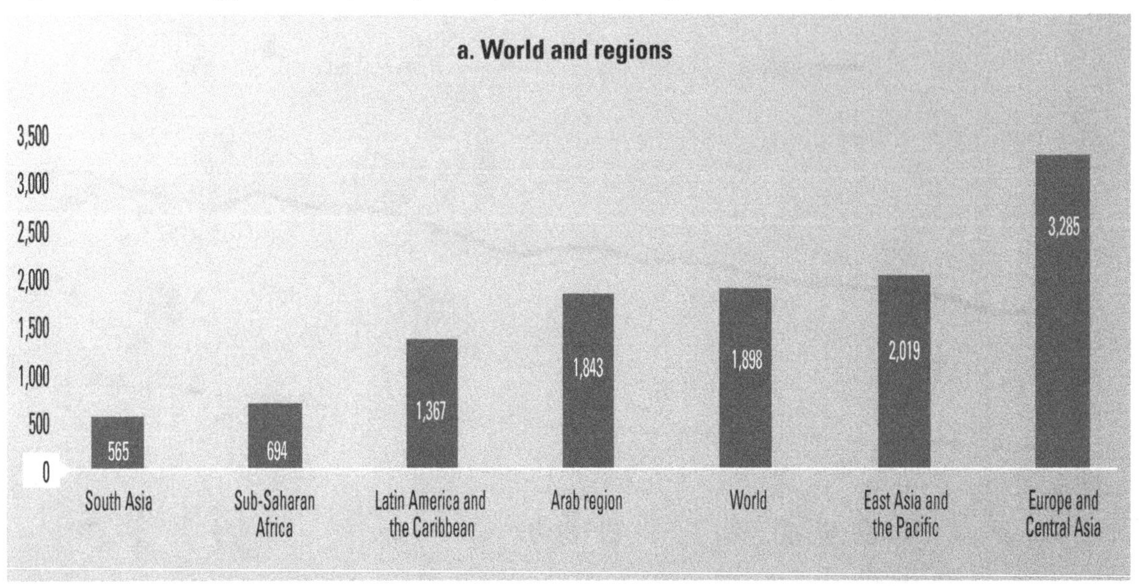

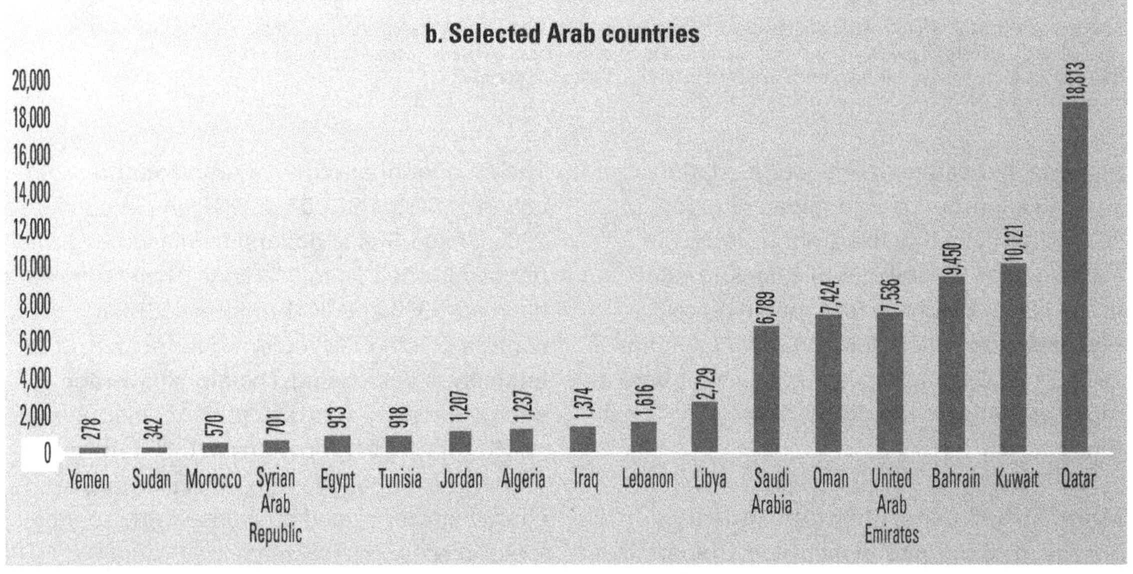

Source: Authors' calculations based on World Bank, World Development Indicators.

in electricity generation remains limited (figure 4.14). Renewable energy other than hydroelectric power contributes less than 1 per cent of electricity generation in the region and is almost exclusively limited to the Maghreb and Mashreq. At the end of 2014, solar (photovoltaic and concentrating solar power) energy was contributing 0.12 per cent of electricity and wind power 0.36 per cent.

Installed renewable energy capacity totals approximately 11 gigawatts, mostly in the form of hydroelectric power (88 per cent in 2014), and concentrated in Egypt, Iraq, Morocco, the Sudan and the Syrian Arab Republic (table 4.1 and figure 4.15). The use of renewables in the region falls below the global average of 8.7 per cent of total energy use provided by alternative energy sources (including hydro and nuclear) in 2011.[45]

Figure 4.12. Energy and electricity consumption, population and GDP (percentage growth relative to 1971)

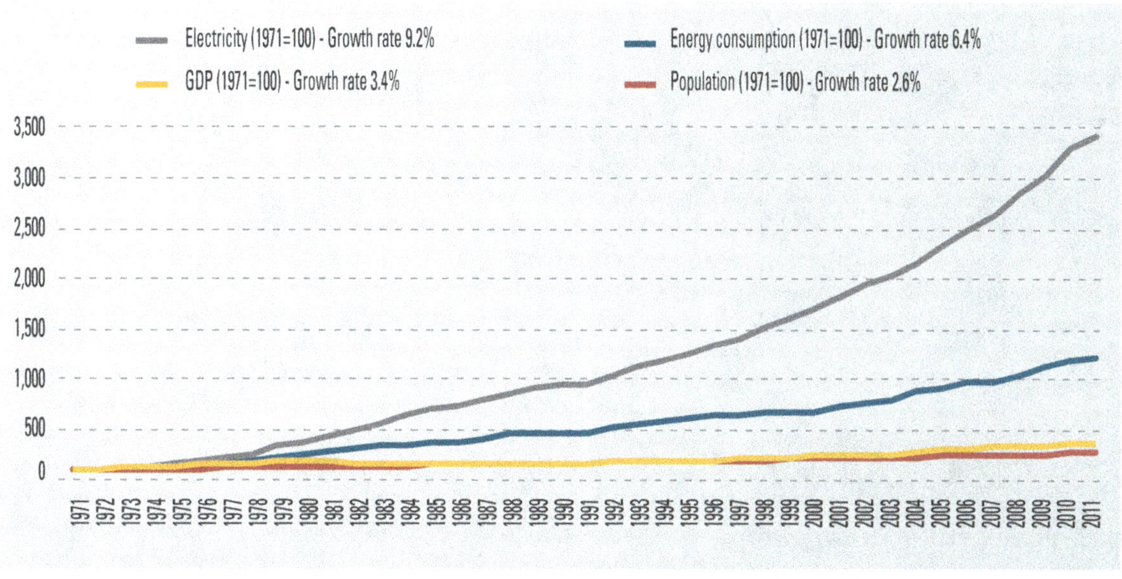

Source: IEA, Energy Balances of Non-OECD Countries. Available from http://www.iea.org/publications/freepublications/publication/energy-balances-of-non-oecd-countries---2015-edition---excerpt.html (accessed 30 August 2015).

Figure 4.13. Energy intensity (tons of oil equivalent per thousand 2005 United States dollars)

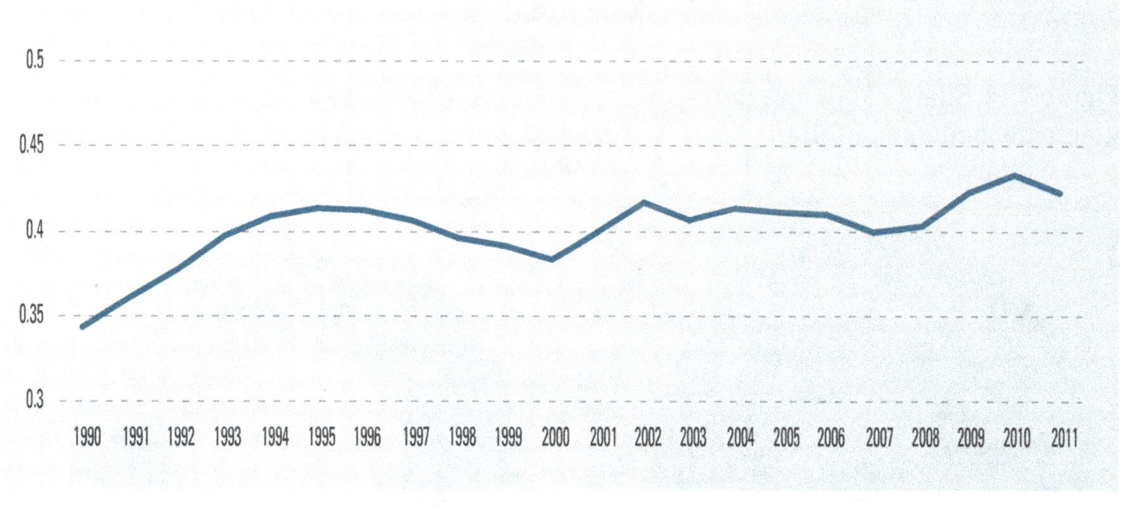

Source: IEA, Energy Balances of Non-OECD Countries (see figure 4.12).

Progress is being made on increasing installed capacity (figure 4.16). Twenty Arab countries have announced renewable energy targets that would total around 106 gigawatts of installed power capacity in Arab countries by 2032 (32 gigawatts photovoltaic, 38 gigawatts concentrating solar power, 30 gigawatts wind, 3.7 gigawatts biomass, and 2.2 gigawatts geothermal).[46] Development is being guided by regional plans such as the Pan-Arab Strategy for the Development of Renewable Energy 2030 and the Arab Renewable Energy Framework.

Table 4.1. Installed renewable energy capacity, 2014 (megawatts)

Country	Total renewable energy	Total (excluding hydro)
Algeria	260.1	32.1
Bahrain	5.5	5.5
Djibouti	1.4	1.4
Egypt	3,385.0	585.0
Iraq	1,867.5	3.5
Jordan	16.5	6.5
Kuwait	1.8	1.8
Lebanon	283.5	1.5
Libya	4.8	4.8
Morocco	2,071.0	326.0
Oman	0.7	0.7
Palestine	1.0	1.0
Qatar	41.2	41.2
Saudi Arabia	7.0	7.0
Sudan	1,647.5	57.5
Syrian Arab Republic	1,151.8	0.8
Tunisia	224.0	158.0
United Arab Emirates	125.5	125.5
Yemen	1.5	1.5
Total	11,097.4	1,361.4

Source: Renewable Energy Policy Network for the 21st Century (REN21) and others, "MENA renewables status report" (Paris, May 2013). Available from www.ren21.net/Portals/0/documents/activities/Regional%20Reports/MENA_2013_lowres.pdf.

Figure 4.14. Share of energy sources in electricity generation, 2014

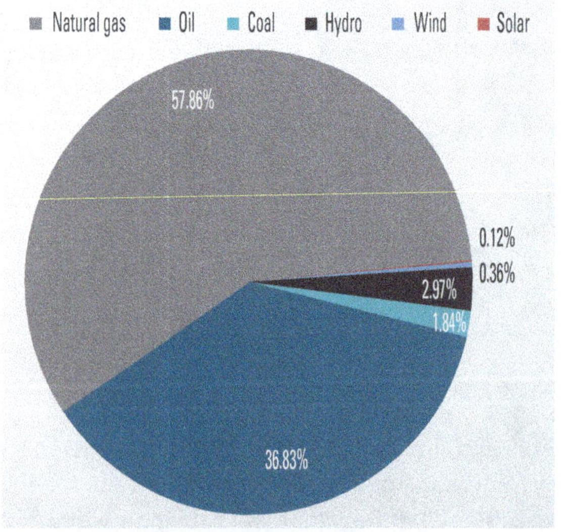

Source: Authors' calculations based on data from the Arab Union of Electricity. Available from http://www.auptde.org/Default.aspx?lang=en (accessed 30 August 2015).

Figure 4.15. Shares of renewable energy sources in installed capacity, 2014

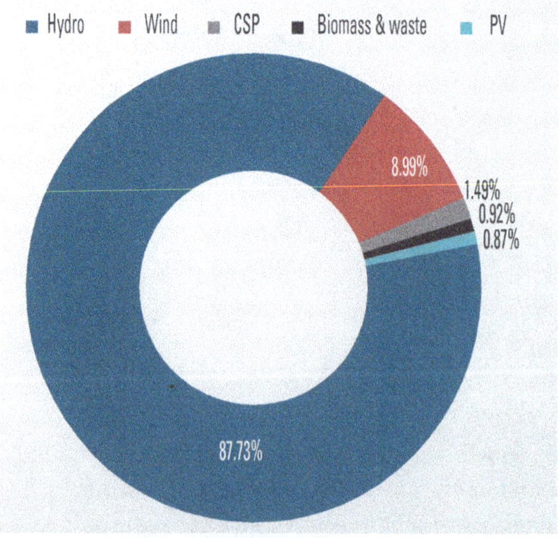

Abbreviations: CSP, concentrating solar power; PV, photovoltaic.
Source: Authors' calculations based on REN21 and others, "MENA renewables" (see table 4.1).

Figure 4.16. Renewable energy (excluding hydroelectric) as a share of total energy consumption

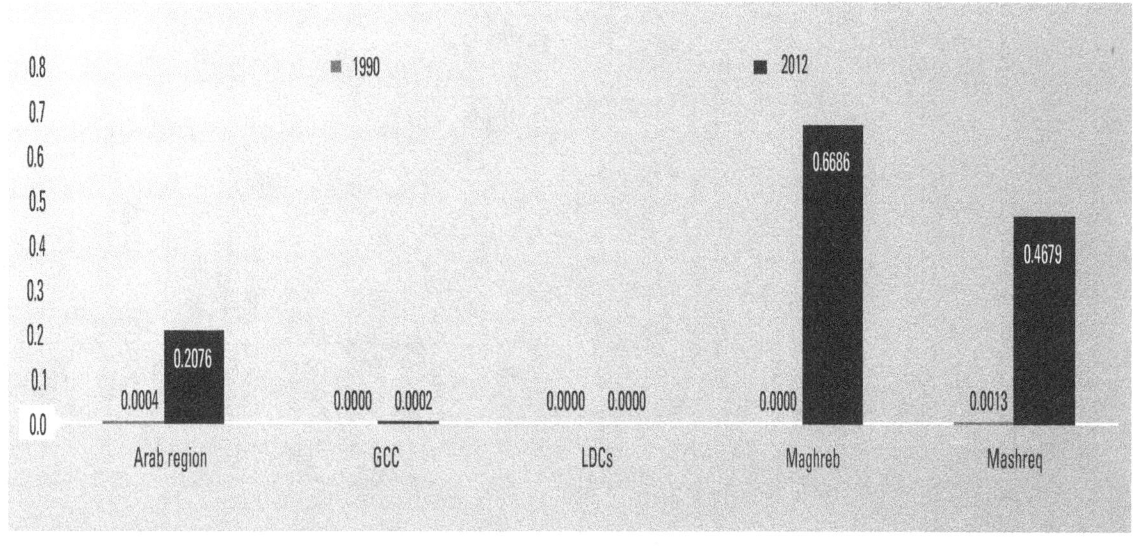

Sources: Authors' calculations based on World Bank, World Development Indicators for renewable energy as a share of total energy consumption (excluding hydroelectric) and IEA, World Energy Statistics and Balances (see figure 4.10)
Notes: Values are weighted against energy use. Data are missing for the Comoros, Djibouti, Mauritania, Palestine and Somalia.

Figure 4.17. Vehicles per kilometre of road

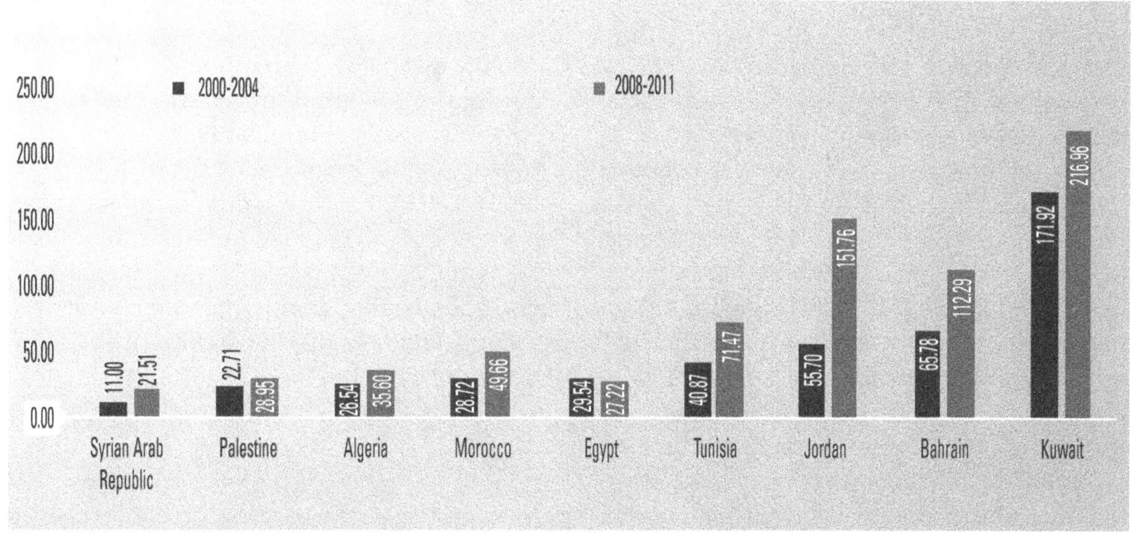

Source: World Bank, World Development Indicators.
Note: This indicator has been discontinued and is no longer available online. Vehicles include cars, buses and freight vehicles but not two-wheelers.

4. Waste and transport

Vehicular use and waste generation are also important indicators of sustainable consumption and production patterns and are analysed below. A comprehensive analysis of sustainable consumption and production cannot be conducted due to

Figure 4.18. Passenger cars per 1,000 people

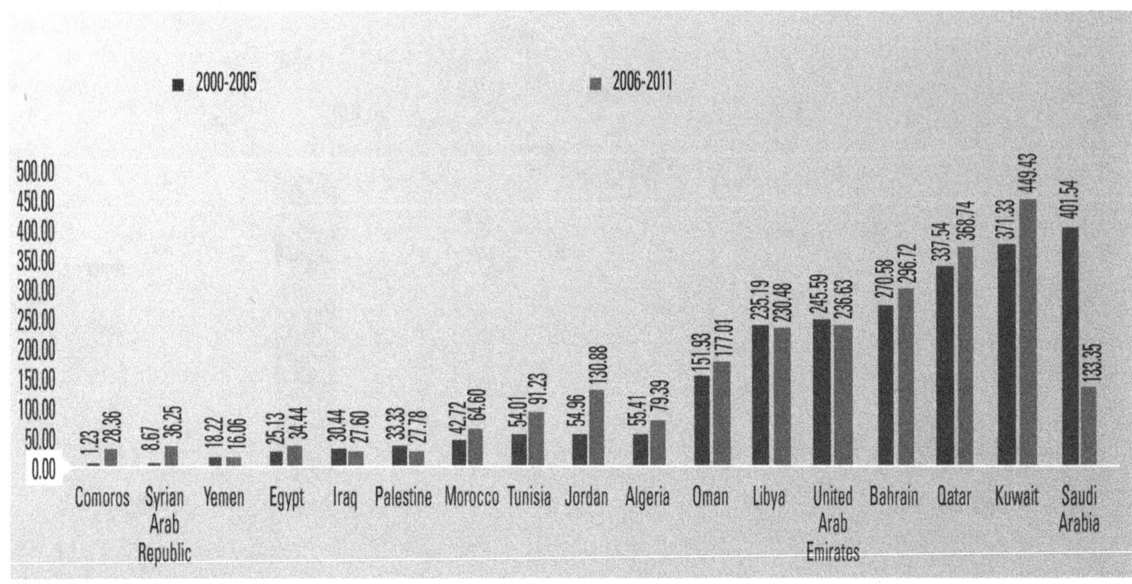

Source: World Bank, World Development Indicators.
Notes: Passenger cars refer to road motor vehicles, other than two-wheelers, intended for the carriage of passengers and designed to seat no more than nine people. For Qatar, Saudi Arabia and Yemen, the 2006-2011 value is from 2012.

significant gaps in data on waste recycling, treatment and disposal (including hazardous waste).

Over the past two decades, changing lifestyles and inadequate public transport have led to a substantial increase in the number of vehicles per kilometre of road in several Arab countries (except in Egypt, which shows a small decrease). In most countries for which data are available, the number is far higher than the global average of 32 as of 2009 (figure 4.17). The greater numbers of cars in circulation is associated with increased fuel consumption, greenhouse gases emissions and traffic congestion. The number of passenger cars per 1,000 people ranges from under 30 in the Comoros to around 450 in Kuwait (figure 4.18). In some cases, the number of passenger cars per 1,000 people has decreased. In Saudi Arabia, the number dropped in 2012 to a third of its value in the early 2000s.

The overall generation of waste per capita decreased between 2000 and 2006, particularly in the Maghreb and Mashreq (figure 4.19). It is unclear, however, to what extent this is due to an absolute reduction in waste or to rapid population growth.

Science, technology and innovation can contribute to building sustainable and resilient societies. Promising research and development in green sectors is being undertaken in the Arab region (box 4.3) and efforts are being made to green sectors (box 4.4). Tangible progress, however, results only when institutional, regulatory, human resource and financial constraints are addressed simultaneously.

B. Sustainable and resilient societies, cities and human settlements

1. Disaster risk reduction

The Arab region is prone to weather volatility, and the frequency of natural disasters, probably as a result of climate change, has increased over the past two decades (figure 4.20). Coupled with a low level of disaster

Figure 4.19. Generation of solid waste (kilograms per person per day)

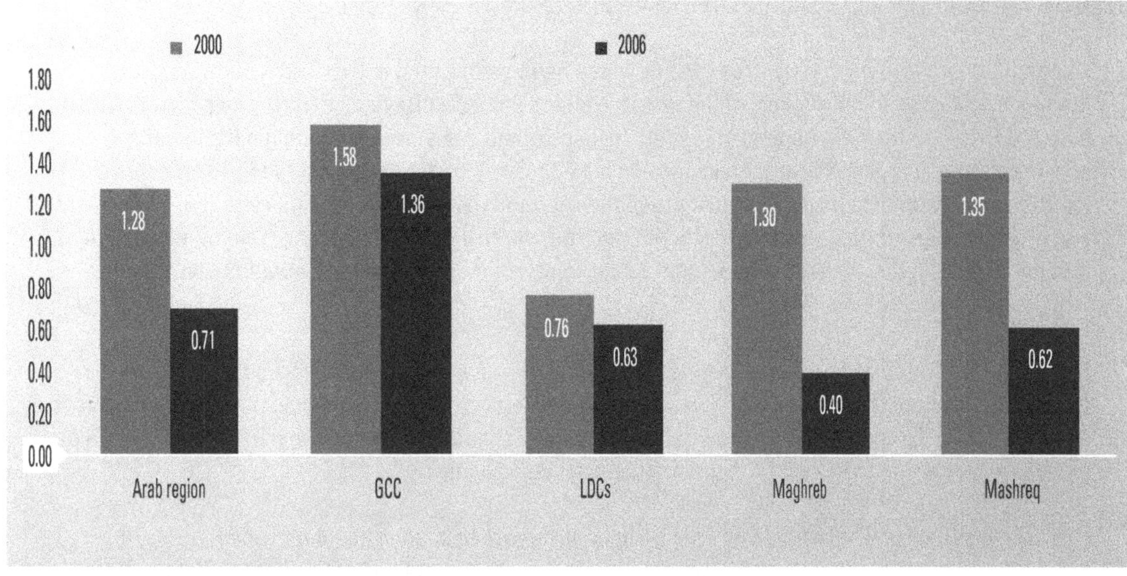

Sources: Authors' calculations based on Daniel Hoornweg and Perinaz Bhada-Tata, "What a waste: a global review of solid waste management", Urban Development Series Knowledge Papers, No. 15 (Washington, D.C., World Bank, March 2012); and Mostafa K. Tolba and Najib W. Saab (eds.), *Arab Environment: Future Challenges* (Beirut, AFED, 2008).
Notes: Values are weighted against total population as taken from World Bank, World Development Indicators. LDC data include only Mauritania and the Sudan. Maghreb data include only Morocco and Tunisia. In the Mashreq subregion, data are missing for Iraq and Palestine.

Box 4.3. Research and development in green sectors: Examples from the Arab region

Important research and development initiatives in green sectors are taking place in the Arab region. In the field of energy, the Clean Combustion Research Center (http://ccrc.kaust.edu.sa/Pages/Objectives-and-Approaches.aspx) of the King Abdullah University of Science and Technology and the Saudi Arabian Oil Company are working to improve combustion technologies by enhancing efficiency, reducing pollutants and capturing carbon emissions.

The Kuwait Institute for Scientific Research (www.kisr.edu.kw/en/research/water) is developing safer and more cost-effective methods of water desalination and treatment, including through the use of advanced membrane technologies, and the Oman-based Middle East Desalination Research Center (http://www.medrc.org/?q=research-initiatives/habs) is applying remote sensing, modelling, and forecasting techniques to manage harmful algal blooms resulting from desalination operations.

In the field of agriculture, the Arab Center for the Studies of Arid Zones and Dry Lands (http://www.acsad.org/index.php/en) is promoting the transfer and use of techniques that combat desertification and the degradation of rangelands, and the International Center for Biosaline Agriculture (http://www.biosaline.org) in the United Arab Emirates is developing nutritious salt, heat and drought tolerant crop varieties that can be planted in degraded and marginal lands.

preparedness, this has led to a substantial increase in the number of lives lost, mainly in the LDCs (figure 4.21). Deaths reported due to disasters were nearly 275 per cent higher in the period 2006-2015 than in the years from 1990 to 1999.[47]

Box 4.4. Greening production in the Arab region

National Cleaner Production Centres (NCPCs) have been established in five Arab countries with donor funding and the technical support of the United Nations Industrial Development Organization (UNIDO) and UNEP. The centres are helping industries to identify and implement technological solutions to address their environmental impact. In Jordan, the NCPC has cooperated with food producers to identify and implement simple, low-cost production methods that have resulted in sizeable energy and water use savings. In Tunisia, 10 hotels benefited from the NCPC, deploying water accounting systems that led to a reduction in water use of up to 70 per cent. For more information about the NCPCs, see http://www.unido.org/ncpc.html.

Since 2012, ESCWA has supported the establishment of six Green Help Desks in Egypt, Jordan, Lebanon, Morocco, Oman and Tunisia (see www.escwa.un.org/sites/gps/index.asp). They complement the work of NCPCs through awareness-raising activities, specialized training and information services to industries wishing to benefit from green economy opportunities.

Financial mechanisms have also been set up in recent years to support the deployment of environmental technologies. In Lebanon, potential investors in green technology (especially in the energy sector) can now benefit from low-cost loans subsidized by the Central Bank (see http://banqueduliban.gov.lb/files/tabs/FinanceUnit.pdf).

Many "green" initiatives in the region are driven by international organizations and need to be expanded at the national and regional levels to make their impact more tangible. Their sustainability is yet to be tested.

Figure 4.20. Disaster occurrences, 1990-2015

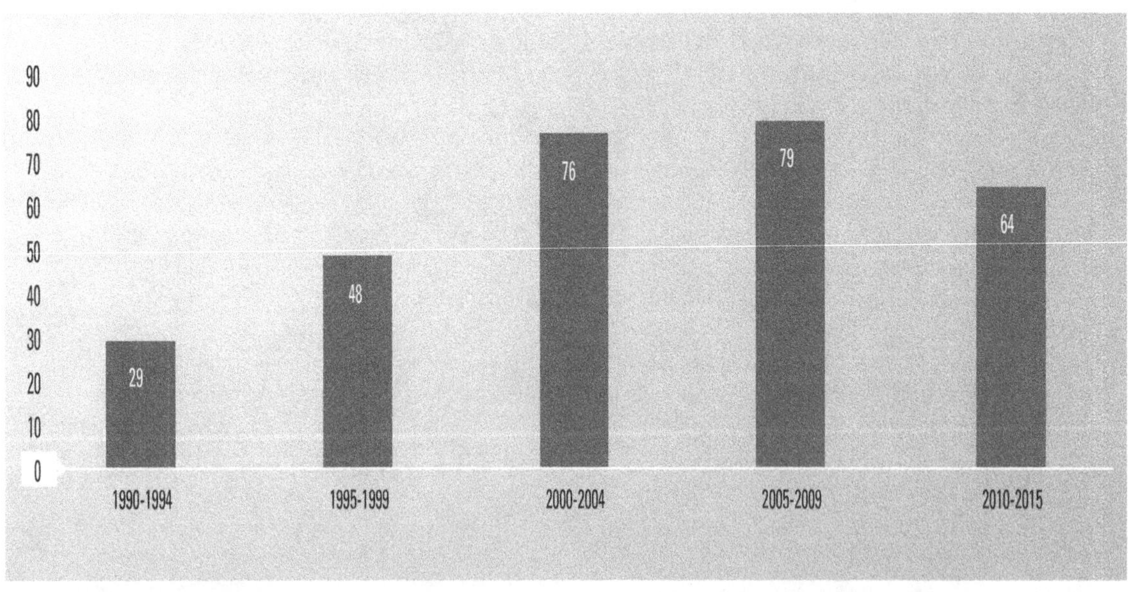

Source: Authors' calculations based on Centre for Research on the Epidemiology of Disasters, The International Disaster database (EM-DAT). Available from www.emdat.be (accessed 7 October 2015).
Note: Values are simple cumulative sums.

Figure 4.21. Deaths due to disasters, 1990-2015

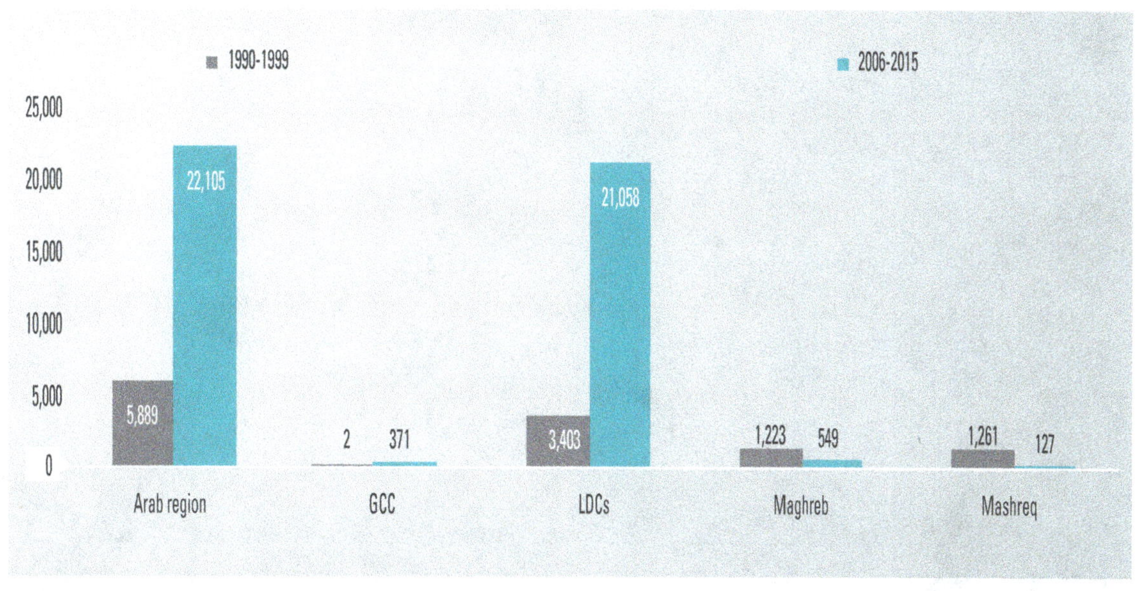

Source: Authors' calculations based on Centre for Research on the Epidemiology of Disasters, EM-DAT (see figure 4.20).
Note: Values are simple cumulative sums.

Figure 4.22. Disaster occurrences, Arab region, 1990-2015

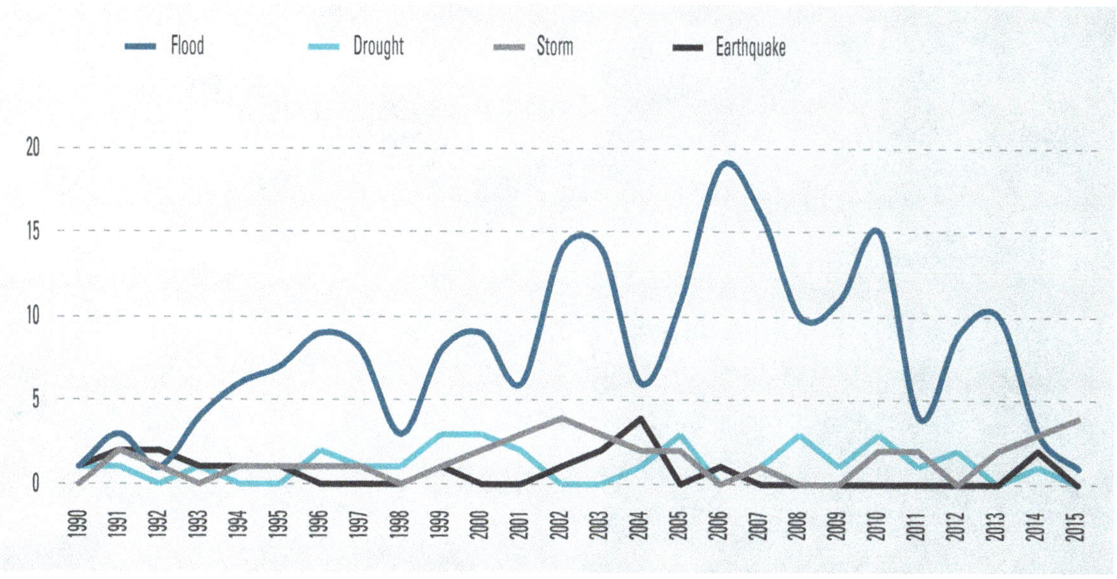

Source: Authors' calculation based on Centre for Research on the Epidemiology of Disasters, EM-DAT.

The increase in reported occurrences of disasters is most pronounced in the case of flooding (figure 4.22), although the number of people affected by disasters has risen most as a result of drought. Earthquakes cause the greatest physical damage. Damage to infrastructure, housing and livelihoods between 1990 and 2015 was estimated at more than $18 billion, including $6.8 billion related to earthquakes, $5.6 billion related to floods and $5.4 billion related to storms (table 4.2).

Table 4.2. Cost and number of affected people by disasters, 1990-2015

Country	Number of people affected[a] and cost (millions of United States dollars)	Type of disaster			
		Drought	Earthquake	Flood	Storm
Algeria	Total affected		241,729	238,442	15
	Total damage		$5,060	$1,480	
Comoros	Total affected		10,000	67,637	9,811
	Total damage			$5	
Djibouti	Total affected	933,008	240,000		775
	Total damage			$2.12	
Egypt	Total affected		92,968	168,498	142
	Total damage		$1,200	$141	$1
Iraq	Total affected		500	73,511	
	Total damage			$1.3	
Jordan	Total affected	330,000		18,000	225
	Total damage			$1	
Kuwait	Total affected			200	
	Total damage				
Lebanon	Total affected			17,000	1,104,575
	Total damage				$155
Libya	Total affected			2,000	
	Total damage			$42.2	
Mauritania	Total affected	3,005,907		173,419	477
	Total damage				
Morocco	Total affected	275,000	13,465	232,896	117,000
	Total damage	$900	$400	$295.2	$300
Oman	Total affected				20,283
	Total damage				$4,951
Palestine	Total affected			14,500	81,121
	Total damage				
Saudi Arabia	Total affected			24,653	
	Total damage			$1,200	
Somalia	Total affected	12,050,000	105,083	2,357,382	142,380
	Total damage		$100	$0.02	
Sudan	Total affected	18,860,000	8,015	4,346,457	30
	Total damage			$533.2	
Syrian Arab Republic	Total affected	1,629,000			352
	Total damage				
Tunisia	Total affected			185,508	
	Total damage			$242.8	
Yemen	Total affected		40,039	399,217	
	Total damage			$1,611	
Total	Total affected	37,082,915	751,799	8,319,320	1,477,186
	Total damage	$900	$6,761	$5,556	$5,407

Source: Authors' calculations based on Centre for Research on the Epidemiology of Disasters, EM-DAT.

[a] Figures for affected people do not include deaths.

The types and impact of disasters vary depending on geography and population concentrations. Large groups in Somalia and the Sudan have been affected by alternating periods of drought and flooding. Earthquakes in Algeria and storms in Oman have been among the most costly disasters in financial terms. Data are, however, missing for damage in several cases, especially in the LDCs.

2. Climate change

(a) Impact and adaptation measures

Due to factors such as elevated solar radiation and heat-absorbent soils, the Arab region is considerably more likely than others to be affected by the rising temperatures predicted under climate change scenarios. Through the Regional Initiative for the Assessment of the Impact of Climate Change on Water Resources and Socioeconomic Vulnerability in the Arab Region (RICCAR), the Swedish Meteorological and Hydrological Institute has generated temperature and rainfall distribution projections for the Arab region up to the year 2100, which predict a general rise in average temperatures during the period 2081-2100 of 1 to 3 degrees Celsius in the medium-case scenario and 2 to 5 degrees Celsius in the worst-case scenario, relative to the baseline 1986-2005. The areas with the highest expected

Figure 4.23. Changes in temperature in 2081-2100 relative to the baseline 1986-2005 for Representative Concentration Pathways (RCPs) 4.5 and 8.5

Temperature (°C) | Annual | CTL: 1986-2005 | SCN: 2081-2100 | rcp45

CTL

SCN-CTL

6 12 18 24 30 36

1 2 3 4 5

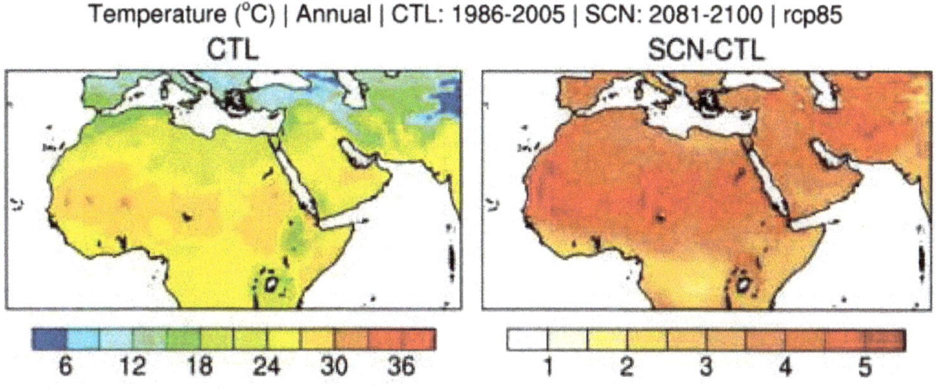

Source: RICCAR, 2015 data.

Note: Representative Concentration Pathways (RCPs) are four greenhouse gas concentration trajectories used for climate modelling.

increases are in the Sahara in North and East Africa, including Morocco and Mauritania (figure 4.23).

The RICCAR climate projections show an increase in the number of hot summer days (annual number of days when maximum temperature - Tmax > 35°C) expected by the end of the century throughout the Arab region (figure 4.24). The results indicate a significant warming trend reaching up to 80 days in the southern Arabian Peninsula in both scenarios and on the west coast of Africa in one of them. The projected increase in summer days will have a major impact on water supply, the health of vulnerable communities, and the duration of peak energy demand periods needed for cooling purposes.

The projections indicate that precipitation in the period from 2081 to 2100 will exhibit greater variability than temperature. In general, average monthly precipitation will fall, particularly in the Atlas Mountains (where the worst-case scenario foresees a drop of up to 10 mm in average monthly rainfall) and in the upper Nile and Euphrates and Tigris river catchments, which is likely to further strain transboundary water cooperation in those basins by the end of the century (figure 4.25).

Changes in precipitation will have a major impact on agricultural communities (box 4.5).

Figure 4.24. Changes in the number of summer days (Tmax > 35°C) in 2081-2100 relative to the baseline 1986-2005 for RCPs 4.5 and 8.5

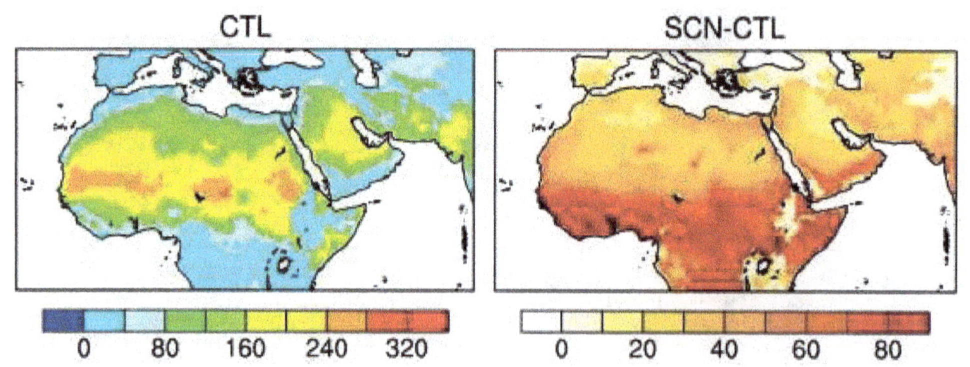

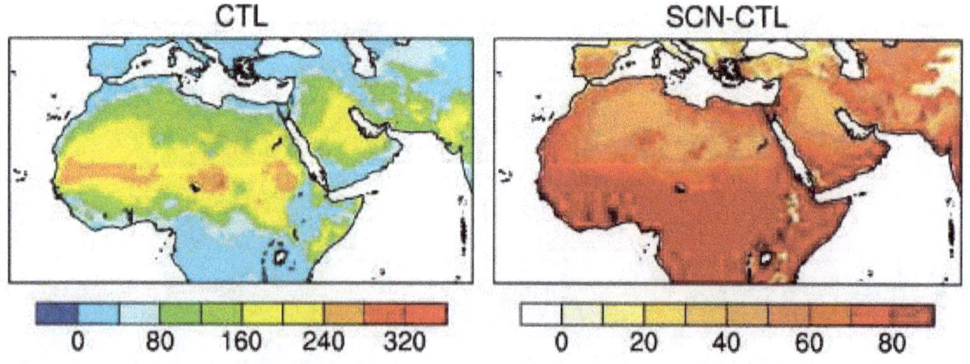

Source: RICCAR, 2015 data.

Figure 4.25. Changes in precipitation in 2081-2100 relative to the baseline 1986-2005 for RCPs 4.5 and 8.5

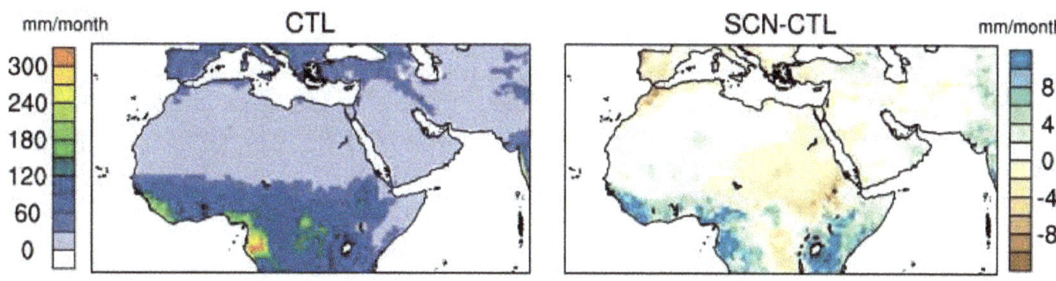

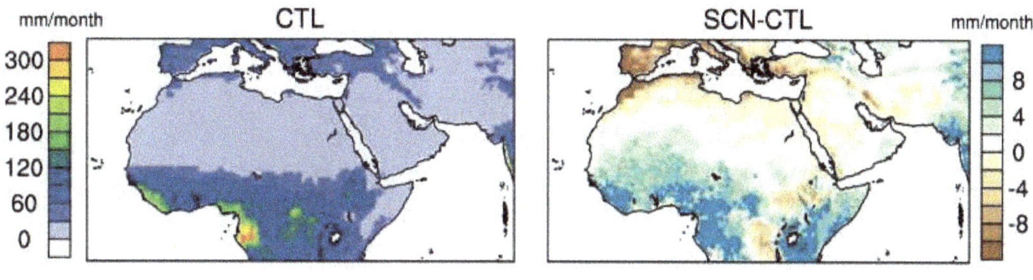

Source: RICCAR, 2015 data.

The effects of drought have already been felt throughout the region. In the 1950s, drought led to the death of most rangeland animals in the northern and eastern parts of the Arabian Peninsula.[48]

Dense urbanization and socioeconomic development of coastal areas make the Arab region especially vulnerable to rising sea levels and coastal flooding caused by extreme weather events. Concentrated urban areas, often with poor infrastructure, line the coasts of the Mediterranean Sea, Red Sea, the Atlantic and Indian Oceans and the Gulf. Such coastal communities are thus directly threatened by climate change, as is low lying agricultural land near the coast.

Much work has been done at the regional level to build resilience to climate-related hazards. The Arab Climate Resilience Initiative aims to promote integrated regional responses to climate change.[49] RICCAR is assessing the impact of climate change on freshwater resources across the Arab region.

It would be beneficial for Arab Governments to integrate climate change measures into national policies and strategies, along with environmental and disaster risk reduction mainstreaming. To be effective, resilience and adaption strategies need to be supported by improved education, awareness-raising and building human and institutional capacity on climate change mitigation, adaptation, impact reduction and early warning.

(b) Greenhouse gas emissions and mitigation measures

Arab States are not bound by the Framework Convention on Climate Change to reduce greenhouse gas emissions. Nevertheless, 10 of them prepared statements of their intended voluntary actions (Intended Nationally

Box 4.5. Climate change migration

Climate change can have a direct impact on people's lives and livelihoods. A clear example is the migration induced by climate change in the Syrian Arab Republic in recent years. Between 2006 and 2011, nearly 60 per cent of the population suffered the worst drought and crop failure in the country's modern history. By 2009, more than 800,000 Syrians had lost their livelihood as a result of drought and, by 2011, almost one million more had become exposed to food insecurity. In 2010, an estimated 200,000 people migrated from their farms to urban areas. What has occurred in the Syrian Arab Republic could well repeat itself elsewhere in the region, as farmers, dependent on rain and scarce water resources, are increasingly placed before the difficult choice of fight or flight.

Sources: Data from The Center for Climate and Security, available from http://climateandsecurity.org (accessed on 15 January 2015); and UNEP, "Climate change in the Arab region", Issues Brief for the Arab Sustainable Development Report (2015), available from http://css.escwa.org.lb/SDPD/3572/Goal13.pdf.

Figure 4.26. Total emissions of greenhouse gases (1,000 metric tons of CO_2)

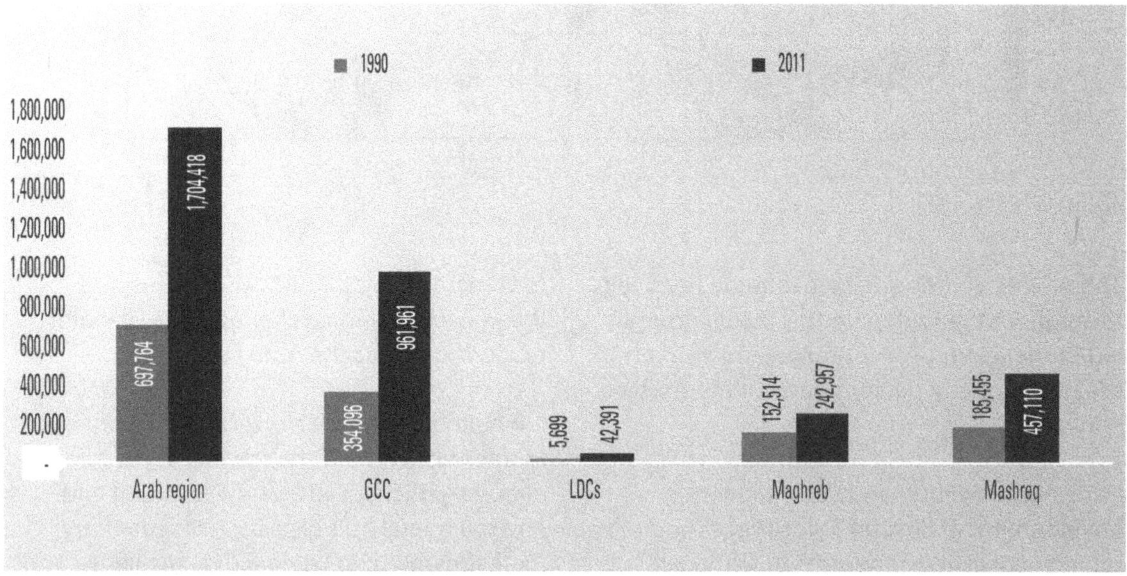

Source: Authors' calculations based on data from the Carbon Dioxide Information Analysis Center (CDIAC).

Determined Contributions) ahead of the twenty-first Conference of Parties (COP21) to the Convention in December 2015.[50]

Total greenhouse gases emission increased by more than 140 per cent in the Arab region between 1990 and 2011 (figure 4.26). To some extent, the increase can be attributed to population growth. Nevertheless, even in per capita terms, emissions increased by more than 50 per cent between 1990 and 2011 (figure 4.27). The regional average of 5.29 metric tons of CO_2 per capita exceeded the global average of 4.9 in 2011.[51] There are large subregional variations: at 20.89 metric tons per capita in 2011, the average for GCC countries is around four times the global average, while Mashreq and Maghreb countries emit about two thirds of the global average. The LDCs are well below regional and global averages, with per capita

Figure 4.27. Emissions of greenhouse gases per capita (metric tons of CO_2)

	1990	2011
Arab region	3.42	5.29
GCC	15.49	20.89
LDCs	0.01	0.67
Maghreb	2.41	2.80
Mashreq	1.95	3.08

Source: Authors' calculations based on data from CDIAC.
Notes: Values are weighted against population as taken from World Development Indictors. Earliest data for Palestine are from 1997.

Figure 4.28. Carbon emissions by sector, 2010 (million metric tons)

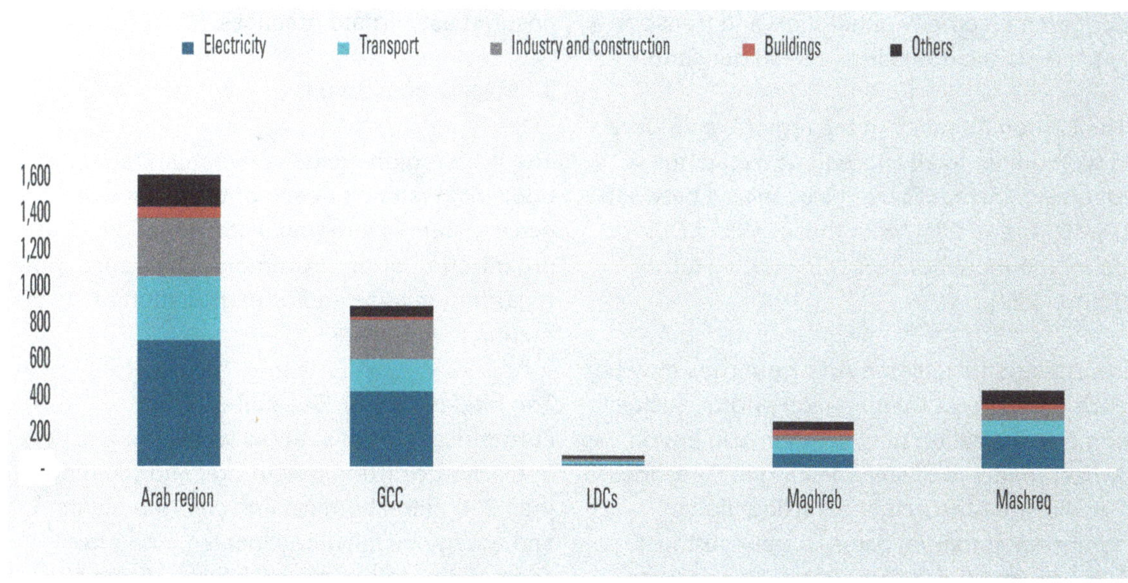

Source: Sherif Arif and Fadi Doumani, "A strategic investment framework for green economy in Arab countries from an energy perspective".
Note: International aviation and marine bunker CO_2 emissions are not included.

emissions less than one eighth of the global average.

By sector, carbon dioxide emissions are primarily attributable to electricity generation, followed by transport, industry and construction, and public and private buildings (figure 4.28). In GCC countries, electricity generation, industry and construction (mainly in relation to refineries and oil derivatives)

Figure 4.29. Emissions of greenhouse gases per dollar of GDP (kilograms CO_2 per $1 GDP PPP)

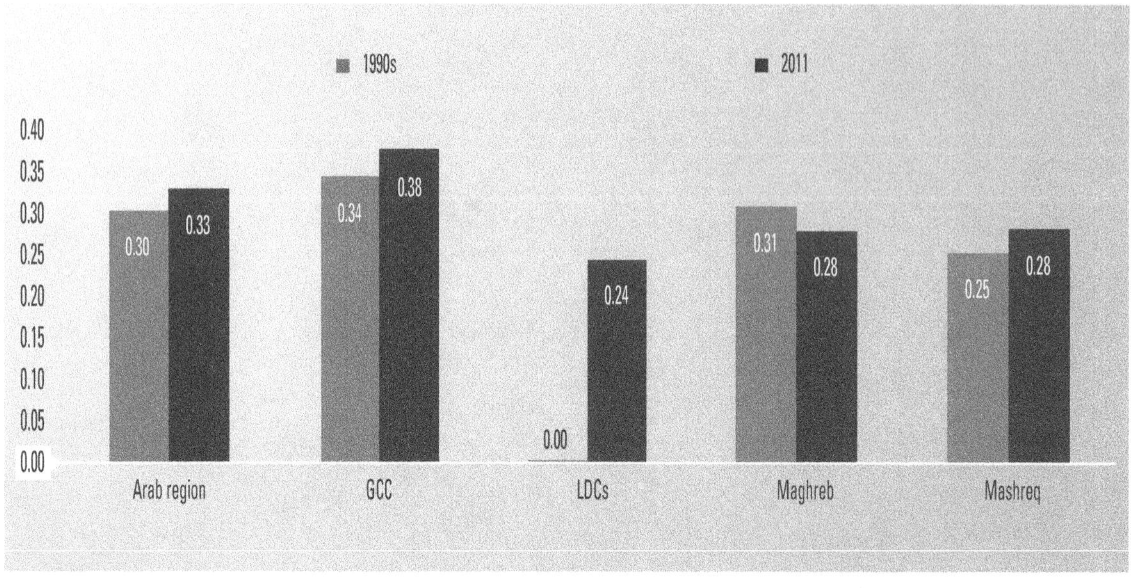

Source: Authors' calculations based on data from CDIAC.
Notes: Values are weighted against GDP PPP (constant 2011 United States dollars) as taken from World Bank, World Development Indicators. Earliest data for Qatar are from 2000. Data are missing for Somalia, the Sudan and the Syrian Arab Republic.

are the larger carbon dioxide emitters (67 per cent). Electricity generation and transport are the main culprits in LDCs (58 per cent).

The carbon intensity of the region's economy is worsening. In all subregions except the Maghreb, increases can be observed between the 1990s and 2011, with those in the LDCs being the most noticeable in relative terms (figure 4.29).

Improvements in some Arab countries may be attributed in part to mitigation efforts, such as: commercialization of wind energy in Egypt; widespread use of solar heating in Palestine, Tunisia and Morocco; the introduction of compressed natural gas as a transport fuel in Egypt; the first concentrated solar power projects in Algeria, Egypt, Morocco and Tunisia; the first two Arab green building councils in the United Arab Emirates and Egypt; Masdar, the first zero-carbon city in Abu Dhabi; and the pioneering carbon capture and storage project in Algeria. Although these efforts remain scattered as individual initiatives, they are a step in the right direction. There remains a lack of overarching policy that would ultimately ensure best climate practices.

3. Marine ecosystems

The Arab region includes five main regional bodies of water. For each of these seas or oceans there is a regional conservation organization or programme. All face challenges regarding misuse and/or degradation of marine resources.[52]

The Mediterranean Sea suffers from eutrophication[53] of shallow waters as a result of discharges from agriculture, and the more than 200 petrochemical and chlorine plants and energy installations located along its coast. Fish production statistics indicate a relatively stable catch in the Mediterranean since the 1980s. Recently, native species (especially in the eastern Mediterranean) have been threatened by exotic Red Sea species entering through the Suez Canal.

The Red Sea and Gulf of Aden region is directly threatened by human activities such

Figure 4.30. Percentage of the population living in coastal areas (at five metres or less above sea level)

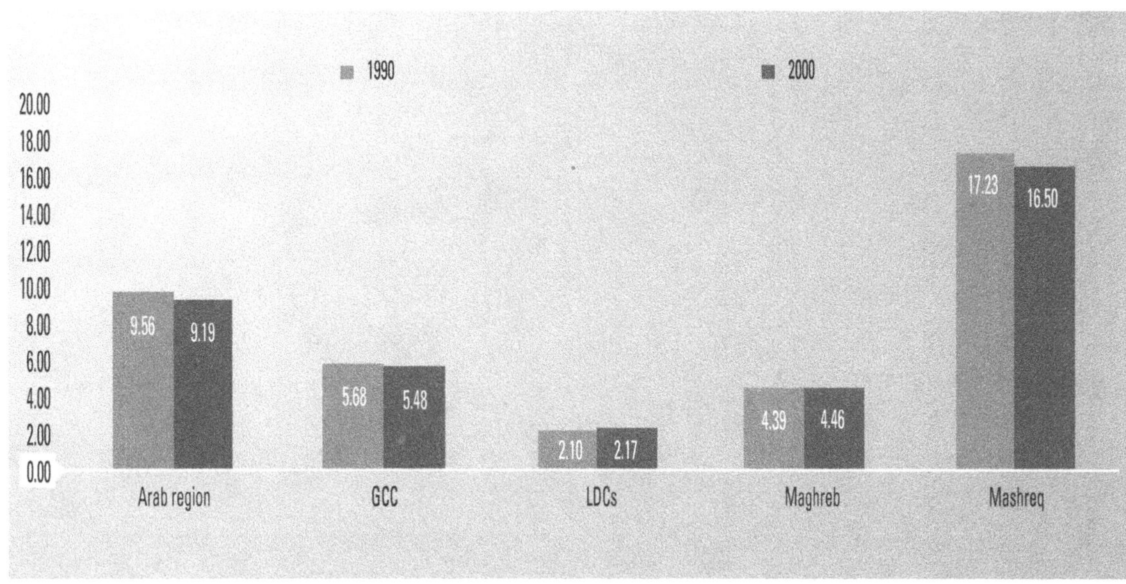

Source: Authors' calculations based on World Bank, World Development Indicators.

as the disposal of domestic and industrial effluent, the unsustainable use of non-living resources and the growing tourism industry. This body of water is particularly sensitive, having some of the highest temperatures and salinity levels in the world. Coral bleaching has already been observed in some areas. Regional cooperation on fisheries is limited and no formal regional stock assessment has been conducted.

The Gulf and Oman Sea area is under exponentially increasing stress due to the high concentration of fossil fuel-related activities, including large numbers of offshore installations, tanker loading terminals and tanker traffic. Several fish species, including kingfish, groupers and shrimp, have been listed a source of concern by FAO.

The Atlantic Ocean and the southwest Indian Ocean are a significant source of fish. For countries such as the Comoros, Mauritania, Morocco, Somalia and Yemen, the fisheries sector is important for food security. Fish production in Somalia and the Comoros seems to have stagnated over the past decades, but no assessments of stocks have been made. Mauritania and Morocco, member countries of the Commission for Eastern Central Atlantic Fisheries, have implemented fisheries management measures in accordance with recommendations of various stock assessments.

In 2000, only 9 per cent of the Arab population resided in coastal areas below five metres above sea level, a slight decrease since 1990 (figure 4.30). Although the proportion of the population has remained stable, the total population in such areas has increased, placing greater stress on sensitive coastal environments.

Average annual fish catch rates for Arab countries increased by more than 180 per cent in 2013 compared with 1990, putting stress on fish stocks in marine bodies in the region (figure 4.31). The annual catch of 795,000 metric tons in the Mashreq countries that year represented an increase of more than 300 per cent since 1990. In the LDCs, the

Figure 4.31. Average annual fish catch (thousand metric tons)

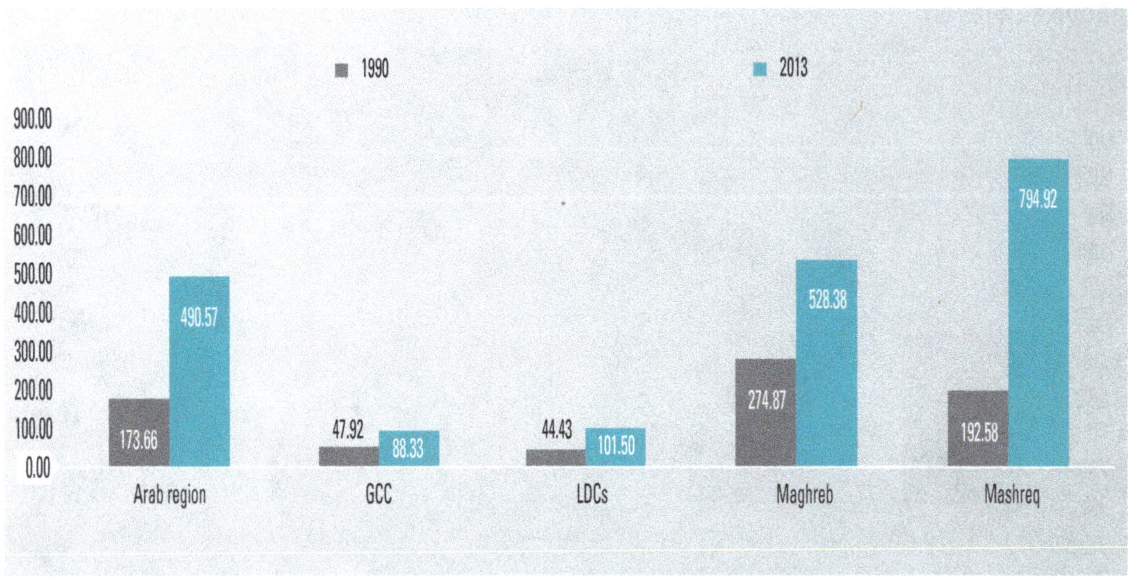

Source: Authors' calculations based on FAO annual fisheries and aquaculture statistics. Available from http://www.fao.org/fishery/statistics/en (accessed 2 November 2015).
Notes: Values are weighted averages against total population, as taken from World Bank, World Development Indicators. Values for the Sudan in the 1990s are for pre-partition Sudan, whereas 2012 and 2013 values do not include South Sudan.

Figure 4.32. Fish catch trends, by body of water (thousand metric tons)

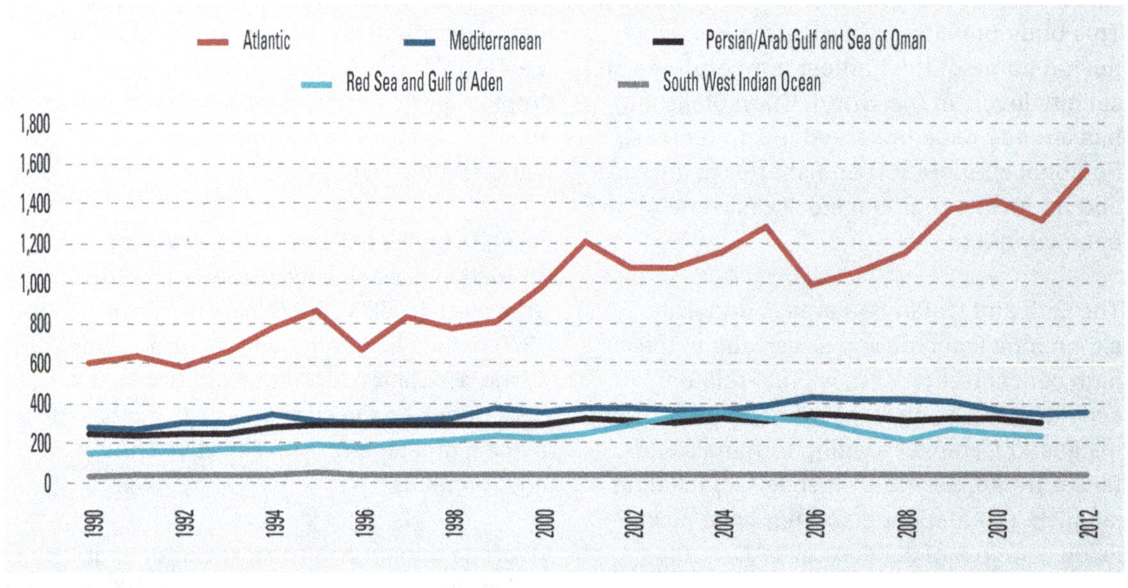

Source: Authors' calculations based on FAO, FishstatJ (Rome, 2014). Available from http://www.fao.org/fishery/statistics/software/fishstatj/en (accessed 2 November 2015).

rise between 1990 and 2013 was nearly 128 per cent. The catch in the Atlantic increased from around 600,000 metric tons in 1990 to 1.56 million metric tons in 2012 (160 per cent increase), representing by far the largest production in the region (figure 4.32).

Increases were also witnessed across other regional bodies of water, including rises of 59 per cent in the Red Sea and Gulf of Aden, 28 per cent in the Mediterranean, and 27 per cent in the Arabian Gulf and Sea of Oman.

4. Terrestrial ecosystems

Extremely arid, the Arab region is dominated by steppe and desert rangelands that constitute more than three quarters of the region's terrestrial ecosystems. Nevertheless, there is great diversity of plant and animal life well adapted to the conditions.

The three phytogeographical regions (Mediterranean, Irano-Turanian and Saharo-Arabian) contain a diverse collection of woody and herbaceous plants, especially annuals and geophytes.[54] Plant biodiversity is greatest in Algeria, Lebanon, Morocco, Somalia, the Sudan, the Syrian Arab Republic and Tunisia, where more than 3,000 species thrive.[55] Plant density is estimated at 1,000-2,000 plant species per 10,000 square kilometres in Jordan, Lebanon, Morocco and the Syrian Arab Republic, and less than 1,000 per 10,000 square kilometres for the remaining Arab countries. There is a density of 21-50 animal species per 10,000 square kilometres in Egypt, Iraq, Jordan, Morocco, the Sudan, the Syrian Arab Republic and Tunisia, 51-100 in Lebanon, and fewer than 20 in the other countries.[56]

Biodiversity degradation in the Arab countries appears to match international trends. According to the International Union for Conservation of Nature and Natural Resources (IUCN), the total number of threatened species in the region stands at over 1,000, with a majority classed as "critically endangered". Of these, 24 per cent are fish, 22 per cent birds and 20 per cent mammals. Djibouti, Egypt, Jordan, Morocco, Saudi Arabia, Somalia, the Sudan and Yemen are host to many threatened species – up to 108 in Egypt.[57] In Yemen, 250 endemic species are threatened with extinction. In Oman, 136 plant species and 46 per cent of all native species are endangered.[58]

Invasive species are a key threat to the region's ecosystems. A total of 551 invasive species have been reported in the region, of which 35 per cent are classified as alien and nearly 51 per cent as native.[59]

The average vegetation cover as a percentage of land area in the Arab region declined from 3.68 per cent in 1990 to 2.84 per cent in 2013 (figure 4.33). That 23 per cent reduction was due in large part to a 33 per cent decrease in the LDCs, while other subregions witnessed relatively small increases.

Rangelands have been affected by overexploitation, with a major change in species composition over the past few decades. According to FAO,[60] severe to very severe human-induced degradation affects up to 30 per cent of the total area of North Africa and 38 per cent of the Arabian Peninsula. Furthermore, between 1970 and 1990 rangelands decreased by 10 per cent in Morocco and Tunisia and 14 per cent in Algeria.[61] Overgrazing remains the major factor in rangelands degradation.

Arab countries have made efforts to preserve their biodiversity, including through the expansion of protected areas (box 4.6). As a percentage of total territorial area, protected areas grew from 3.21 per cent in 1990 to 9.28 per cent in 2012, an increase of around 190 per cent (figure 4.34). Despite that increase, protected areas in the Arab region remain below the global average of 14 per cent in 2012.[62] A regional assessment of biodiversity and ecosystem services is urgently needed if the Arab countries are to strengthen the link between science and policy when it comes to conservation and the sustainable use of biodiversity.

ESCWA and other United Nations bodies could, in conjunction with the Intergovernmental

Figure 4.33. Average vegetation coverage (percentage of land area)

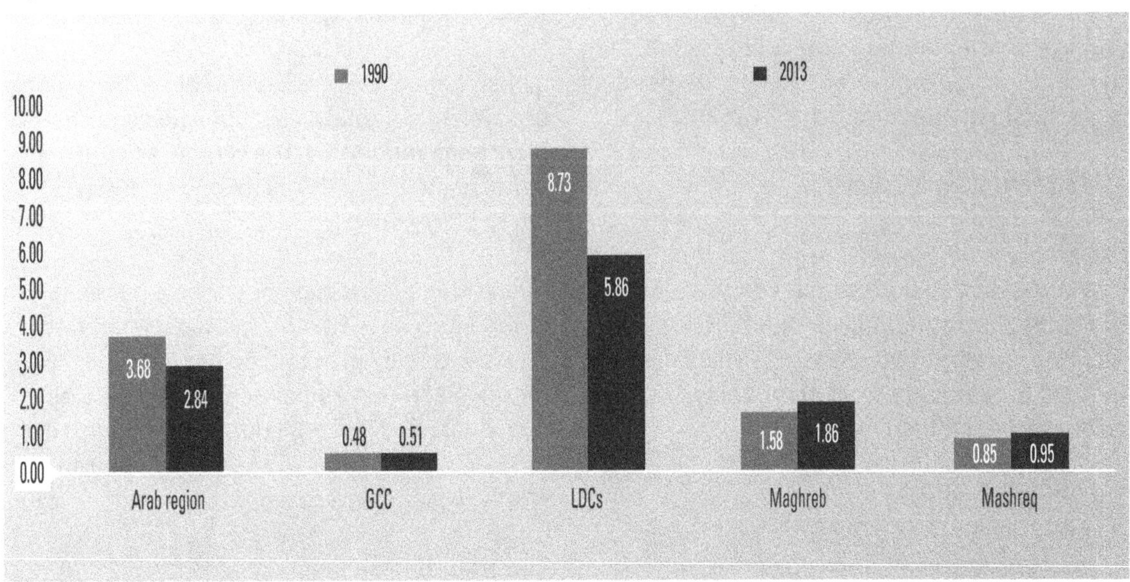

Source: Authors' calculations based on FAO, FAOSTAT (accessed 2 November 2015).
Note: Values are weighted against land area, as taken from FAOSTAT.

Box 4.6. Integrating conservation with development in the Dana Wildlands in Jordan

In the mid-1990s, Jordan, with funding from the World Bank and the Global Environment Facility, launched the project on Conservation of the Dana Wildlands and the Azraq Oasis and Institutional Strengthening of the Royal Society for the Conservation of Nature. It was designed to improve management of the Dana Biosphere Reserve and pioneered the concept of community engagement in protected areas. Through an incentive-based approach, traditional livelihood options such as goat grazing were replaced with opportunities in industries such as ecotourism. The project was successful in generating income, and was gradually welcomed by the local population. The Dana project set the bar for biodiversity protection efforts by demonstrating the significance of integrating socioeconomic factors in conservation projects to ensure their acceptability and long-term sustainability.

Source: UNEP, "Terrestrial ecosystems and biodiversity in the Arab region", Issues Brief for the Arab Sustainable Development Report (2015). Available from http://css.escwa.org.lb/SDPD/3572/Goal15.pdf.

Platform on Biodiversity and Ecosystem Services (www.ipbes.net), develop a capacity-building programme for national stakeholders. It would focus on conducting national ecosystems assessments, in addition to pilot and demonstration projects that benefit from local knowledge. The Arab region could also benefit from thematic assessments of marine and coastal ecosystems, and land degradation and restoration, such as have been carried out in other regions.

A regional assessment of biodiversity and ecosystems could help to mobilize multidisciplinary teams from regional and national research institutions, build partnerships with institutions in developed countries, contribute to knowledge

Figure 4.34. Terrestrial and marine protected areas (percentage of total territorial area)

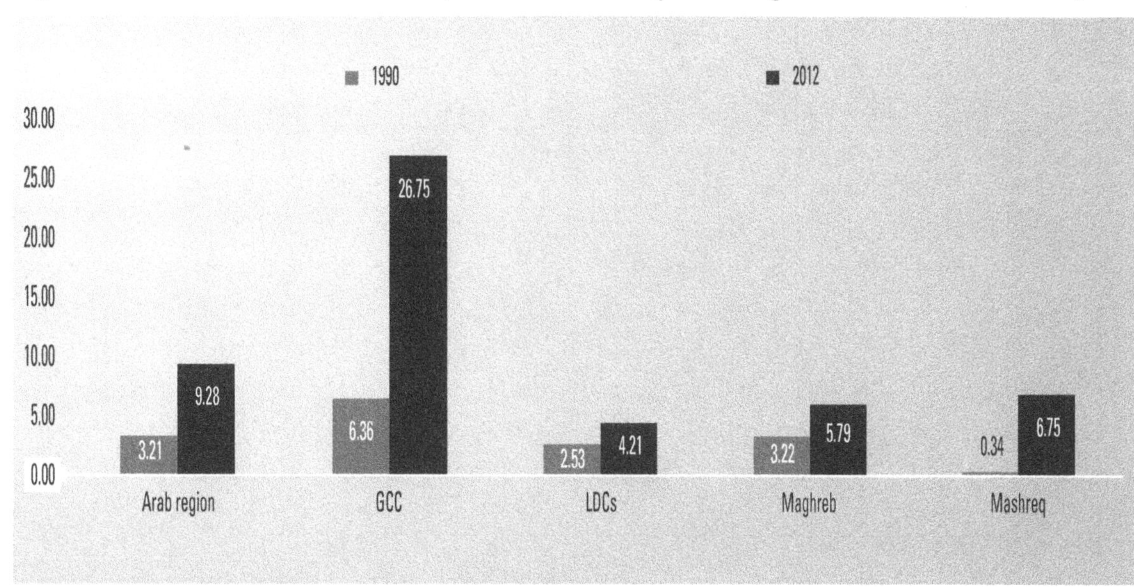

Source: Authors' calculations based on World Bank, World Development Indicators (accessed 2 November 2015).
Notes: Values are weighted against total surface area. Earliest data for Yemen are from 1994. Latest data for the Sudan are from 2011.

generation and sharing, and ensure access to data and information. It would be instrumental in determining a sustainable development baseline and examining the contribution of ecosystems to sustainable development.

5. Peace, Governance and Institutions

"We are determined to foster peaceful, just and inclusive societies which are free from fear and violence. There can be no sustainable development without peace and no peace without sustainable development."

Preamble of the 2030 Agenda for Sustainable Development

5. Peace, Governance and Institutions

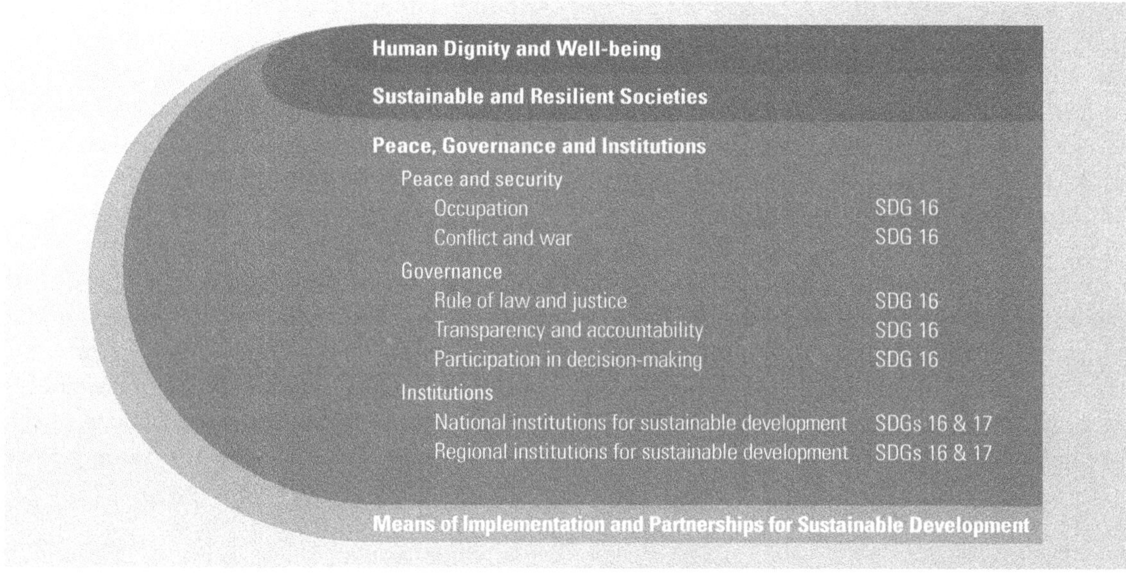

The achievement of peace, good governance and effective institutions is a critical component of the 2030 Agenda for Sustainable Development. They are addressed specifically by SDG 16 (SDG 17 also partly addresses institutional issues) but have a key role to play in the achievement of the other goals. None of the SDGs can be achieved where there is violence, the people have no voice, Governments cannot be held to account, societies are unfair and the justice system does not work.

The importance of those issues in the Arab region, plagued by political instability, internal conflicts, war and ongoing occupation, has become clearer still in recent years. A former United Nations Secretary-General, Mr. Kofi Annan, once said: "Humanity will not enjoy security without development, it will not enjoy development without security, and it will not enjoy either without respect for human rights".

In 2015, the Arab region ranked as the least peaceful part of the world, suffering as it does under the Israeli occupation of Palestine and the dramatic worsening of conflicts in Iraq, Libya, the Syrian Arab Republic and Yemen.

There have been improvements in some areas of governance in some Arab countries, such as the holding of free and fair elections. However, in other respects, such as freedom of expression, matters have worsened. The record on fairness and justice is mixed and the matter of legal identity remains of particular concern.

Several countries provide good examples of capacity to implement strategies with broad ownership, harmonize short-term actions with long-term priorities, coordinate across ministries, and make full use of evidence. Regional mechanisms are being established and strengthened in order to support national stakeholders in this work.

This chapter is largely based on expert reports on governance, human rights and institutions for sustainable development.[1]

A. Peace and security

Violence and instability are becoming the greatest obstacles to achieving sustainable development in the Arab region. In fragile States and those affected by conflict and violence, people are twice as likely to be undernourished than in other developing countries and the number of children not in school is three times as high. Conflict sets back GDP growth, in some cases by decades, and can add another 20 per cent of the population to those living below the poverty line.[2] If occupation and insecurity persist, sustainable development will be impossible.

1. Occupation

The Israeli occupation of Palestinian and other Arab lands is the only remaining case of military occupation in the world today. For decades, Israel has repeatedly, and with almost total impunity, violated international humanitarian and human rights laws, including the denial of the Palestinian people's rights, particularly their right to freedom and self-determination. Israeli practices have severely curbed their right to development, causing in fact a process of "de-development" (reversal of development gains). This is not to mention the regional repercussions of the occupation and the resulting wars that have affected the entire Arab region. Achieving the 2030 Agenda in Palestine will be impossible until Israel ends its occupation, an independent Palestinian State is established and the right to return of Palestinian refugees is recognized. The role of the international community in enforcing international law and supporting development in Palestine is crucial.

(a) Occupation and de-development in Palestine

Israeli violations of international humanitarian law and human rights law are widely documented.[3] The Israeli blockade and repeated offensives against Gaza are a stark example of such violations (box 5.1). Although Israel is party to the Fourth Geneva Convention relative to the protection of civilian persons in time of war, its forces have used excessive force against Palestinian civilians, killing more than 10,000 Palestinians since 1987. Between 2000 and 2014, 1,918 Palestinian children were killed by Israeli forces and settlers. Israeli security forces have used torture and various forms of ill-treatment against detainees. It is reported that 125 Palestinian prisoners died due to torture or ill-treatment up until 2013. Minors are not spared, with the United Nations Children's Fund (UNICEF) documenting 107 cases of ill-treatment of Palestinian children in 2013, 11 of whom were under the age of 14.

Forced displacement of Palestinians and the destruction and confiscation of their property by the Israeli authorities continue. Some 135,000 Palestinians have been evicted from their homes since 1967 and, until 1993, around 250,000 Palestinians had their residency permits revoked, leading to their de facto exile. Between 1967 and 2010, some 24,800 buildings were demolished in occupied Palestinian territory. Successive Israeli Governments have continued to build settlements on expropriated Palestinian lands in the occupied territory since 1967. By mid-2014, the number of Israeli settlers in the West Bank, including East Jerusalem, was estimated to have reached 700,000, quadrupling since the Oslo Accords.[4] Israeli policies regarding the settlements in the occupied Palestinian territory have resulted in the emergence of dual legal regimes that discriminate between people living within a single territory based on religion.[5] Barrier zones surrounding some settlements have created additional restrictions on the mobility of Palestinians, which is already severely constrained due to the separation wall, Israeli checkpoints and other obstacles and administrative and military measures.

The Israeli occupation has hampered access by Palestinians to water, food, health and education, which are among the basic human rights. Since 1967, Israel has controlled all shared water resources in the West Bank (surface and groundwater) and exploited 85 per cent of them.[6] The destruction in 2014 of the only power plant in Gaza left 1.5 million residents without access to adequate water supplies. In 2013, one in every three households in the occupied Palestinian territory was considered to be food insecure, and more than half the population of Gaza depends solely on humanitarian food distribution.[7] Palestinians are frequently denied access to adequate medical care. Pregnant women are particularly affected, with more than 67 Palestinian mothers giving birth at Israeli checkpoints during the past 15 years. There is a shortage of educational facilities in the West Bank and those that exist are inadequate. Around 10,000 Palestinian students attend makeshift "schools" under tents or in tin shacks. In East Jerusalem, 2,200 more classrooms are needed to accommodate students.

Economic development in Palestine is hampered by "frequent military strikes and the destruction of infrastructure, isolation from global markets, fragmentation of domestic markets and confiscation and denial of access to national natural resources".[8] Following the 2014 military offensive in Gaza, the Palestinian economy suffered once more: per capita GDP shrank by 3.3 per cent, unemployment increased by 3 per cent and the fiscal deficit widened. During the first quarter of 2015, Israel withheld clearance revenue – the largest source of public revenue for the Palestinian Government – thus aggravating an already bleak economic situation. Forced dependence on electricity and water imports from Israel further saps Palestinian resources. This process of "de-development" undermines donor support, which is already insufficient and in decline.[9]

(b) Impact of the occupation beyond Palestine

The occupation of Palestine has created a protracted refugee situation. More than three million Palestine refugees (out of a total of 5.2 million Palestinian refugees in the world), registered with the United Nations Relief and Works Agency for Palestine Refugees in the Near East (UNRWA), live in dire conditions in camps in Lebanon, Jordan and the Syrian Arab Republic.[10] A socioeconomic survey of Palestinian refugees in Lebanon[11] reported that two thirds of them are poor, one third suffer from chronic illnesses, and 15 per cent are severely food insecure. They face social and economic exclusion and unemployment among them exceeds 50 per cent (higher still for women). Eight per cent of children aged 7-15 years do not attend school and only half those aged 16 and above do so. Fighting in the Syrian Arab Republic has damaged most Palestinian camps and severely affected the 560,000 refugees living there. Many of them have been displaced, either within the country or abroad.

The Israeli occupation and ensuing wars have had a profound effect on the region as a whole, hindering regional integration and sustainable development by diverting resources away from development, and weakening governance. Partly as a result of the Israeli occupation and related conflicts and instability, the Arab region spends more on weapons (4.15 per cent of GDP) than any other in relative terms, placing a great strain on public finance.[12] Some scholars believe that occupation and the resulting wars have hindered the promotion of democratic governance in several Arab States and fuelled religious extremism, giving them an excuse to "prioritize" resistance against Israel and the containment of extreme religious elements at the expense of granting their own people basic human rights.[13]

Box 5.1. Blockades and repeated offensives cripple Gaza

The 1.7 million Palestinians in Gaza have lived under blockade since 2007, with severe socioeconomic consequences. Three military offensives since 2009 have taken a heavy human toll. More than 1,700 civilians were killed in the 2009 offensive and almost 1,500, including 500 children, in the 2014 summer offensive. In 2009, almost half of the health facilities in Gaza were damaged or destroyed. During the 2014 offensive, 17 hospitals, 56 clinics and 32 ambulances were damaged, and 16 medical workers lost their lives while on duty. The education system was similarly crippled, with 26 schools destroyed and 122 damaged, 69 of them run by UNRWA. The pace of reconstruction has been extremely slow for a number of reasons, including Israeli restrictions on the import of construction material.

The impact on the economy is substantial. Unemployment in Gaza reached 44 per cent in 2014, the highest level on record. The middle class is effectively non-existent and most households depend on humanitarian aid. The United Nations Conference on Trade and Development (UNCTAD) estimates that the cost of the three offensives to Gaza is in the order of three times its annual GDP. Including indirect costs lifts the estimate considerably. In 2012, the United Nations predicted that Gaza could be "unliveable" by 2020 if current trends continued, a view restated by UNCTAD in 2015.

Sources: Economic and social repercussions of the Israeli occupation on the living conditions of the Palestinian people in the Occupied Palestinian Territory, including East Jerusalem, and the Arab population in the occupied Syrian Golan (A/70/82–E/2015/13); *Palestine, the Occupation and the Fourth Geneva Convention: Facts and Figures* (E/ ESCWA/ECRI/2014/Booklet.1); Report on UNCTAD assistance to the Palestinian people: developments in the economy of the occupied Palestinian territory (TD/B/62/3); United Nations Country Team in the occupied Palestinian territory, *Gaza in 2020: A Liveable Place?* (Jerusalem, Office of the United Nations Special Coordinator for the Middle East Peace Process, August 2012, available from www.unrwa.org/userfiles/file/publications/gaza/Gaza%20in%202020.pdf).

2. Conflict and war

The Arab region is the least peaceful in the world, according to the Global Peace Index (figure 5.1). Topping the list of least peaceful countries in the world in 2015 was the Syrian Arab Republic, followed by Iraq, Afghanistan, South Sudan, Central African Republic, Somalia and the Sudan. According to ESCWA, 11 out of 22 Arab countries have suffered at least one internal conflict since 2009 (figure 5.2).

The Global Peace Index considers three main categories: militarization, safety and security, and ongoing conflict. The Arab region and North America are the most militarized regions in the world (figure 5.3).
In terms of ongoing conflict, South Asia is still considered worse than the Arab region as a whole, although the Syrian Arab Republic, the Sudan, Somalia and Iraq are among the 10 worst countries globally in that category.

The situation in the Arab region deteriorated in 2015 across many subindicators because of the dramatically worsening situations in Iraq, Libya, the Syrian Arab Republic and Yemen, where challenges to central Governments have been complicated by internationalization of those conflicts, sectarian divisions and the expansion of the so-called Islamic State group (figure 5.4).[14] Libya and Djibouti were among the top five countries with the most dramatic increases in violence in 2015.[15]

According to the Global Terrorism Index report for 2014, the Arab region has undergone a steep increase in recent years in the Maghreb and Mashreq, while the level of terrorism in LDCs remained relatively high (figure 5.5).[16] From 2000 to 2013, about half the world's suicide attacks took place in the Arab region (more than 45 per cent of them in Iraq and the Syrian Arab Republic). Citizens of the Arab region also suffer from the violence associated with occupation and brutality against non-violent political protesters.

Figure 5.1. Changes in Global Peace Index score

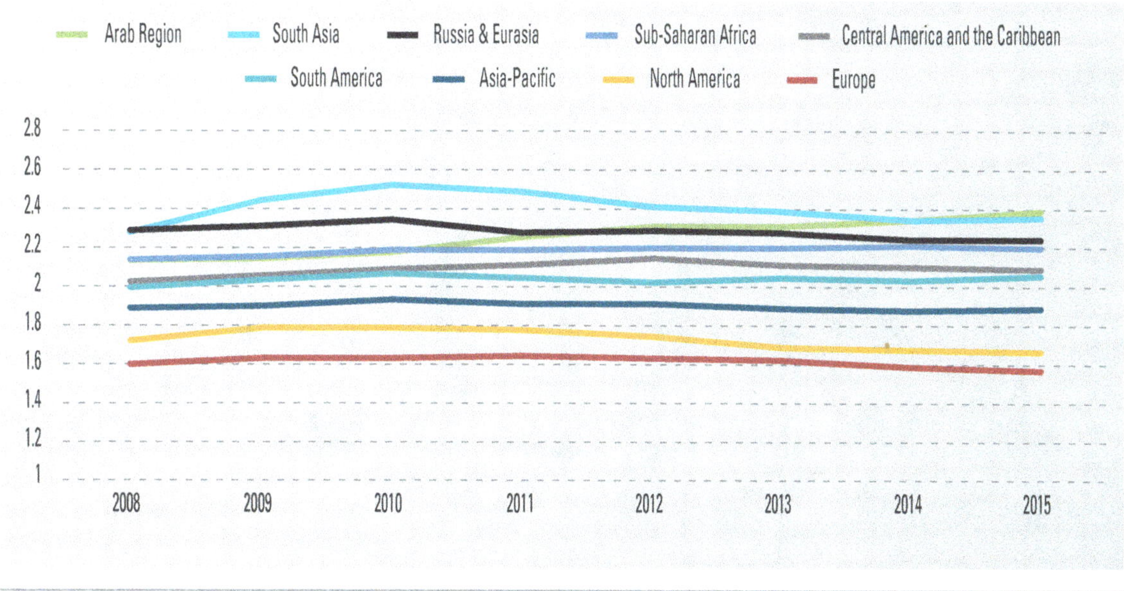

Sources: Authors' calculations based on data from the Institute for Economics and Peace, Global Peace Index, available from www.visionofhumanity.org (accessed 2 November 2015); and email correspondence with the Institute.

Figure 5.2. Incidence of conflict (percentage of countries suffering from at least one internal conflict between 2009 and 2014)

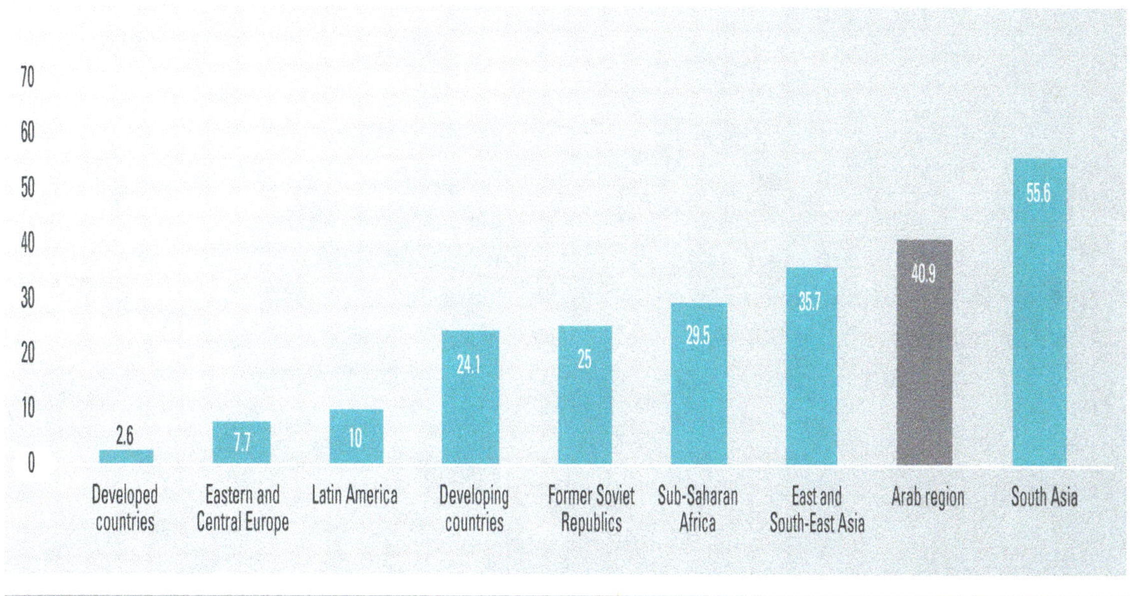

Source: Authors' calculations based on data from Uppsla Conflict Data Program (UCDP)/Peace Research Institute Oslo (PRIO) Armed Conflict Dataset. Available from www.prio.org/Data/Armed-Conflict/UCDP-PRIO (accessed 2 November 2015).

Conflict and political violence in the region have taken a heavy toll in fatalities and caused massive displacement. The Global Peace Index estimates conflict-related fatalities for 2014 at 71,667 in the Syrian Arab Republic, 18,489 in Iraq, 3,836 in Yemen, 3,060 in Libya, and 360 in Lebanon. Millions have been forcibly displaced as refugees and

Figure 5.3. Global Peace Index domain scores, 2015

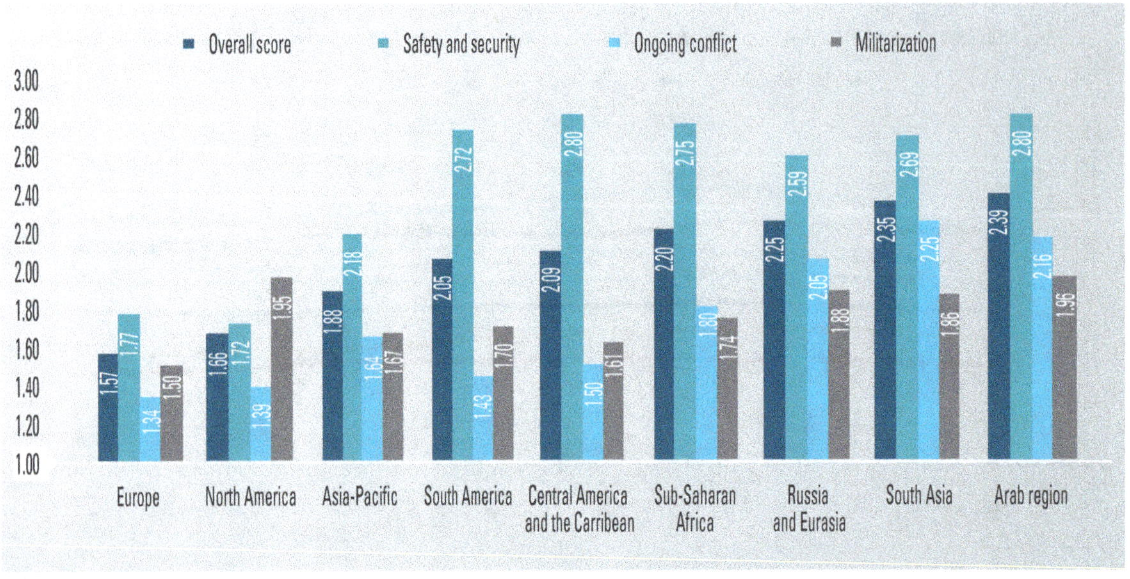

Source: Authors' calculations based on data from the Institute for Economics and Peace and email correspondence with the Institute.
Notes: Country groupings used in the Global Peace Index (GPI) were maintained, except for the Arab region, as it is not available in the original GPI classification. Each domain score is a simple average of domain scores of the countries making up the country grouping.

Figure 5.4. Global Peace Index, 10 largest indicator score changes for the Arab region, 2008 to 2015

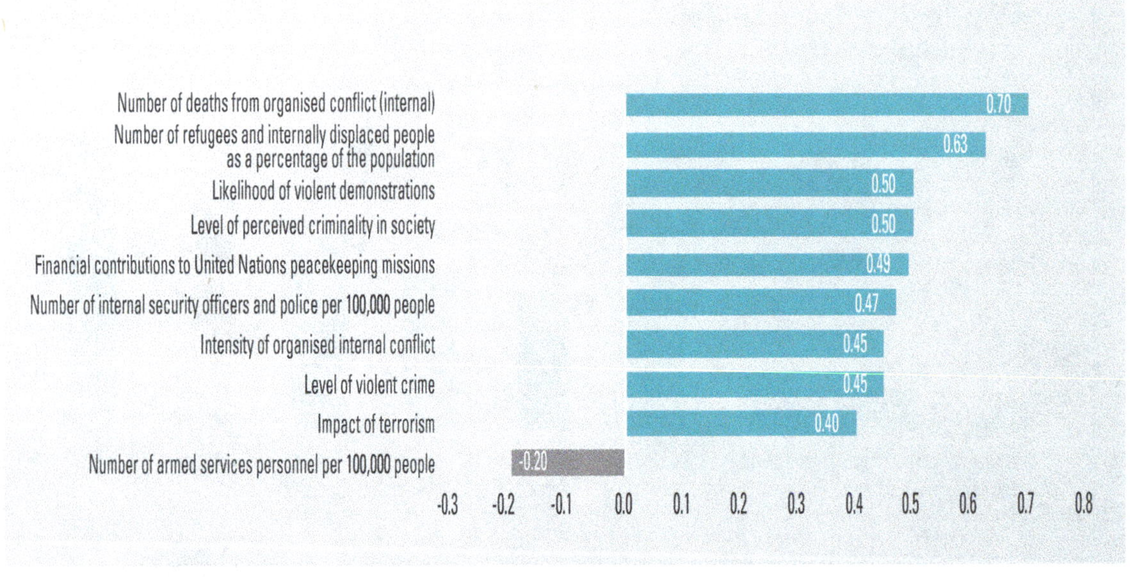

Source: Authors' calculations based on data from the Institute for Economics and Peace and email correspondence with the Institute.

internally displaced persons (IDPs), which has resulted in a loss of productivity (as in most cases they are unable to work), and has placed great strain on host countries in terms of natural resources and the environment, infrastructure, social conflict, and the financial cost to host Governments of providing services.

Figure 5.5. Global Terrorism Index, Arab subregions

Mashreq
Maghreb
LDCs
GCC

10.00
9.00
8.00
7.00
6.00
5.00
4.00
3.00
2.00
1.00
0.00

2006 2007 2008 2009 2010 2011 2012 2013

Source: Authors' calculations based on data from the Global Terrorism Index. Available from www.visionofhumanity.org/#page/indexes/terrorism-index (accessed 15 October 2015).
Notes: Scores range from 0 (no impact) to 10 (highest impact). The index does not include data for the Comoros or Palestine.

Figure 5.6. Refugees and IDPs by country of origin, 2014

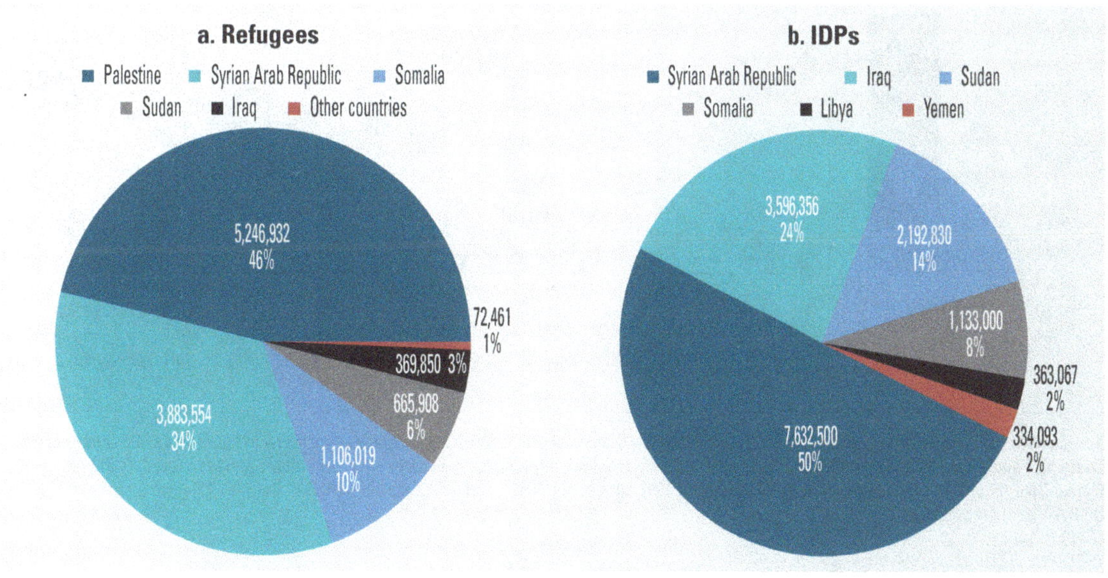

Sources: Authors' calculations based on data from the United Nations High Commissioner for Refugees (UNHCR) Statistical Online Population database, available from www.unhcr.org/pages/4a013eb06.html; and UNRWA in figures as of 1 January 2015, available from http://www.unrwa.org/sites/default/files/unrwa_in_figures_2015.pdf.
Note: Data for Palestine are a sum of UNHCR and UNRWA figures.

As of 2014, refugees from the region exceed 11 million persons (figure 5.6 (a)). This represents 58 per cent of the global total (27 per cent from Palestine, 20 per cent from the Syrian Arab Republic, 6 per cent from Somalia, 3 per cent from the Sudan and 2 per cent from Iraq).

Figure 5.7. Refugee population

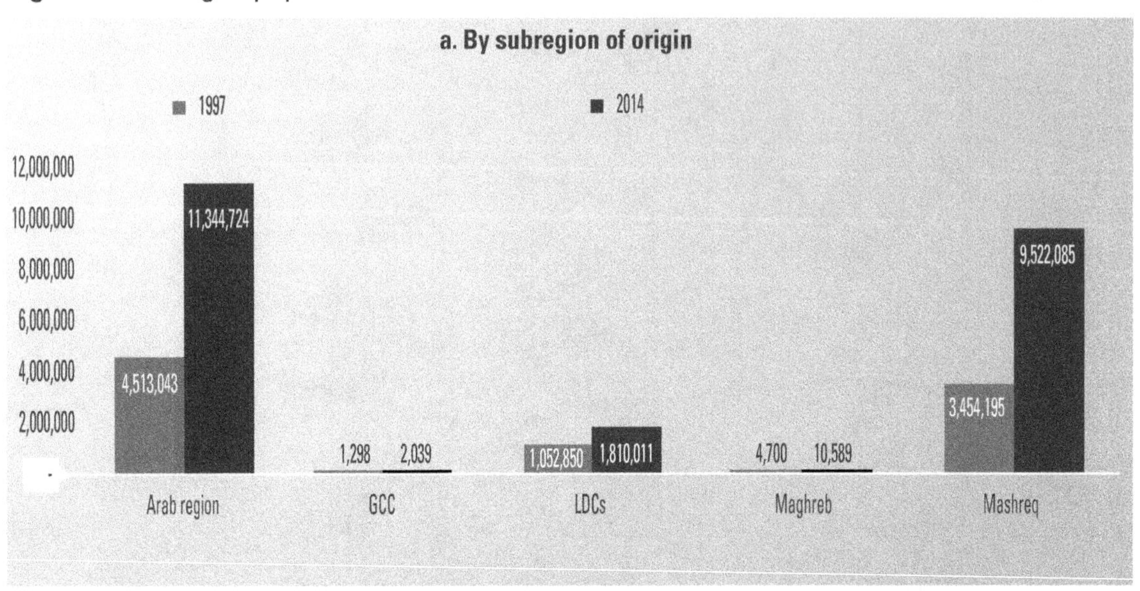

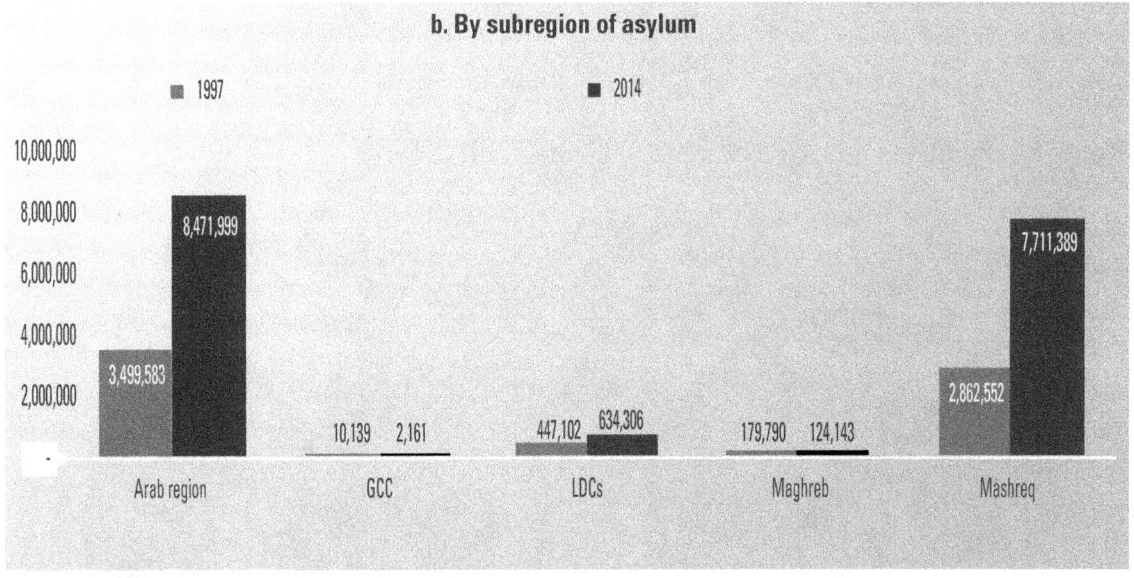

Sources: Authors' calculations based on data from the UNHCR Statistical Online Population database, UNRWA in figures as of 1 January 2015 (see figure 5.6); and McGill Palestinian Refugee ResearchNet, available from http://prrn.mcgill.ca/background/table1.htm (accessed 27 October 2015).
Notes: Data for 1997 for Palestine refugees are a sum of 1997 data from UNHCR and 1992 data from McGill. Data for 2014 are a sum of UNHCR and UNRWA data for that year.

At 15 million (figure 5.6 (b)), IDPs in the region account for 46 per cent of the world total (24 per cent in the Syrian Arab Republic, 11 per cent in Iraq, 7 per cent in Somalia and 4 per cent in the Sudan).

At the end of 2014, there were around 3.9 million Syrian refugees, with more than 630,000 registered in Jordan – almost 10 per cent of the population – and more than 1,170,000 registered in Lebanon – more than a quarter of the population.[17] UNRWA reports 5.1 million registered Palestinian refugees.[18] Figure 5.7 shows the trends in the Arab region between 1997 and 2014. The refugee crisis continues to affect mostly the Mashreq

Figure 5.8. Internally displaced persons

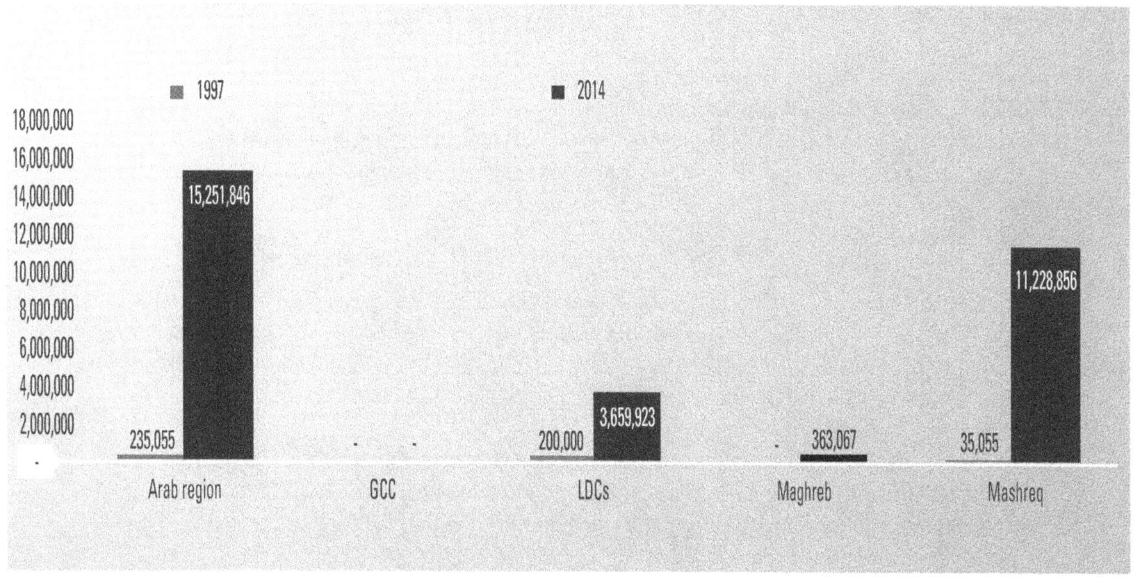

Source: Authors' calculations based on data from the UNHCR Statistical Online Population database (see figure 5.6).

subregion, and most refugees appear to remain in the region.

More than 7.6 million Syrians and 3.6 million Iraqis were reported to be IDPs, making the Mashreq the subregion with the highest figures worldwide, followed by the LDCs, with 2.2 million Sudanese and 1.1 million Somali IDPs. Figure 5.8 shows the trends in the Arab region between 1997 and 2014. In line with the 1951 Convention relating to the Status of Refugees and the human development goals of UNRWA, host countries should work more closely with national, regional and international aid agencies and allow them to implement their programmes.

B. Governance

Arab States are often referred to as rentier systems - sharing rents with the people in exchange for political acquiescence. Some have been able to maintain stability through revenue redistribution but the question remains whether the system is sustainable.

One common rent-sharing mechanism is the provision of civil service jobs, with limited expectations for performance.[19] The civil service thus becomes a means of avoiding the need for government accountability rather than for the provision of quality public services. Such systems are also characterized by unfair pay scales, over-staffing and rigid hierarchies.

What the United Nations Development Programme (UNDP) termed the "deficit of freedom and good governance" in its 2004 Arab Human Development Report needs to be addressed if the region is to achieve sustainable development. Good governance is a key SDG and a necessary enabler of all of the other goals.

Measuring governance is challenging and a plethora of indicators for doing so have emerged over the past two decades. Some focus on rules and procedures, some on their implementation and still others on the economic, social, environmental and other impacts of governance. Indicators can provide valuable information but they can also be misused, skewed to favour a certain ideology, behaviour, policy or institutional

Box 5.2. ESCWA framework for monitoring governance

In its *Arab Governance Report: Governance Challenges in Countries Undergoing Transition* (E/ESCWA/ECRI/2013/4), ESCWA defines democratic governance as a system of collectively binding traditions, rules and policies that regulate a society and that are created, modified and controlled by its members through participative and representative arrangements, based on respect for human rights and equal rights and obligations. Contestation, inclusiveness, the division of powers and institutional capacity are crucial for democratic governance.

The main building blocks of democratic governance are: clear constitutional and human rights principles; political stability and the absence of violence; institutional effectiveness and accountability; inclusiveness and transition-related reforms; and economic governance and effective service delivery. These are rendered operational through the eight pillars depicted in the figure below.

Each country defines its priorities and chooses among the pillars and subcategories those that require urgent attention. The resulting framework will thus be adapted to national priorities and help to identify policy actions that could improve governance. It is expected, however, that many essential variables will require the collection of primary data.

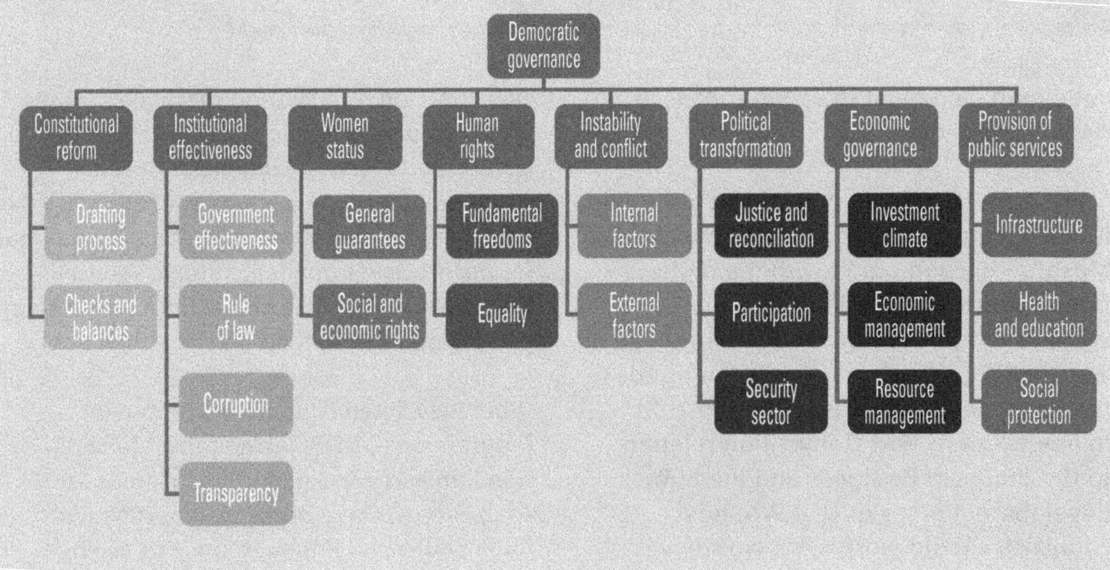

design. When many variables are combined into one broad indicator, the composite indicator is often vague. ESCWA has proposed a comprehensive framework for monitoring democratic governance, focussing on regional specificities and priorities (box 5.2).

The remainder of this chapter highlights governance issues referred to in SDG 16 and which are of special relevance to the Arab region.

1. Rule of law and justice

Rule of law and justice include a range of issues. Three are highlighted here: corruption, legal identity and the functioning of the justice system.

(a) Corruption

Corruption hinders sustainable development by shifting government priorities and financial resources towards the private interests of the powerful. It has been asserted that corruption in Arab countries that underwent uprisings is exemplified by "the ruling elites, including extended family and select cronies, who captured both the polity and key segments of the economy [...] to control the accumulation and distribution of resources and jobs to perpetuate their power and amass illicit wealth".[20] Many studies have examined the costs of corruption. One revealed that, between 2002 and 2006, an average of $111 billion per year flowed illicitly out of the region due to corruption, crime and tax evasion.[21] Studies also show that the poor pay the heaviest price due to those losses.[22]

Transparency International's Corruption Perceptions Index (CPI) shows that the Middle East and North Africa area is widely seen as corrupt. Some countries rocked by the 2011 uprisings had the worst scores on the index prior to the uprisings.[23] Similarly, the Arab region as a whole scores 3.5 out of 10 for separation of powers on the Bertelsmann Stiftung Transformation Index (BTI)[24] – far below the global average of 5.3.

Unclear and overly complex non-standard bidding documents, lengthy procurement processes, bribery and other opportunities for corruption abound in the region. Systems of checks and balances are needed in the public sector to prevent corrupt individuals from taking advantage of positions of power. Civil servants need to be schooled to serve the public fairly and equitably in accordance with the law. Action must be taken against those who do not. In many Arab countries, this does not occur. A United Nations study of six Arab countries noted "a significant gap between policies and practices, particularly for reporting on and investigating wrongdoing".[25]

The Global Competiveness Index provides rates for three specific aspects of corruption – favouritism in decisions of government officials, diversion of public funds and irregular payments and bribes. Among the 15 Arab countries included in the 2014-2015 Global Competiveness Index survey, nine scored better than the worldwide mean score in terms of favouritism and diversion of public funds, and eight scored better than the worldwide mean score in terms of irregular payments and bribes. However, in all three categories most Arab countries have seen a deterioration since 2010.

(b) Legal identity

Denial of citizenship is widespread in the Arab region and affects several groups including Palestinians, the Bidun and children whose fathers are not citizens of the country concerned. For example, the Citizenship and Entry into Israel Law of 31 May 2003 suspended the possibility of Palestinians from the occupied Palestinian territory of obtaining Israeli residence permits or citizenship in Israel, including through family reunification. The effect of this discriminatory law is that thousands of Palestinian families must separate, emigrate or live illegally in Israel under constant threat of arrest and deportation. The Bidun ("those without" nationality) group is concentrated in the Gulf countries. During the 1980s, many had their rights revoked by law and have consequently been unable to work, travel, receive education or health benefits, register marriages or, in most cases, even obtain a driver's license. Improvements have been made since 2000 and several thousands have been granted citizenship.[26]

Thirteen of the 27 countries around the world in which men and women do not have an equal right to pass citizenship on to their children (or spouse) are in the Arab region. UNHCR distinguishes various categories. Countries that allow some safeguard against the child's statelessness (for example, if the father is unknown or stateless himself) include

Figure 5.9. Rule of Law Index: Civil justice

	Egypt	Jordan	Lebanon	Morocco	Tunisia	United Arab Emirates
Factor 7: Civil Justice	0.39	0.62	0.45	0.51	0.52	0.63
7.1 People have access to affordable civil justice	0.39	0.53	0.48	0.43	0.48	0.46
7.6. Civil justice is effectively enforced	0.16	0.58	0.47	0.49	0.48	0.67

Source: World Justice Project 2015. Available from http://worldjusticeproject.org/rule-of-law-index (accessed 22 July 2015).
Note: Index ranges from 0 (worst) to 1 (best).

Figure 5.10. Rule of Law Index: Criminal justice

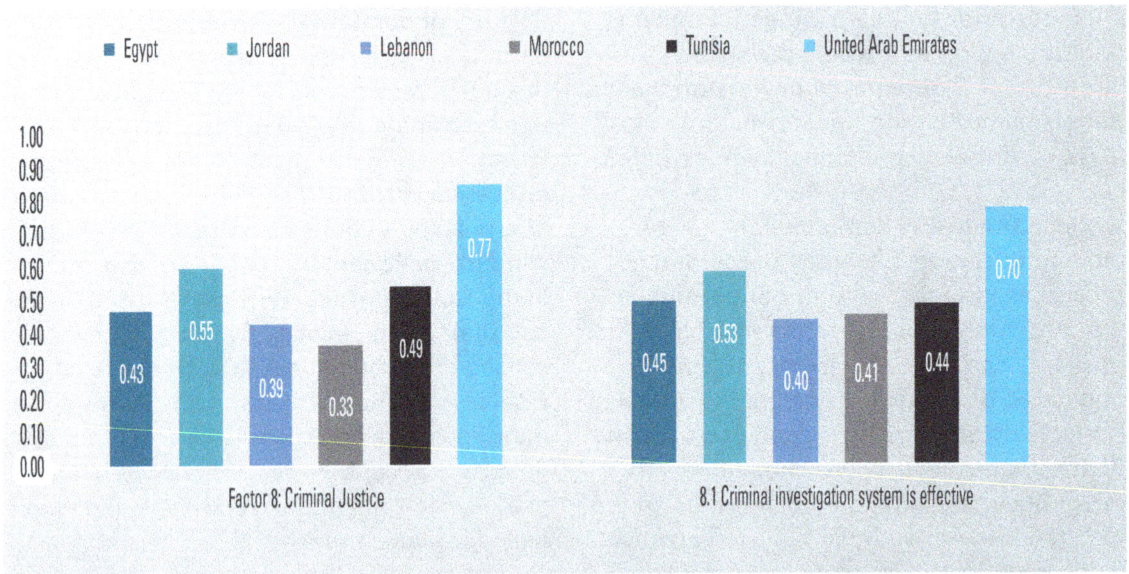

Source: World Justice Project 2015 (see figure 5.9).
Note: Index ranges from 0 (worst) to 1 (best).

Bahrain, Iraq, Jordan, Libya, Oman, Saudi Arabia, the Sudan, the Syrian Arab Republic and the United Arab Emirates. Countries that provide no (or extremely limited) exceptions include Kuwait, Lebanon, Qatar and Somalia.[27]

(c) The justice system

In addition to the fairness of laws, the administration of justice must be effective so that people may resolve grievances in a peaceful manner. Effectiveness refers to the system's capacity to investigate, adjudicate and enforce judgments in a timely and impartial manner. Accessibility includes general awareness of available remedies, the availability and affordability of legal advice and representation, and the absence of excessive or unreasonable fees and hurdles.

The World Justice Project's Rule of Law Index provides ratings for only six Arab countries: Egypt, Jordan, Lebanon, Morocco, Tunisia and the United Arab Emirates. The United Arab Emirates and Jordan score highest on civil and criminal justice (two of the index factors). The United Arab Emirates scores well on enforcement of civil justice, but much lower on access to affordable civil justice. By contrast, Egypt scores significantly higher on access to affordable civil justice than on enforcement (figures 5.9 and 5.10).

Access to justice typically is limited for people in situations of vulnerability, among them migrant workers (box 5.3).

The role of the police and armed forces in law enforcement and security also warrants special attention in the Arab region, particularly in countries affected by conflict and terrorism. Their activities are well defined under international law, including the human rights treaties and the Code of Conduct for Law Enforcement Officials,[28] and are based on the need to respect fundamental rights of people under all circumstances, including when placing them under arrest and during interrogation. Suspicion must be based on tangible evidence. Torture is strictly prohibited.

This is particularly important within the Arab region where many countries are in conflict or post-conflict situations and suffer directly from terrorism. Bypassing the rule of law and violating human rights in an effort to restore order and confront terrorism is counter-productive, and may have the unintended consequence of driving victims of such violations into the arms of terrorism. Counter-terrorism measures adopted by a number of Arab countries have included the implementation of broad and vague antiterrorism laws that have adversely affected whole populations by legalizing undefined periods of pretrial detention, the death penalty, curbs on freedom of expression, and telephone tapping.[29]

Box 5.3. Access to justice by vulnerable groups: Migrant workers

Regulation of the labour market and migrant labour is a prerogative of the State, but legislation governing employment must be consistent with human rights. In many Arab countries, that is not the case. The sponsorship system applied in some countries ties migrant workers legally to their employers and is thus open to abuse. The system gives employers excessive liberties to "protect their investment", including by holding workers' passports.

The situation of migrant domestic workers in the region, the vast majority of whom are women, has been heavily criticised, including by United Nations' human rights bodies. Domestic workers are often not covered by national labour laws and face difficult working conditions, such as low pay, deprivation of freedom of movement, the withholding of passports and lack of legal recourse.[a]

Source: Fateh Azzam, "A human rights approach to sustainable development in the Arab Region".
[a] See, for example, the Concluding Observations of the Committee on Economic, Social and Cultural Rights regarding Kuwait (E/C.12/1/Add.98, paras. 15-18) and the concluding observations of the Committee on the Elimination of Discrimination against Women on Oman, Saudi Arabia and the United Arab Emirates (CEDAW/C/OMN/CO/1, paras. 27 and 42; CEDAW/C/SAU/CO/2, p. 7; CEDAW/C/ARE/CO/1, para. 36).

Box 5.4. Nascent independent government bodies

Several independent bodies are mandated to monitor and investigate government conduct in some Arab States. They include: the Independent Election Commission and the Anti-Corruption Commission in Jordan; the Commission of Integrity in Iraq; the Instance Nationale de la Lutte Contre la Corruption in Tunisia; the Instance Centrale de la Prévention de la Corruption in Morocco and the State Audit Institution in the United Arab Emirates, which is mandated to ensure that public funds are used in compliance with federal law and oversees the effective management of the State budget. Such institutions are still in their infancy and they are often criticized for being independent more in name than in practice.

Source: Lamia Moubayed, "From government to governance: how will the Arab region meet the goals of sustainable development in the post-2015 period" (Beirut, 2015, E/ESCWA/ECRI/2015/WP.3).

Figure 5.11. Selected Worldwide Governance Indicators, 2014

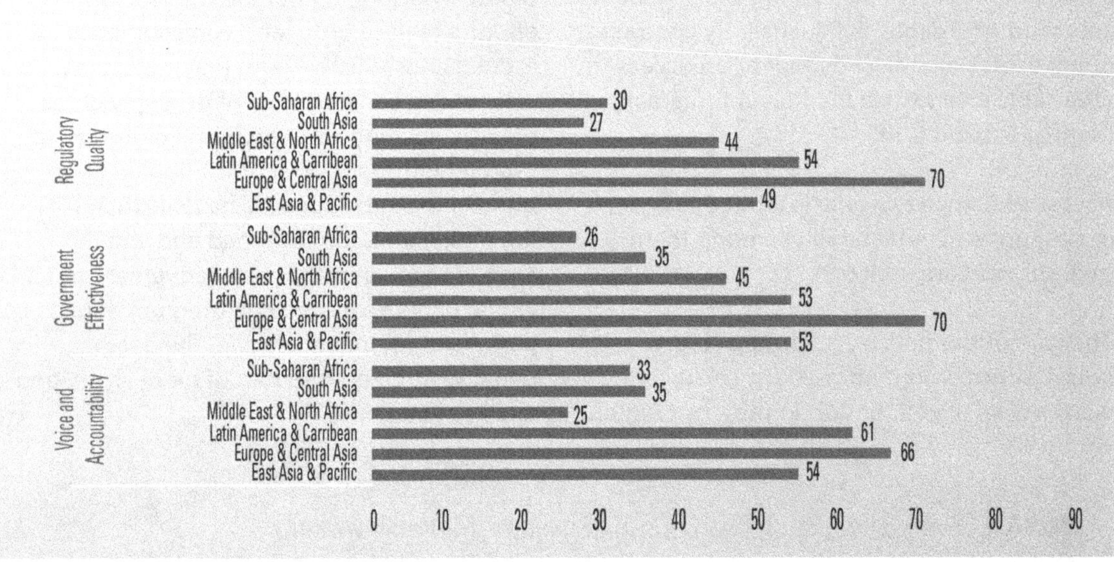

Source: World Bank, Worldwide Governance Indicators. Available from http://info.worldbank.org/governance/wgi/index.aspx#reports (accessed 13 October 2015).

2. Transparency and accountability

Transparency in policymaking is essential for citizens to know what their leaders are doing. In this regard, the situation in the region, as deducted from the Global Competitiveness Index, is mixed. While half the Arab countries have improved transparency in recent years, the other half have slid backwards.[30]

In terms of budget accountability and comprehensiveness, the Middle East and North Africa (MENA) area rates better than the average for low income countries but not as well as middle-income countries (box 5.4). Based on the Public Expenditure and Financial Accountability Index, the region's public financial management systems are roughly comparable to those of other countries at similar income levels, although the region's deficiencies are evident in areas such as credibility of the budget and accounting, recording and reporting.[31] Similarly, the International

Figure 5.12. Bertelsmann Stiftung Transformation Index (BTI): Extent to which environmental concerns are taken into account in macro- and microeconomic terms

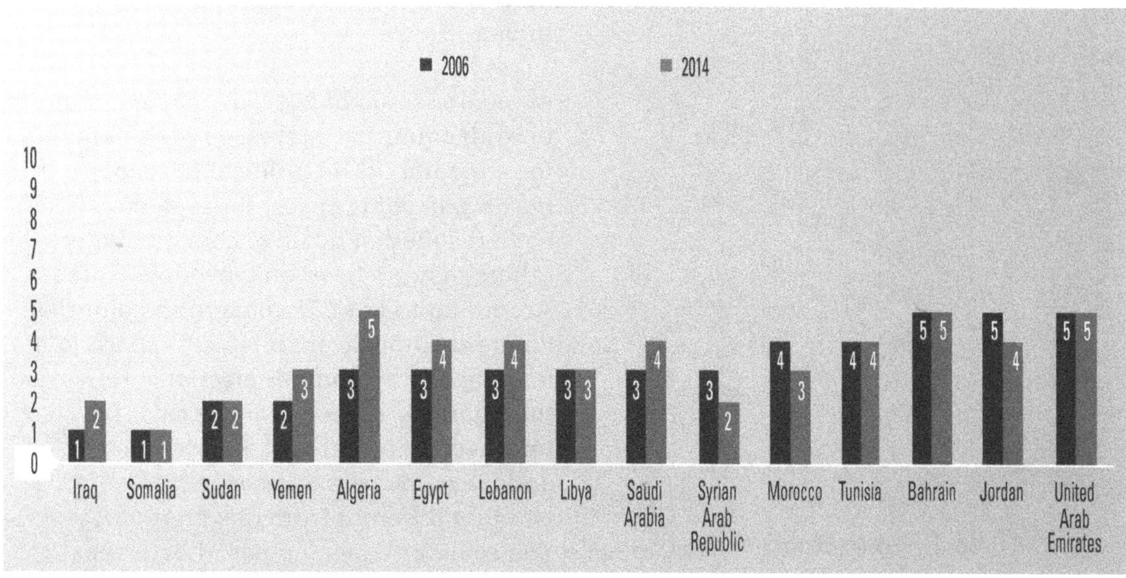

Source: Bertelsmann Stiftung, BTI. Available from http://www.bti-project.org/ (accessed 2 November 2015).
Note: Index ranges from 1 (worst) to 10 (best).

Monetary Fund (IMF) Budget Institutions Index finds that, although the MENA area ranks comparatively well overall, there are deficiencies with regard to budget implementation, sustainability and credibility, and transparency.[32] In the Open Budget Index of 2015, most of the 11 Arab countries considered ranked as providing minimal or no budget transparency (only Jordan, with a score of 55 out of 100, and Tunisia, with 42, ranked as having "some" transparency).

The region's poor ranking cannot be explained by lack of technical competence. Figure 5.11 shows that, while the MENA area ranks lowest in the world in terms of voice and accountability, its rankings are close to world averages in terms of the competence-related indicators of regulatory quality and government effectiveness.

In addition to government accountability and technical competence, the BTI assesses the extent to which policymaking addresses environmental sustainability. Somalia has the lowest score possible and in the cases of Jordan, Morocco and the Syrian Arab Republic, performance has declined since 2006. All Arab countries score below 5 out of 10, reflecting a lack of integration of environmental concerns into economic policy (figure 5.12).

3. Participation in decision-making

Voice and accountability are associated with higher levels of development. In the Arab region, this association has tended to be weak. Although the level of development in Arab countries varies widely in terms of per capita GDP, all are below global averages in terms of voice and accountability (figure 5.13). Furthermore, popular dissatisfaction in that regard has been among the primary causes of often violent political instability.

According to article 21 of the International Covenant on Civil and Political Rights, all citizens have the right to participate

Figure 5.13. Per capita income and voice and accountability

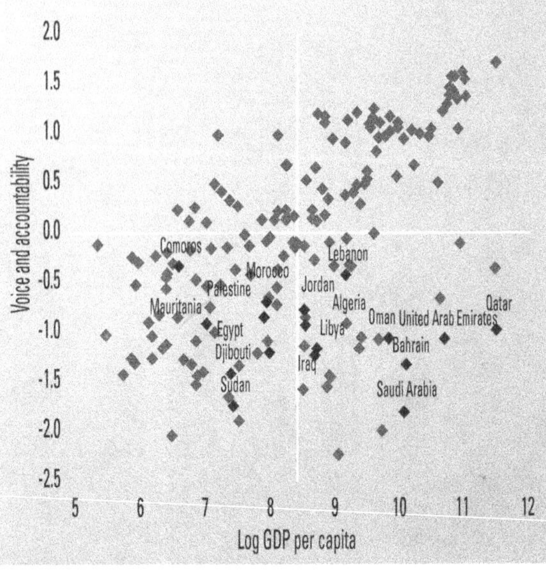

Source: Authors' calculations based on World Bank, World Development Indicators (accessed 16 October 2015).
Note: Light blue dots represent non-Arab countries.

in public affairs, generally understood as participation directly or through representatives chosen in fair and free elections. However, democratic participation equally encompasses the notion of the right to express views on policy. Participation broadens the legitimacy of policies, development plans and projects, and ensures that priorities reflect the needs of a given region or locality. It also implies that all competing interests are represented. While not all of those interests may be met in the end, open debate contributes to the public perception that the interests of the broadest possible majority take priority.

The benefits of participation extend to the implementation of plans. For example, efforts to deal with pollution, climate change and water scarcity cannot succeed without the involvement of civil society. In addition to raising public awareness of environmental issues, they can encourage people to engage in preventing pollution, recycling and conserving water. Their participation is crucial if State policies are to bear fruit.

In the uprisings of 2011, people in a number of Arab countries expressed their demand for a greater say in political decision-making. In some cases, those demands have resulted in positive change, but in others matters have only become worse. According to the BTI, most Arab countries have seen improvements with regard to the holding of free and fair elections. However, the figures are open to interpretation. Improvements were recorded in Tunisia and Libya, but the two cases could not be more different from one another. The score of Libya increased between 2006 and 2014 because its elections were well administered, despite the fact that participation was low and armed conflict ensued afterwards. Some countries continue to hold the lowest score possible. The index is less clear with regard to changes in the role of civil society. While the extent to which the Governments allow civil society to participate in the political process has improved, there was a general deterioration in terms of "civil society traditions" (social capital and the number of actively engaged civic associations).

In the Arab region, legislation on free expression is generally vague and draws red lines around criticism of policy and the Head of State. Human rights reports frequently contest the legality of arrests and trials of people for alleged crimes under such laws.

Although the rights of association and assembly have been bolstered in most Arab countries since 2006, they remain at the lowest possible levels in Saudi Arabia, Somalia and the Syrian Arab Republic (figure 5.14).[33] In fluid situations such as those prevailing in a number of

Figure 5.14. BTI: Extent to which individuals can form and join independent political parties or groups and extent to which these groups associate and assemble freely

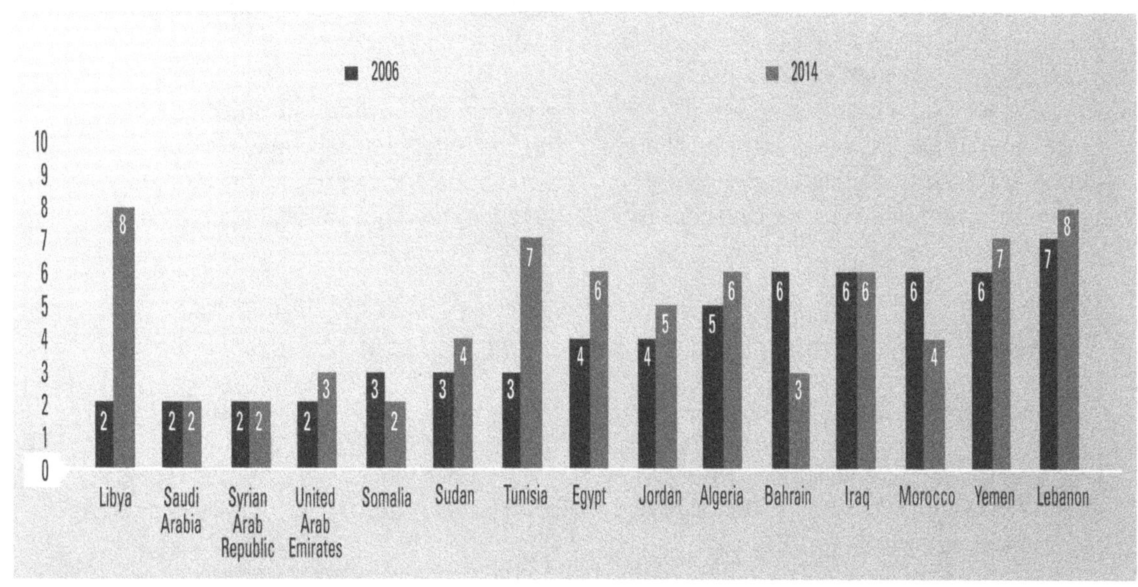

Source: Bertelsmann Stiftung, BTI. Available from http://www.bti-project.org/ (accessed 2 November 2015).
Note: Index ranges from 1 (worst) to 10 (best).

Arab countries, assessments can change dramatically over short periods of time.

C. Institutions

The SDGs need to be included in national development planning if they are to be achieved. Regional institutions also play an important role in consolidating national efforts, disseminating information and facilitating peer learning. Adequate follow-up and review mechanisms will be key at all levels.

1. National institutions for sustainable development

National development planning in Arab countries has rarely focused on sustainable development. Box 5.5 provides a selected list of recent documents and presents some of the lessons learned from national experiences. Recent assessments of national planning experiences have highlighted the importance of broad ownership, strategic prioritization, coordination across ministries, and the full use of evidence. Sustainable development requires a balance between its various economic, social and environmental objectives, which in turn necessitates continuous dialogue among representative and credible actors.

(a) Ownership

National ownership is fundamental. National development strategies require a country-driven process promoting partnerships between government, domestic stakeholders and development partners. Taking into account the views of different institutions, interest groups and non-governmental organizations (NGOs), from various parts of the country increases the quality of strategies and policies and encourages support for them when they are carried out.

Mechanisms for enhancing stakeholder consultation can come in the form of national councils or advisory bodies, or less structured forums, ad-hoc advisory groups, expert panels and focus groups. Sustainable development experts tend to prefer the creation of dedicated national councils,[34] made up of representatives of government, civil society, academia and business. However, a range of different approaches may be most useful for involving stakeholders in strategic planning with a view to obtaining the outcomes that citizens most care about. Consultations can constitute an independent review function to ensure accountability and to recommend corrective or adaptive actions.[35]

In the Arab countries, ad-hoc dialogues, forums, intersectoral consultations and workshops are common. Unfortunately, they have largely been characterized by a lack of

Box 5.5. Examples of recent national development strategies and lessons learned

Notable examples of national development strategies in Arab countries in recent years include:

- Qatar's National Vision 2030 (2009) and National Development Strategy 2011-2016
- Saudi Arabia's tenth national development plan and economic long-term vision 2024 (in preparation)
- The United Arab Emirates' National Agenda Vision 21; National Green Growth Strategy; and Abu Dhabi Economic Vision 2030
- Jordan's National Resilience Plan 2014-16 (2014) and national vision 2030 (in preparation)
- Lebanon's national sustainable development strategy (in preparation)
- Bahrain's 2030 National Planning Development Strategy (2007)
- Development Strategy of the New Tunisia (2012); National Sustainable Development Strategy 2016-2020 (2014); Guidance note for the strategic development plan 2016-2020 (in preparation)
- Iraq's National Development Plan 2010-2014 (2010)
- Egypt's Strategic Framework for Economic and Social Development to 2022 (2012)
- Algeria's National Strategy for the Fight against Poverty (2005-2015) and Five-Year Plan (2010-2014)
- The Sudan's Interim Poverty Reduction Strategy Paper (2012)
- Djibouti's Poverty Reduction Strategy Paper (2009)
- Morocco's National Sustainable Development Strategy (2015)

A number of lessons learned can be distilled from these experiences:

- Linking national strategies to international goals is helpful in increasing the volume of development aid received, but no single set of policies is applicable in all countries. Attention needs to be paid to specific national issues.
- Broad ownership of plans increases their effectiveness and can be enhanced through extensive consultations.
- Sustainable development requires a long-term strategy and short-term action planning. The sequencing and speed of reforms, in particular, affects success. Sustainability requires an intergenerational view.
- It is essential to coordinate planning and implementation between ministries and sectors. Clear institutional arrangements are important to provide ministerial accountability and coordination. High-level leadership is essential.
- Plans benefit from evidence during strategy development and – perhaps even more so – implementation, to allow policymakers to monitor progress against indicators, modify plans as needed and allow for accountability.

Source: Cameron Allen, "The institutional framework of sustainable development in the Arab region", Expert Report for the Arab Sustainable Development Report (Beirut, 2015, E/ESCWA/SDPD/2015/Technical Paper.3). Available from http://css.escwa.org.lb/SDP-D/3572/3-Instituions.pdf.

sustained engagement with stakeholders or understanding of key sustainable development issues by the stakeholders themselves, and by their poor communication and negotiation skills. However, Tunisia has made strides towards stronger participation and ownership (box 5.6) and in Morocco, an economic, social and environmental council (www.cese.ma), with representatives from the public and private sectors, NGOs and academic institutions, has been set up.

(b) Strategic prioritization

The Arab countries have varying capacity for setting and maintaining priorities in planning (figure 5.15). Perhaps one of the biggest challenges is to align a long-term vision with short-term, sector-specific action plans. Such "multi-tiered" planning is essential and a good example from the region is Qatar's planning framework (box 5.7). Morocco's National Sustainable Development Strategy was developed through a participatory process and is based on four main principles (box 5.8).

Countries affected by conflict encounter particular difficulties. Lebanon has embarked on the formulation of a national sustainable development strategy despite the prevailing climate of political instability and spillover effects from the civil war in the neighbouring Syrian Arab Republic. The strategy contains clear objectives (box 5.9).

(c) Coordination

Consistency between sectors and ministries is essential. During the planning phase, trade-offs and synergies among sector plans need to be identified and negotiated. Implementation must

Box 5.6. Participation and national sustainable development planning in Tunisia

Since the early 1990s, Tunisia has pioneered the establishment of institutions for sustainable development. The National Commission for Sustainable Development headed by the Prime Minister was created in 1993. Three years later, the national Agenda 21 action plan was developed and subsequent five-year development plans included considerations of sustainability. Those endeavours were largely State-led and development policies still had shortcomings. Since the transition that ensued after the 2011 uprising, the role of civil society has become more prominent. The new Constitution adopted in January 2014 explicitly enshrines the principles of sustainable development and the economic, social and environmental rights of citizens.

A new sustainable development strategy was prepared between 2012 and 2014 in a context of acute political, social and economic challenges, wide regional disparities, and a growing demand for real participation by citizens and stakeholders. Creation of the strategy comprised four steps: (a) a draft strategy document was prepared by national consultants, under the Ministry of Environment; (b) workshops were held in various regions to discuss it; (c) national consultations took place involving experts and consultants from public administrations, academic institutions, civil society and the private sector; and (d) a national conference on the "foundations of sustainable development" (Les Assises Nationales du Développement Durable) was organized in early October 2014.

The conference resulted in the adoption of the strategy, which addresses six priority areas (production and consumption patterns; management of natural resources, ecosystems and adaptation to climate change; quality of life and pollution control; land use planning, the city and transportation; education, innovation and knowledge management; and environmental governance for sustainable development). The findings of the conference and the final version of the strategy will be incorporated into the next development plan (2016-2020).

Source: Mounir Majdoub, report prepared for ESCWA (Beirut, 2015).

Figure 5.15. BTI: Government's record of setting and maintaining strategic priorities

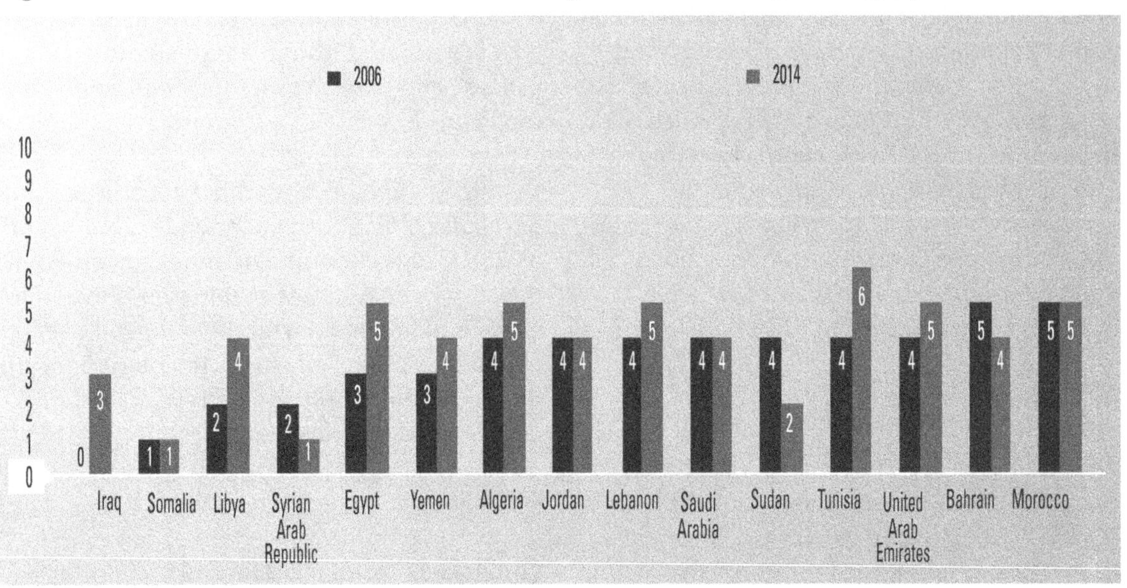

Source: Bertelsmann Stiftung, BTI. Available from http://www.bti-project.org/ (accessed 2 November 2015).
Note: Index ranges from 1 (worst) to 10 (best).

Box 5.7. Qatar's multi-tiered planning process

Qatar has laid out a long-term planning framework (National Vision 2030), a medium-term action plan (National Development Strategy 2011-2016) and medium-term sectoral strategies. The vision sets clear long-term goals concerning four specific pillars. The national strategy aims to coordinate sectoral and enterprise strategies and contains priority development plans for 14 sectors, with corresponding targets to be achieved by 2016. The targets of the national strategy are themselves a subset of those contained in 14 comprehensive sector strategy reports. The annual budget is the Government's main instrument for short-term economic management and the strategy lends the budget a forward-looking and results-based orientation, aligning major investments with the country's overarching development goals.

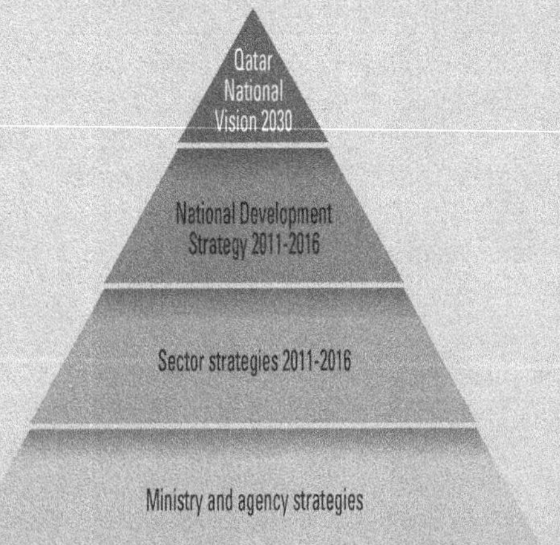

- Defines long-term goals
- Defines initiatives for achieving goals of the Qatar National Vision 2030
- Defines sectoral priorities incorporated into the National Development Strategy 2011-2016
- Defines ministerial plans for implementing sectoral strategies

Source: Qatar General Secretariat for Development Planning, *Qatar National Development Strategy 2011-2016: Towards Qatar National Vision 2030* (Doha, 2011). Available from www.gsdp.gov.qa/gsdp_vision/docs/NDS_EN.pdf.

Box 5.8. Morocco's National Sustainable Development Strategy

Morocco's National Sustainable Development Strategy was developed through broad consultation with the public sector, private businesses and civil society. It has four main principles:

1. Efficient economy: An efficient economy is a driving force for sustainable development. Sectoral strategies and proactive policies should be consistent with economic development objectives. Obstacles to competitiveness need to be removed through systematic intersectoral convergence and better integration of social and environmental considerations. A circular economy can be truly green.
2. Human development and social cohesion: Policies are required to reduce disparities with regard to access to health care and free and quality education for all. Poverty reduction plans should target the most deprived sectors of society, including rural populations who protect natural resources such as water reserves and forests, and prevent desertification.
3. The environment: Environmental matters should not be addressed in emergency situations alone. Environment initiatives can help to foster sustainable growth and green jobs.
4. Culture: Promotion of national culture will make it possible to maintain traditional social specificities. All segments of the population, including people living in remote areas, can help to promote the development of their cultures.

Source: مريم حوزين، التنمية المستدامة في المغرب، وثيقة خلفية: التقرير العربي حول التنمية المستدامة (بيروت، 2015)
http://css.escwa.org.lb/SDPD/3572/MoroccoAr.pdf.

Box 5.9. Lebanon's national sustainable development strategy

The Ministry of Planning in Lebanon began work on its first national sustainable development strategy in March 2015. The country already had strategies for key sectors such as social development, territorial planning, industrial development and human rights. They were studied and objectives were identified for a national strategy, in alignment with the SDGs. Those objectives include:

- Development of human capital and a labour force of international standards
- Consolidation of social cohesion
- Provision of everyday necessities
- Promotion of economic growth
- Preservation of natural and cultural heritage
- Good governance
- Repositioning of Lebanon on the Arab, Mediterranean and international maps

Three key challenges to the eventual success of the national strategy were identified:

- Ensuring ownership and the commitment of key stakeholders to the strategy
- Enhancing existing institutions responsible for aspects of sustainable development, such as coordinating, mainstreaming, monitoring and reporting on progress
- Mobilizing the required funding and support of international partners for implementation of the strategy

Source: Mounir Majdoub, report prepared for ESCWA, 2015.

Figure 5.16. BTI: Extent to which the Government can harmonize conflicting objectives in a coherent policy

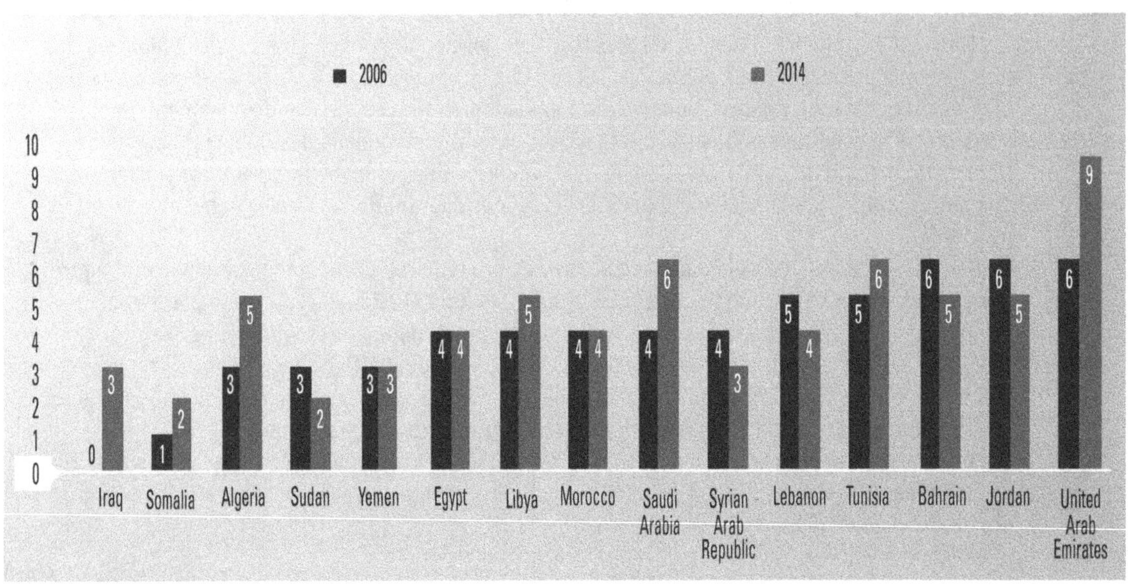

Source: Bertelsmann Stiftung, BTI. Available from http://www.bti-project.org/ (accessed 2 November 2015).
Note: Index ranges from 1 (worst) to 10 (best).

Figure 5.17. BTI: Extent to which Government is effective in implementing its own policies

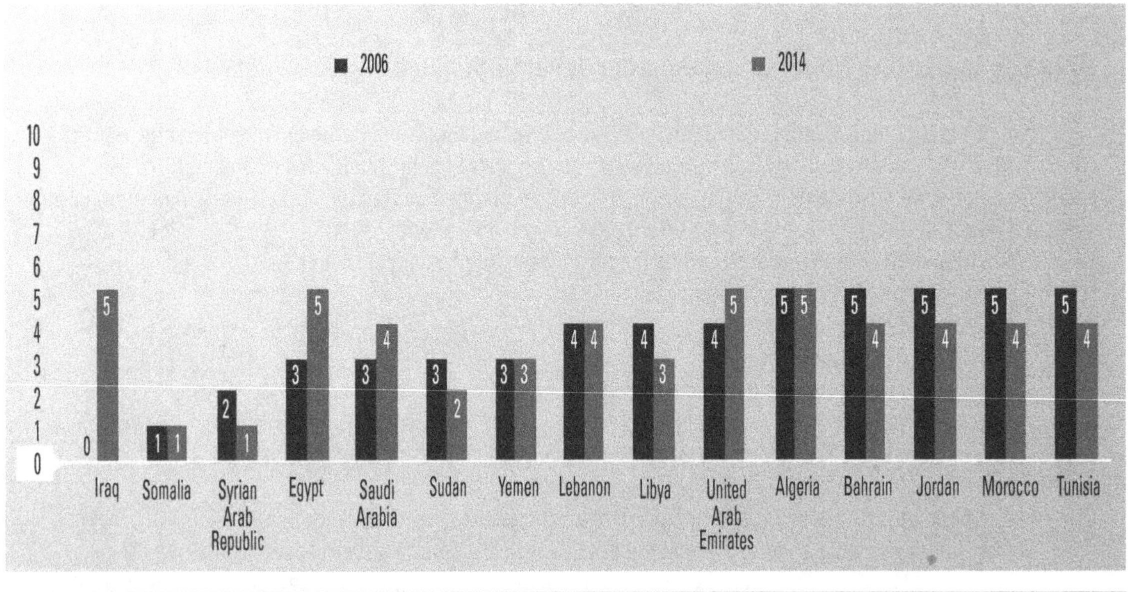

Source: Bertelsmann Stiftung, BTI. Available from http://www.bti-project.org/ (accessed 2 November 2015).
Note: Index ranges from 1 (worst) to 10 (best).

be coordinated in order to ensure accountability and avoid overlaps or gaps in ministerial mandates. On planning and implementation, Somalia, the Sudan and the Syrian Arab Republic score particularly poorly among the 15 Arab countries included in the BTI study (figures 5.16 and 5.17). The United Arab Emirates scores particularly highly on policy coordination.

Box 5.10. Jordan's Higher National Committee for Sustainable Development

The Higher National Committee for Sustainable Development in Jordan was formed in 2002. It is chaired by the Minister of Planning and International Cooperation, whose deputy is the Minister for the Environment. It includes representatives from 22 government and non-government institutions and meets quarterly. The Committee is mandated to:

- Participate in setting national priorities and ensure planning consistency
- Mainstream environmental concerns into national plans and sectoral strategies
- Endorse action and financing plans, and local development and decentralization frameworks
- Approve policy documents and enhance the application of good governance principles
- Review and amend legislation in line with sustainable development requirements
- Review and endorse national reports on progress in sustainable development

Three subcommittees on economic, social and environmental issues prepare concept papers and periodic progress reports, contribute to awareness-raising campaigns and propose executive action plans. However, the role of the Committee could be bolstered as part of Jordan's drive to transform itself into a green economy.

Source: محمد الخصاونة، التنمية المستدامة في المملكة الأردنية الهاشمية، وثيقة خلفية: التقرير العربي حول التنمية المستدامة (بيروت، 2015)، http://css.escwa.org.lb/SDPD/3572/Jordan.pdf.

A comprehensive planning process requires a cross-ministerial coordination mechanism linked to budgetary processes in order to make decision-making effective and to foster timely implementation. Such a mechanism could come in the form of an interministerial steering or oversight committee, a planning commission, or some kind of national sustainable development body. The most successful examples are overseen by the Head of State, involve high-level representation from a wide range of ministries, include subnational or local government representatives, and are tasked with the drafting and carrying out of a national development strategy. Coordination mechanisms require strong and technically capable secretariats or planning departments. Jordan provides a good example (box 5.10).

National Governments may set country-level goals and the mandates to support them, but it is often local governments that are responsible for implementing them. Devolution of decision-making to the local level can be encouraged through subnational and local plans that are linked to centralized economic planning.

(d) Use of evidence and the science-policy interface

Evidence is needed to provide an objective basis for policy and any subsequent modifications, and to ensure accountability. On its own, evidence guarantees nothing, but the exchange of knowledge between experts (scientists) and policymakers aimed at enriching decision-making is increasingly seen as a critical aspect of governance.

A precondition for evidence-based policy is the availability of sustainable development data, which in turn requires national statistical capacity and a willingness by policymakers to be innovative and flexible. This is covered in chapter 6.

A wide range of evidence-based analytical approaches, models and tools have been developed to support robust policy design. Scenario analysis is increasingly used in

Box 5.11. Examples of evidence-based analytical approaches

Scenario modelling for MDG simulations in Arab countries
The World Bank's Maquette for MDG Simulations (MAMS) is a dynamic CGE model that has been extended to cover the generation of outcomes in terms of growth, MDGs, and the educational make-up of the labour force, as well as the interaction of these outcomes with other aspects of economic performance. It also uses methodologies at the microlevel to identify determinants of MDG achievement and to quantify effects on poverty and inequality. The modelling is based on a social accounting matrix for each country, which is designed to form a consistent and comprehensive accounting framework for addressing alternative MDG strategies. Studies using MAMS have been completed in Egypt, Morocco, Tunisia and Yemen. For more on MAMS, see http://go.worldbank.org/XSQTI86EN0.

Saudi Arabia – CGE modelling and dashboard monitoring tool
ESCWA and other United Nations agencies are helping the Ministry of Economy and Planning in Saudi Arabia to lay out its tenth national development plan. Assistance is being provided to formulate indicators and scenarios that connect national goals and sectoral objectives to enable effective follow-up. The Ministry will be provided with a CGE model for formulating development policies and a dashboard tool to monitor progress.

combination with quantitative modelling. In the Arab region, computable general equilibrium (CGE) modelling is being used by Saudi Arabia for its national development strategy. CGE modelling and bottom-up simulation models have been used in the United Arab Emirates to support its Green Growth Plan. A dynamic CGE model has also been used in Egypt, Morocco, Tunisia and Yemen (box 5.11).

The extensive work done at the country level provides examples of evidenced-based analytical approaches. They include national assessment reports prepared in the lead-up to Rio+20 in 2011-2012, voluntary presentations under the Annual Ministerial Review mechanism of the United Nations Economic and Social Council, national MDG progress reports, environmental performance reviews, investment policy reviews, trade policy reviews, trade sustainability impact assessments, national reports on multilateral environment agreements, capacity needs assessments, technology needs assessments, development policy reviews and World Bank MAMS reports, national human development reports, United Nations development action frameworks and common country assessments, Intergovernmental Panel on Climate Change national communications, country strategy papers (for example, of multilateral development banks) and Human Rights Council universal periodic reviews. Annex IV provides an inventory of major global and Arab regional assessments, publications and databases relating to each of the 17 SDGs.

It is important to monitor implementation progress and consider modifications in plans along the way.[36] Monitoring and reporting has improved significantly in the region in the context of the MDGs. Most Arab countries have produced regular national MDG progress reports and some, including Iraq, Morocco, Saudi Arabia and Tunisia, also prepare occasional sustainable development reports. However, national statistical capacity remains heavily reliant on international organizations. That said, some countries have

Box 5.12. Monitoring and reporting

United Arab Emirates
The United Arab Emirates National Agenda and the United Arab Emirates Vision 2021 include a set of clear, quantitative targets and indicators across six goals: the competitive knowledge economy; sustainable environment and infrastructure; public safety and a fair judiciary; cohesive society and preserved identity; world-class health care; and first-rate education. The agenda provides a concise visual framework for monitoring progress and accountability.

Tunisia
The National Observatory for Environment and Sustainable Development is in charge of environmental statistics and sustainable development monitoring. The country's first indicator report was published in 2003 with 36 indicators. The 2014 report includes 46 indicators organized into 9 sustainable development challenges.

Iraq
Since 2010, the Iraqi Central Statistics Organization has published annual environment and sustainable development indicator reports. The 2013 version comprises 69 environmental indicators.

Morocco
In Morocco's fourth sustainable development indicators report, issued in 2014, 56 indicators across 14 themes cover economic, social and environmental issues. For each indicator, the report highlights trends and progress in past decades and provides analysis of key actions needed.

Sources: United Arab Emirates, "National Key Performance Indicators", Vision 2021, available from www.vision2021.ae/en/national-priority-areas/national-key-performance-indicators (accessed 2 November 2015); Iraq, "Central Statistical Organization", available from www.cosit.gov.iq/en/env-stats/environmental-statistics (accessed 2 November 2015); and Morocco, "Indicateurs du développement durable au Maroc", quatrième rapport national, available from www.environnement.gov.ma/PDFs/Rapport_national_IDD_2014.pdf

done commendable jobs on monitoring their national plans (box 5.12).

The Abu Dhabi Global Environmental Data Initiative is a world-class project to improve environmental monitoring data using remote sensing techniques, mobile phone records and other modern technologies. Another example of modern technology use is Geographic Information Systems, which has been integral in the development of spatial master plans in countries such as Algeria and Bahrain.

2. Regional institutions for sustainable development

Progress on sustainable development goals is reviewed above all at the country level. At the regional level, the focus is on identifying regional trends, obstacles, commonalities, best practices and lessons learned.

Institutions in the Arab region that may participate in the review process include: the League of Arab States; ESCWA, the Economic Commission for Africa (ECA), the UNDP Regional Bureau for Arab States, the UNEP Regional Office for West Asia and other United Nations agencies coordinated by the Regional Coordination Mechanism. NGOs can also make an important contribution (box 5.13). Subregional institutions that fall wholly or partially within the Arab region, such as the Gulf Cooperation Council, African Union, and Union for the Mediterranean promote regional integration for development (box 5.14).

Box 5.13. Development and environment NGOs

- Arab NGO Network for Development (ANND): a regional network of NGOs working in 10 Arab countries and with 23 members advocating for social and economic rights in the Arab region. It works in three main areas: (a) development policies; (b) social and economic reform agendas and the role of international and regional organizations; and (c) economic and trade liberalization and its social and economic implications.
- Centre for Environment and Development in the Arab Region and Europe (CEDARE): an intergovernmental organization established in 1992 to advocate for sound governance in the interests of the environment, by building human resources and institutional capacity, advancing applied research and environmentally friendly technologies, and acting as a catalyst for joint action between the Arab region, Europe and the international community.
- Arab Forum on Environment and Development (AFED): a regional NGO that prepares independent periodic reports on the state of the environment in Arab countries, with several major reports issued to date, most recently on energy, food security and sustainable consumption.
- Arab Network for Environment and Development: network of NGOs focusing on the integration of environment and development. It opened the door to NGOs to attend the Council of Arab Ministers Responsible for the Environment meetings after obtaining observer status in the League of Arab States in 1995.

Box 5.14. Subregional organizations

- The Gulf Cooperation Council (GCC) was established in 1982 and is considered the most successful example of integration in the Arab region. Its six member countries (Bahrain, Kuwait, Oman, Qatar, Saudi Arabia and the United Arab Emirates) have focused on harmonization of regulations in economic and trade affairs (GCC Customs Union and Common Market), joint projects in education, science and technology, and cooperation in security and other political affairs.
- The Arab Maghreb Union (AMU) was founded in 1989 by Algeria, Libya, Mauritania, Morocco and Tunisia, with the aim of promoting the movement of goods, unifying customs systems and gradually liberalizing the movement of goods, services and factors of production. However, its efforts have been hampered by political problems.
- The African Union includes several North African Arab countries. It works on sustainable development through the African Union Commission, the New Partnership for Africa's Development (NEPAD), and the African Monitoring of the Environment for Sustainable Development (AMESD).
- The Mediterranean Strategy for Sustainable Development (MSSD) provides a regional response to the sustainable development agenda and SDGs for Mediterranean countries.

In addition to these institutions, a multitude of regional and subregional partnerships, funds, networks and organizations work on aspects of sustainable development. Some have been listed in chapter 6.

(a) The League of Arab States

The League of Arab States was established as a regional intergovernmental organization in 1945 and is the only such institution

Box 5.15. The Bahrain Document

The Bahrain Document contains recommendations on implementing the SDGs in accordance with the priorities of the Arab region. It was submitted by ESCWA as the regional input to the third session of the High-level Political Forum on Sustainable Development in New York in July 2015. Occupation, lack of peace and security, poverty, extremism, terrorism and refugee flows were identified in the document as key stumbling blocks in the region. It reaffirmed the intent of the Arab States to end the Israeli occupation of all Arab lands, working with the international community to achieve peace, security and inclusive sustainable development. It stressed the need for the international community to shoulder its share of responsibility and help refugee host States to maintain their development gains and care for refugees. It called for the development of effective institutions, the mobilization of resources and improved statistical capacities. The need to manage natural resources efficiently and adopt measures to reduce risks caused by natural hazards was also underlined

Source: Bahrain Document, Adopted at the Second Session of the Arab High-Level Forum on Sustainable Development, Manama, 7 May 2015. Available from http://css.escwa.org.lb/SDPD/3572/ForumOutcome.pdf.

comprising all 22 Arab countries. Its aim is to "draw closer the relations between member States and coordinate their political activities with the aim of realizing a close collaboration between them, to safeguard their independence and sovereignty, and to consider in a general way the affairs and interests of the Arab countries".[37]

The League holds summits for Heads of State once a year. The League Council is its main executive body and is composed of representatives (usually foreign ministers) of all member States. There are 13 specialized ministerial councils and a General Secretariat, which conducts administrative and executive work. A permanent Arab Parliament has recently been developed, with members drawn from the parliaments of member States.

Despite technical, political and financial constraints, the League has notched up important accomplishments, including several related to sustainable development. In 2002, the Council of Arab Ministers Responsible for the Environment adopted the Sustainable Development Initiative in the Arab Region. It was recently updated to incorporate the results of the 2012 United Nations Conference on Sustainable Development (Rio+20), with a new Arab Strategic Framework for Sustainable Development (2015-2025). Sessions of the Arab Economic and Social Development Summit have been held every two years since 2009 and have led to the establishment of a $2 billion fund to finance small and medium enterprises and the adoption of an Arab Strategy for the Development of Renewable Energy Applications (2010-2030).

(b) The United Nations in the Arab region

The work of United Nations bodies in the Arab region is coordinated by the Regional Coordination Mechanism (RCM). RCMs were established in line with resolution 1998/46 of the Economic and Social Council of 31 July 1998, and the United Nations regional commissions act as their secretariats. The first meeting of the RCM in the Arab Region was convened by ESCWA in 1999. Since then, meetings have been held once or twice a year. The participation of the League of Arab States in its meetings since 2006 effectively extended the mandate of the RCM to all 22

Arab States.[38] Six thematic working groups were set up, focussing on the MDGs (and, subsequently, the transition to the SDGs), food security, climate change, statistics, the Annual Ministerial Review, and migration.

Representatives of the United Nations Country Office in Lebanon may attend RCM meetings as observers. Meetings are also open the Economic Commission for Africa and multilateral institutions like the World Bank and the International Monetary Fund. The Islamic Development Bank and other regional financial institutions are also invited.

ESCWA has worked hard with regional partners to coordinate a united position on the SDGs and implement the conclusions of Rio+20, including the development of a "green economy road map".

(c) Arab Forum on Sustainable Development

The recently established Arab Forum on Sustainable Development, which has held two sessions (in 2014 and 2015), is designed to create a regional link between the global High-level Political Forum on Sustainable Development and implementation at the national level. As well as coordinating with international and regional bodies, it will engage with ministries and a broad range of non-State actors, including civil society. Its multi-stakeholder engagement distinguishes it from other formal regional institutions, which are primarily intergovernmental. At its May 2015 session, the Forum debated the status and financing of sustainable development in the Arab region, implementation challenges and institutional frameworks. It culminated in the release of the Bahrain Document (box 5.15).[39]

6. Means of Implementation and Partnerships for Sustainable Development

Photovoltaic panels, solar water heaters, simple geothermal heating and cooling, and biodigester as installed at the Advancing Research Enabling Communities Center in Lebanon

"We are determined to mobilize the means required to implement this Agenda through a revitalized Global Partnership for Sustainable Development, based on a spirit of strengthened global solidarity, focussed in particular on the needs of the poorest and most vulnerable and with the participation of all countries, all stakeholders and all people."

Preamble of the 2030 Agenda for Sustainable Development

6. Means of Implementation and Partnerships for Sustainable Development

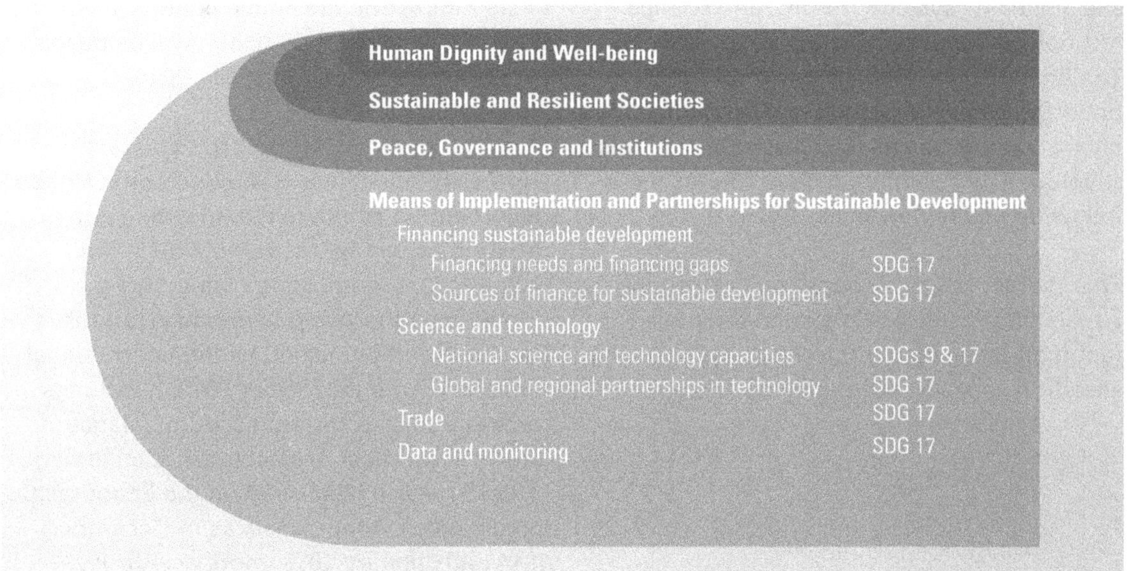

Achieving sustainable development will require the mobilization of significant financial resources, science and technology in order to spur economic growth and employment. States will have to hone their capacity to adapt new scientific findings and technology, just as the international community will have to facilitate knowledge transfer. Intraregional and international trade will be a key to reaping the benefits of comparative advantages and economies of scale. Statistical capacity is crucial to enabling policymakers to make full use of data and monitoring to formulate evidence-based policies.

The Arab countries will need to bridge a large financing gap through tax and subsidy reforms and by rationalizing military expenditure. International flows, including official development assistance (ODA), foreign direct investment (FDI), intraregional investment and remittances, constitute a sizeable source of finance for several Arab countries. However, the general downwards trend over the past several years raises questions about the extent to which they can continue to rely on such flows. Green finance offers opportunities that only few Arab countries have fully tapped. Trade can be an engine of development, but the region's share of global non-oil exports remains modest and the region is the least economically integrated in the world.

In spite of efforts to develop science, technology and innovation in the Arab region, it remains mostly a user of technology. The little knowledge generated does not benefit industry because the region's economies are weak and undiversified. Statistical capacity is limited and many Arab countries were unable to report fully on the 45 MDG indicators using official national data.

The 2015 Addis Ababa Action Agenda encapsulates the need for a new framework for mobilizing the resources required to achieve the 2030 Agenda.[1] It complements the means of implementation targets included under SDG 17 and identifies seven action areas: domestic public resources; domestic and international private business and finance; international development cooperation; international trade as an engine for development; debt and debt sustainability; systemic issues; and science, technology, innovation and capacity-building. The Agenda also contains recommendations on three specific initiatives: a technology facilitation mechanism (discussed later in this chapter); a global infrastructure forum; and a follow-up and review mechanism.

This chapter is largely based on background papers and issues briefs prepared for this report on the subjects of technology, financing, statistical capacity and trade.[2]

A. Financing sustainable development

The full range of national and international public and private sources of finance must be mobilized in a coordinated and optimal fashion and the financing itself – not just what is being financed – needs to be sustainable.

1. Financing needs and financing gaps

The funding requirements of sustainable development and resource gaps can be estimated in various ways and depend on the particulars of each case. ESCWA estimates that $3.6 trillion will be required for selected Arab countries to achieve sustained economic growth between 2015 and 2030.[3] Resources will also be needed to repair past and ongoing environmental and conflict-related damage. The cost of environmental degradation in the region has been estimated at 5 per cent of GDP,[4] and that of conflict at more than 2 per cent of foregone GDP in each year of internal conflict.[5]

Shorter-term investment estimates prepared by the McKinsey Global Institute[6] and the International Energy Agency (IEA)[7] accord special priority respectively to infrastructure and energy (with a focus on energy efficiency and renewable energy). According to McKinsey, the Arab countries need to spend between $110 billion and $150 billion a year in the coming five years on investments in non-energy infrastructure. In the energy sector, the IEA estimates that $105 billion will be needed in the Middle East during 2014-2020.[8]

In preparation for this report, two scenarios were developed in an ESCWA commissioned document[9] to estimate the financing gap in the Arab region for the period 2015-2016. Scenario I depends on the latest forecasts provided by the World Economic Outlook Database and published by the International Monetary Fund in October 2014. It includes forecasts for the current account balance and GDP for most Arab countries, including LDCs. Scenario II is based on the Economist Intelligence Unit forecasts as of December 2014 and January 2015, more accurately reflecting the impact of falling oil prices. Table 6.1 shows the estimated financing gap for the Arab countries in 2015 and 2016 for both scenarios.[10]

Between 13 and 15 Arab countries are expected to have a financing deficit for 2015 and 2016 and the total financing gap is estimated to range between $80 billion and $85 billion annually. The second scenario, based on more recent oil price projections, results in a lower financing gap given that it is experienced mainly by net oil importers that stand to benefit from a drop in oil prices. In contrast, the total surplus in scenario I exceeds $250 billion, and drops sharply to around $100 billion in scenario II.

That upper middle-income countries should have a higher financing gap than their lower middle-income counterparts or LDCs (figure 6.1) can be explained by the fact that higher development requirements are not necessarily a spending priority in

Table 6.1. Estimated financing gap

	Country	Scenario I (billions of United States dollars)		Scenario II (billions of United States dollars)	
		Financing gap/ surplus 2015	Financing gap/ surplus 2016	Financing gap/ surplus 2015	Financing gap/ surplus 2016
UMI	Algeria	-9.98	-12.12	-15.88	-17.50
HI	Bahrain	2.86	2.57	1.35	0.77
LDC	Comoros	-0.11	-0.12	-0.11	-0.12
LDC	Djibouti	-0.76	-0.92	-0.76	-0.92
LMI	Egypt	-17.57	-21.72	-11.45	-13.64
UMI	Iraq	3.14	0.40	0.66	3.18
UMI	Jordan	-6.34	-5.06	-4.60	-5.26
HI	Kuwait	82.28	82.51	59.27	56.10
UMI	Lebanon	-9.91	-10.45	-12.67	-12.49
UMI	Libya	-12.45	-5.08	-2.49	-3.05
LDC	Mauritania	-3.14	-2.76	-3.14	-2.76
LMI	Morocco	-9.09	-8.92	-6.80	-7.30
HI	Oman	5.23	3.05	-0.05	0.65
LMI	Palestine	NA	NA	NA	NA
HI	Qatar	58.73	50.82	17.07	17.58
HI	Saudi Arabia	73.73	63.70	-5.73	0.26
LDC	Somalia	NA	NA	NA	NA
LDC	Sudan	-6.22	-6.29	-6.22	-6.29
LMI	Syrian Arab Republic	-4.51	-4.20	-4.51	-4.20
UMI	Tunisia	-4.79	-4.39	-5.70	-5.74
HI	United Arab Emirates	51.79	50.17	28.36	19.27
LDC	Yemen	-0.44	-0.64	-0.44	-0.64
Number of Arab countries with financing gap		13	13	15	13
Total financing gap ($billion)		85.32	82.69	80.19	79.92
Number of Arab countries with financing surplus		7	7	5	7
Total financing surplus ($billion)		277.76	253.22	106.71	97.81

Source: Sherine El Sharkawy, "Financing sustainable development in the Arab region".
Notes: Organisation for Economic Co-operation and Development (OECD) classifications: high income (HI); upper middle-income (UMI); lower middle-income (LMI); and least developed country (LDC). Scenario I is based on International Monetary Fund (IMF) forecasts dated October 2014 for current account balance and GDP, except for the Syrian Arab Republic, for which Economist Intelligence Unit forecasts were used. Principal repayments and disbursements of private debt were estimated in light of historical average levels. Net investment and portfolio flows were estimated as per the historical average to GDP. Scenario II is based on Economist Intelligence Unit forecasts dated December 2014 and January 2015 for current account balance and GDP, except for the Comoros, Djibouti, Mauritania, the Sudan and Yemen, for which IMF forecasts were used. Principal repayments and disbursements of private debt and net private investment and portfolio flows are estimated in a similar manner to Scenario I.

LDCs, where the pursuit of less ambitious development objectives is likely to continue. This is an important limitation of the analysis, which also does not reflect the financing needs associated with post-conflict reconstruction. The determination of the additional anticipated growth in needed finance - above the current forecasts - should be done on a country-specific, non-arbitrary basis, depending on prioritized sustainable development goals to arrive at a more accurate estimate. Another limitation is the

Figure 6.1. Financing gap/surplus according to income group, 2015-2016 (billions of United States dollars)

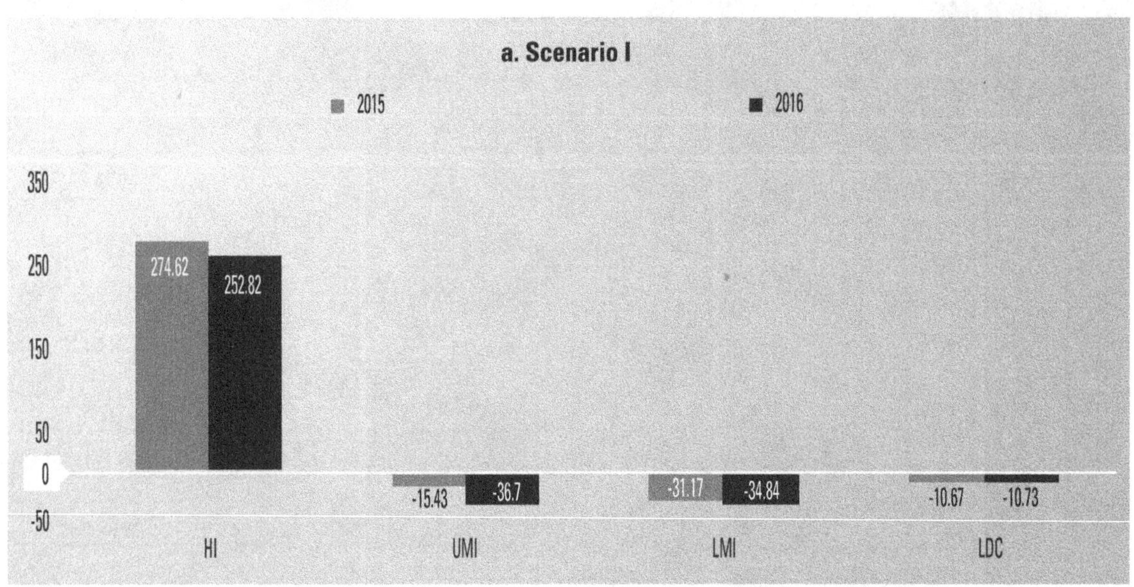

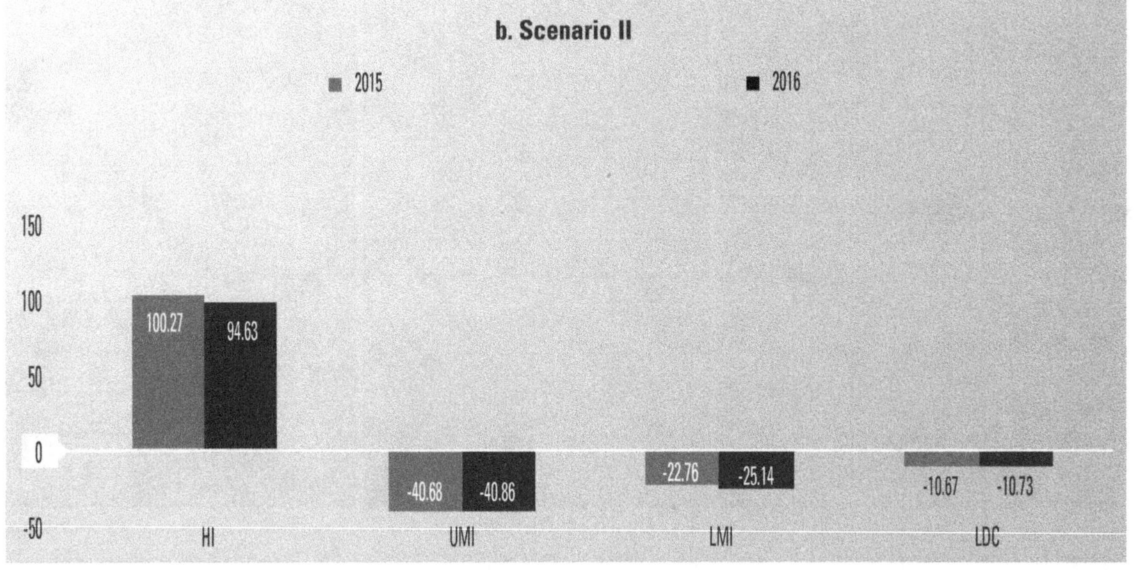

Source: Sherine El Sharkawy, "Financing sustainable development in the Arab region".
Notes: HI (GCC countries); UMI (Algeria, Iraq, Jordan, Lebanon, Libya and Tunisia); LMI (Egypt, Morocco, Palestine, and the Syrian Arab Republic) and LDC (the LDC grouping as referred to in this report).

unavailability of forecast data on Somalia and Palestine. Accounting for those factors would yield a still higher financing gap estimate for Arab countries. However, other factors could lower the estimate. Synergies between sectors could lead to more efficient use of resources in the achievement of more than one sustainable development goal. The estimates provided here are thus purely indicative.

2. Sources of finance for sustainable development

All possible sources of finance will need to

be mobilized. Major public sources include taxes and tariffs, public debt and ODA. Private sources include foreign direct investment and remittances.

(a) Public sources of finance

Domestic revenue collection can be raised significantly by improving tax systems, fighting tax evasion, reforming subsidies, correcting inequalities and combating corruption. The IMF estimates that many Arab countries present low "tax effort",[11] signifying the need for tax reform (figure 6.2). The estimate is based on a comparison between the country's tax revenues with a peer average (countries with similar per capita income) and the maximum tax receipts that other countries with similar characteristics have achieved (called the tax capacity).[12] The difference between the collected tax revenues and the tax capacity points to technical inefficiencies in tax collection and administration and deliberate policy decisions, such as allowing for tax exemptions.[13] Noticeable differences between countries can be observed. Some lower middle-income Arab countries, including Morocco and Tunisia, have worked to increase their tax effort and perform better than the world average for middle-income countries. High-income Arab countries have done much less compared to the world average.

Inefficient tax collection and administration sometimes indicates significant illicit cash flows and a large informal sector. A recent study found that firms in Tunisia connected with the old regime evaded at least $1.2 billion in import duty between 2002 and 2009.[14] Moreover, about one third of the region's GDP is undeclared.[15]

Fuel subsidies and military expenditure represent a serious drain on State budgets in the region and a high opportunity cost in the form of lost returns from spending on sustainable development.

To assess the opportunity cost of fossil fuel subsidies, figure 6.3 compares expenditure on them with public capital spending, and expenditure on education and health as a

Figure 6.2. Tax effort, 2013

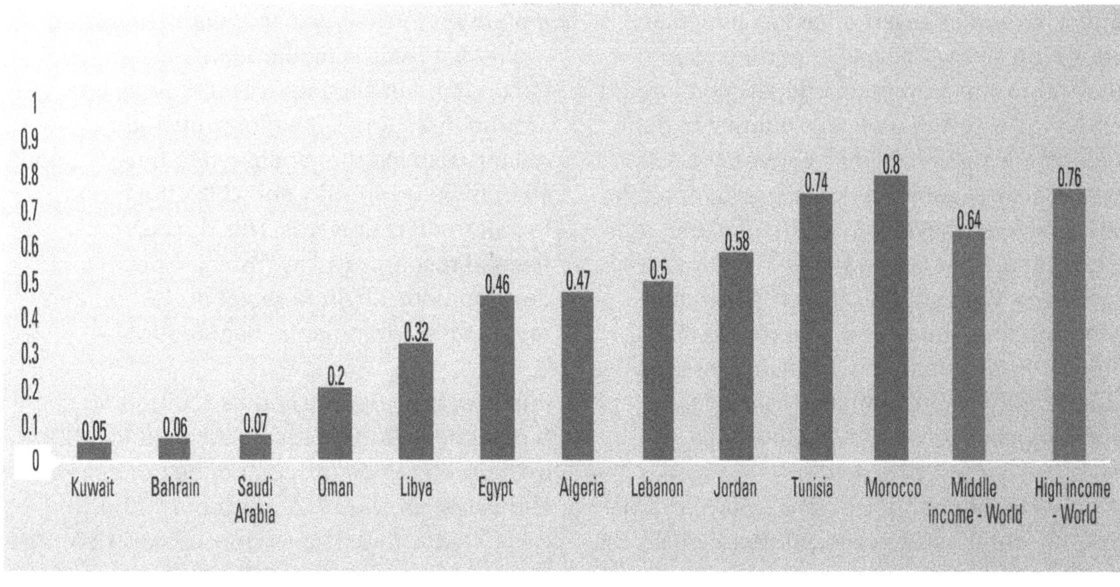

Source: Ricardo Fenochietto and Carola Pessino, "Understanding countries' tax effort", IMF Working Paper, No. 13/244, (Washington, D.C., IMF, November 2013). Available from www.imf.org/external/pubs/ft/wp/2013/wp13244.pdf.

Figure 6.3. Energy subsidies, capital spending and expenditure on education and health (percentage of GDP, 2011)

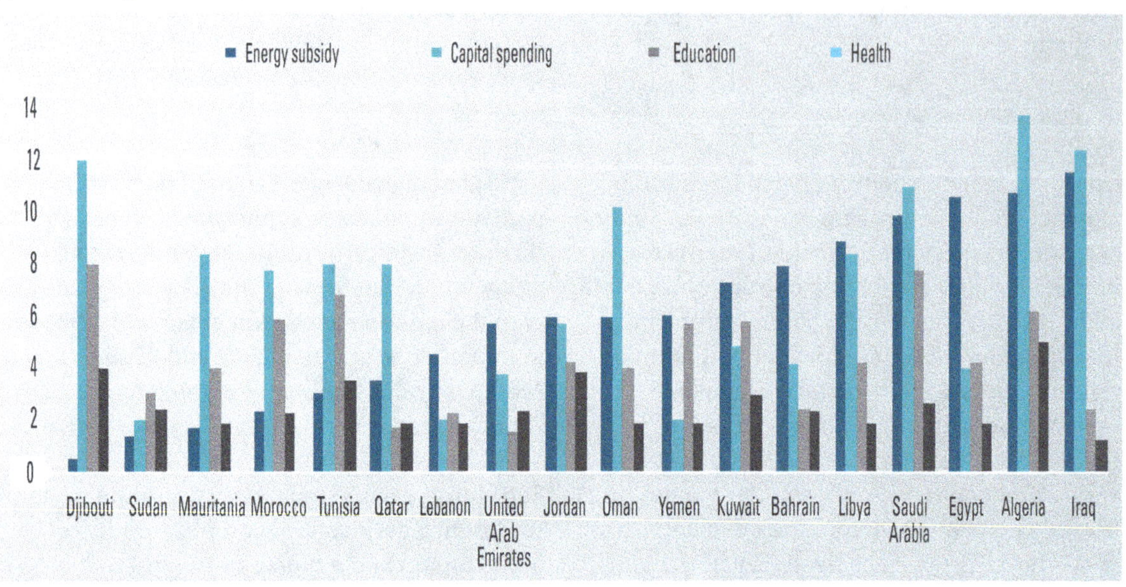

Source: Sherif Arif and Fadi Doumani, "A strategic investment framework for green economy in Arab countries from an energy perspective".
Note: Data were taken from IMF datasets and were not available for the Comoros, Palestine, Somalia or the Syrian Arab Republic.

percentage of GDP. Spending on fuel subsidies in most GCC countries, Algeria, Iraq and Jordan exceeds or almost matches capital spending, indicative of allocation inefficiencies and disincentives to switch to cleaner energy. In Bahrain, Lebanon, Yemen and, especially, Egypt, subsidies dwarf other key budgetary allocations. In net oil/gas importing countries, they represent a drain on budgets and foreign exchange reserves and pose a threat to debt repayment sustainability. In Egypt, the $20.3 billion energy subsidies were greater than the $19.2 billion fiscal deficit in 2010. In 2013, the Government initiated a series of energy price increases. Conversely, Djibouti, Mauritania, Morocco, the Sudan and, to a certain extent, Tunisia were able to reduce their subsidies significantly when compared to capital spending and social sector allocations.

A growing number of Governments (particularly in GCC countries) is looking at replacing across-the-board subsidies that strain budgets, distort market signals and benefit mainly middle to higher income brackets with targeted subsidies. Morocco, for instance has one of the lowest energy subsidies relative to GDP (2.3 per cent of GDP for fuel products) in the region and is embarking on a green growth path.

Military expenditure in the Arab region amounted to 6.84 per cent of GDP in 2014 (figure 6.4). This is higher than the military expenditure in all other world regions and around three times the global average. While military expenditure appeared to have dropped sharply between 1991 and 2009, the more recent trend is upwards. This directs much needed resources away from socioeconomic development, environmental protection and reversing environmental degradation.

Public debt is a prime source for funding budget deficits. Average public debt to GDP in the Arab region (excluding the LDCs, Iraq and Palestine) was 31.2 per cent in 2014,[16] compared with the 26.4 per cent world average for developing countries. Public debt to GDP is increasing in most Arab countries (figure 6.5) and is unsustainable in several cases.

Figure 6.4. Military expenditure (percentage of GDP)

	1991	2009	2014
East Asia and the Pacific	1.47	1.73	1.79
Latin America and the Carribean	1.56	1.41	1.30
Europe and Central Asia	2.49	1.92	1.81
Sub-Saharan Africa	2.82	1.62	1.36
World	2.93	2.63	2.31
South Asia	3.27	2.82	2.41
Arab region	11.58	5.36	6.84

Source: World Bank, World Development Indicators.

Figure 6.5. Public debt-to-GDP ratio (percentage)

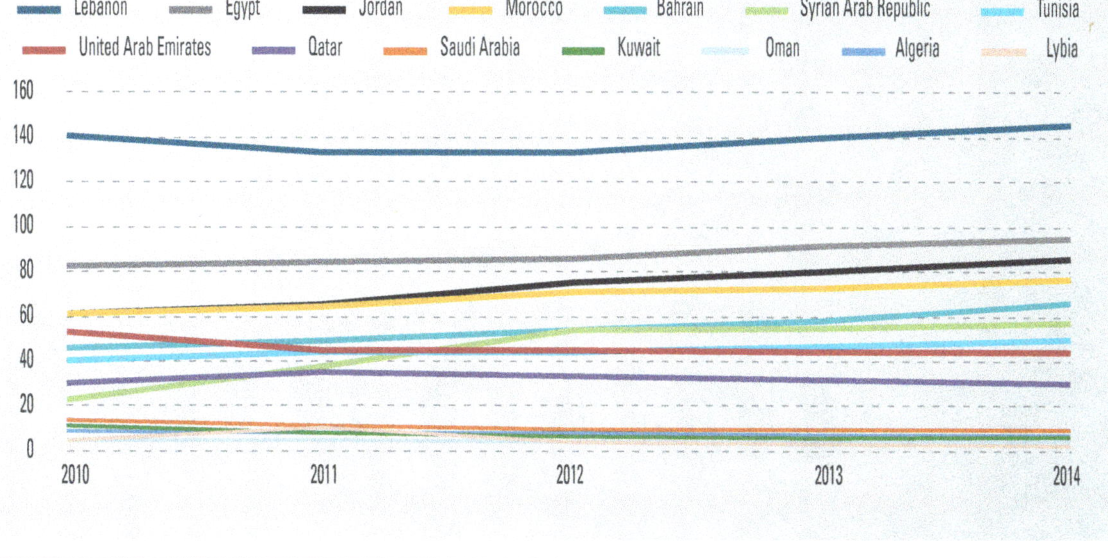

Source: Sherine El Sharkawy, "Financing sustainable development in the Arab region".

Support from other Governments and international organizations is another major source of development financing. However, the target of 0.7 per cent of donor countries' gross national income (GNI) in ODA for developing countries, including 0.15 to 0.20 per cent for LDCs, has not been achieved. Global interdependence is a strong argument for international cooperation on sustainable development, including its funding and policy coordination. In reality, ODA patterns reflect a combination of interdependence, need and political interests.

Figure 6.6. ODA received, 2013

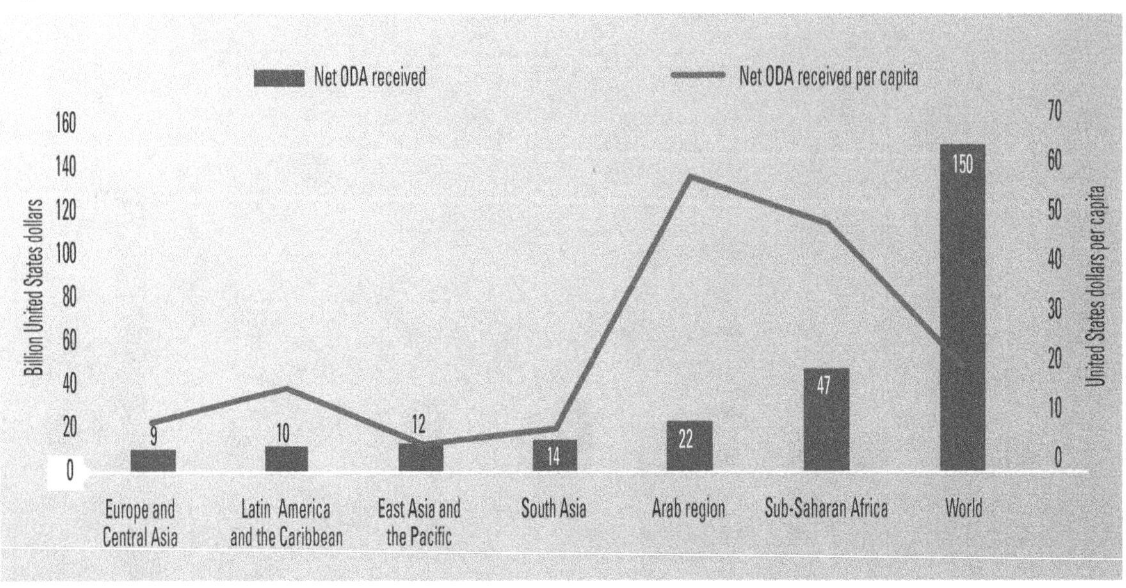

Source: World Bank, World Development Indicators.

Figure 6.7. Net ODA received per capita, selected Arab countries, 2013 (United States dollars)

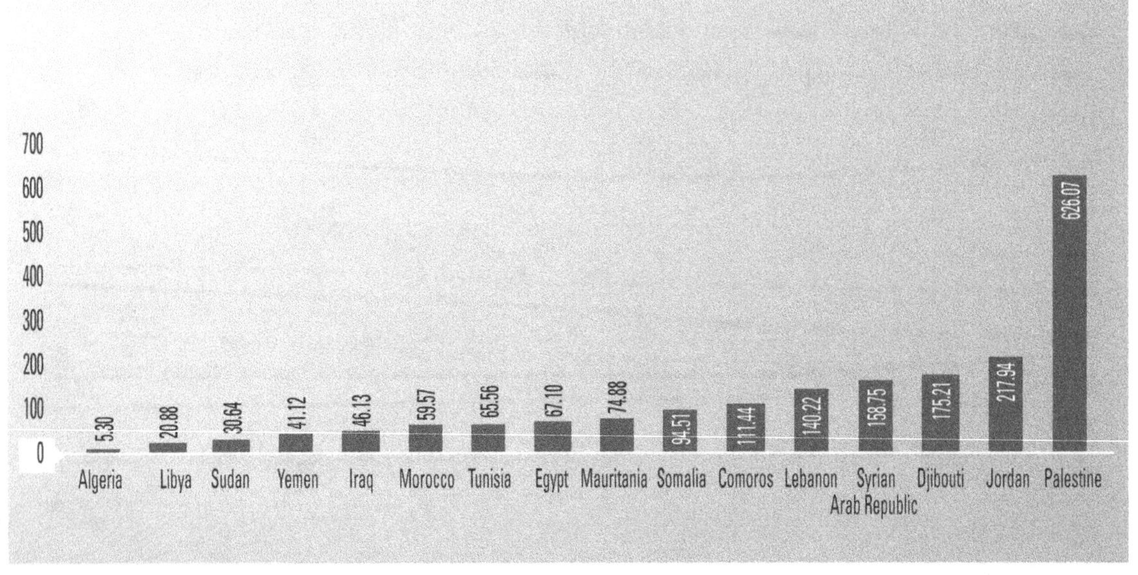

Source: World Bank, World Development Indicators.

In 2013, the Arab region received $22 billion in ODA (figure 6.6), of which $5.5 billion went to Egypt, the most received by any country in the world. On a per capita basis, the region received $60 in the same year, more than any other region of the world and around three times the global average. Palestine received $626 per person, the seventh highest figure in the world (figure 6.7). However, recurrent military offensives and destruction of infrastructure mean that the aid has not resulted in development. Moreover, it is estimated that

Figure 6.8. Net ODA received, Arab region (constant 2012 United States dollars - billions)

35
30
25
20
15
10
5
0
1990 1991 1992 1993 1994 1995 1996 1997 1998 1999 2000 2001 2002 2003 2004 2005 2006 2007 2008 2009 2010 2011 2012 2013 2014

Source: World Bank, World Development Indicators.

Figure 6.9. Cumulative financing operations of Arab development institutions by region, 2013

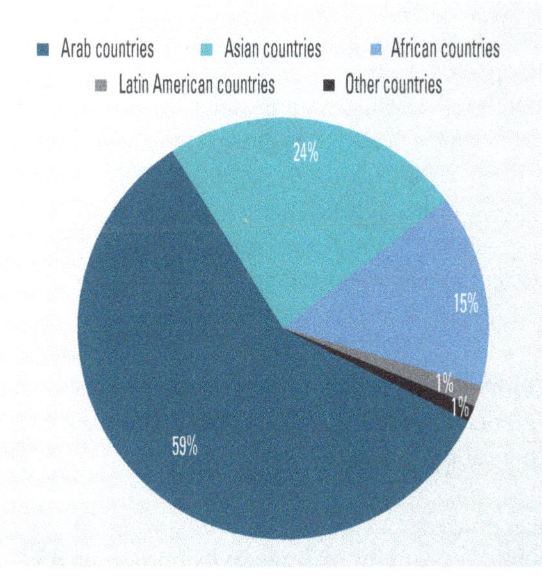

Source: الأمانة العامة لجامعة الدول العربية وآخرون، التقرير الاقتصادي العربي الموحد 2014 (أبو ظبي، صندوق النقد العربي، 2014).
Note: Institutions include: Islamic Development Bank, Abu Dhabi Fund for Development, Organization of the Petroleum Exporting Companies (OPEC) Fund for International Development, Saudi Fund for Development, Arab Fund for Economic and Social Development, Kuwait Fund for Arab Economic Development, Arab Monetary Fund and the Arab Bank for Economic Development in Africa.

the majority of international aid intended to support Palestinians, effectively benefits the Israeli economy.[17] Elsewhere in the region, conflicts are also undermining the efficacy of donor support and diverting resources from development to humanitarian causes.

ODA to countries in the Arab region in 2013 was showing an upwards trend (figure 6.8), having fallen from a peak in 2005 (channelled mainly to Iraq).

Some Arab countries, in particular Kuwait, Saudi Arabia and the United Arab Emirates, are donors (figure 6.9). Their donations exceeded 0.7 per cent of GNI between 1975 and 2010.[18] Aid, a sizeable portion of it to other Arab countries, has been routed through national and regional development funds (box 6.1).

Despite their significant role in financing development in the Arab region (especially infrastructure projects in energy and transport), the share of Arab development funds in total ODA going to Arab countries

Box 6.1. Selected Arab and Islamic development funds

- Arab Gulf Programme for Development (AGFUND; http://agfund.org): a non-profit organization that supports sustainable human development efforts targeting the neediest groups, especially poor women and children, in developing countries. It cooperates with development organizations, NGOs and other institutions, and channels financial assistance through 17 United Nations specialized agencies.
- Arab Fund for Economic and Social Development (www.arabfund.org): focuses on funding public and private investment projects and providing grants and expertise. Based in Kuwait, the fund also promotes closer cooperation between Arab countries by funding regional projects.
- Organization of Petroleum Exporting Countries (OPEC) Fund for International Development (www.ofid.org): fosters social and economic development, particularly in poor countries, and advances South-South cooperation by providing concessional loans for investment projects, programmes, and balance of payments and budget support.
- Islamic Development Bank (www.isdb.org): participates in equity capital and grant loans for productive projects and enterprises, and provides financial assistance to member countries and Muslim communities worldwide.
- Kuwait Fund for Arab Economic Development (www.kuwait-fund.org): supports economic development in Arab and other developing countries through loans, guarantees and technical assistance, and contributes to regional and international institutions.
- Saudi Fund for Development (www.sfd.gov.sa): finances projects in developing countries through soft loans and promotes national non-oil exports by providing finance and insurance products.
- Abu Dhabi Fund for Development (www.adfd.ae): provides economic assistance to developing countries in the form of concessional loans, grants and equity in investment projects (primarily basic infrastructure projects in transport, water, electricity and irrigation).
- Arab Monetary Fund (www.amf.org.ae): hosted by the United Arab Emirates, the fund aims mainly to help Arab countries to maintain the equilibrium of their balance of payments through the provision of short-term and medium-term credit.
- The Arab Bank for Economic Development in Africa (www.badea.org): located in Khartoum, the bank counts 18 Arab member countries and aims to strengthen Arab-African solidarity by financing economic development in African countries and providing technical assistance.

has been highly volatile, often as a result of political considerations and oil price swings.[19] Overall, there has been a downward trend since the 1970s, with noteworthy spikes in 1990 and 2008.[20]

(b) Private sources of finance

Private means of finance include FDI, remittances, portfolio investments and domestic savings. Portfolio investment accounts for less than 1 per cent of GDP in the Arab region and will not be discussed in detail. Domestic savings and other aspects of the financial system are discussed elsewhere in this report.

FDI inflows can be particularly beneficial when accompanied by new technologies and production techniques. In the Arab region, however, most FDI has been in low technology sectors that generate few new jobs: oil, real estate and construction.[21]

In 2013, the United Arab Emirates and Saudi Arabia received the highest FDI in absolute

Table 6.2. Inward FDI and ease of doing business, 2013

Country	FDI (billions of United States dollars)	FDI/GDP (percentage)	Ease of doing business ranking
United Arab Emirates*	10.5	2.50	22
Saudi Arabia	9.3	1.25	49
Egypt	5.6	2.04	112
Morocco	3.4	3.22	71
Kuwait*	2.9	1.57	86
Iraq	2.9	1.28	156
Lebanon	2.8	6.39	104
Libya	2.8	6.39	188
Sudan	2.2	3.27	160
Jordan	1.8	5.34	117
Algeria	1.7	0.80	154
Oman	1.6	2.02	66
Mauritania	1.2	27.73	176
Tunisia	1.1	2.32	60
Bahrain	1.0	3.02	53
Djibouti	0.3	19.64	155
Palestine*	0.2	1.75	143
Somalia	0.1	NA	NA
Comoros	0.01	2.12	159
Yemen	-0.1	-0.37	137
Qatar	-0.8	-0.42	50
Syrian Arab Republic	NA	NA	175

Source: World Bank, Doing Business 2015. Available from http://data.worldbank.org/data-catalog/doing-business-database (accessed 2 November 2015).
Note: For countries marked with an (*), 2012 data were used due to unavailability of 2013 data.

terms, which tallies with their high ranking in terms of ease of doing business. Djibouti and Mauritania received high FDI relative to their GDP, despite ranking poorly in terms of their business environment (table 6.2).

According to the World Development Indicators, FDI as a percentage of GDP is relatively low in the Arab region – about 1.7 per cent of GDP, compared with 2.9 per cent worldwide. As a share of total inflows to developing economies, FDI levels in the region rose from around 4 per cent ($1.3 billion) in 1990 to a peak of 17 per cent ($97 billion) in 2008, only to drop back to 6 per cent ($44 billion) in 2014 - the sixth consecutive decline since 2008 (figure 6.10). Inward investment to the Arab region has declined substantially since 2008, initially triggered by the financial crisis of 2008 and subsequently due to increased political and social instability in the region. By contrast, FDI to other developing country regions reverted to an upward trend following the recessionary dip.

Figure 6.10. Inward foreign direct investment (United States dollars at current prices and exchange rates - billions)

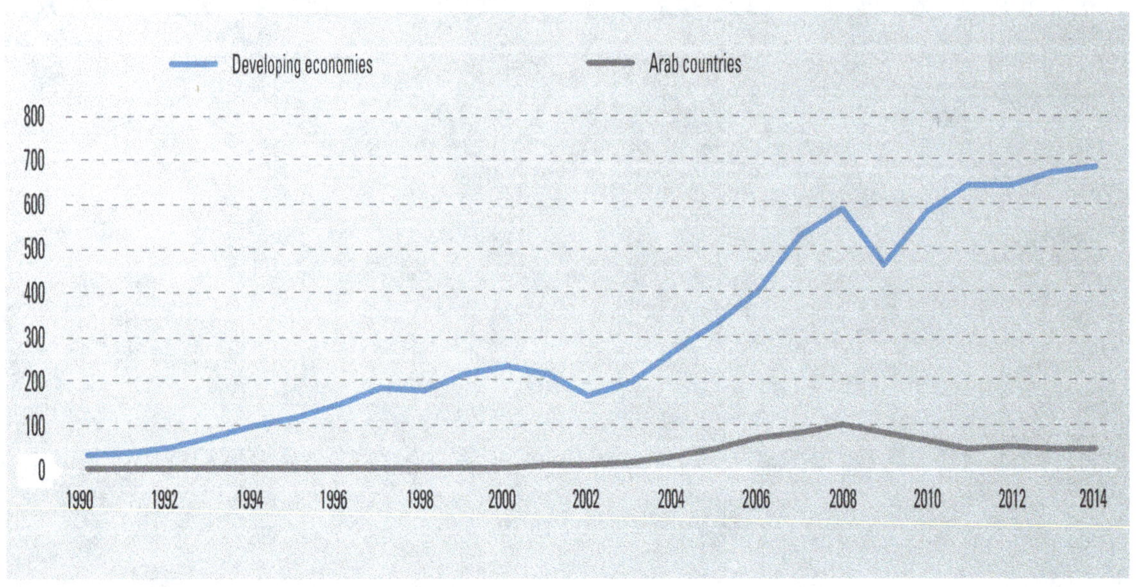

Source: UNCTAD, UNCTADstat. Available from http://unctadstat.unctad.org/EN (accessed 27 October 2015).

Figure 6.11. Arab intraregional investment (current United States dollars - billions)

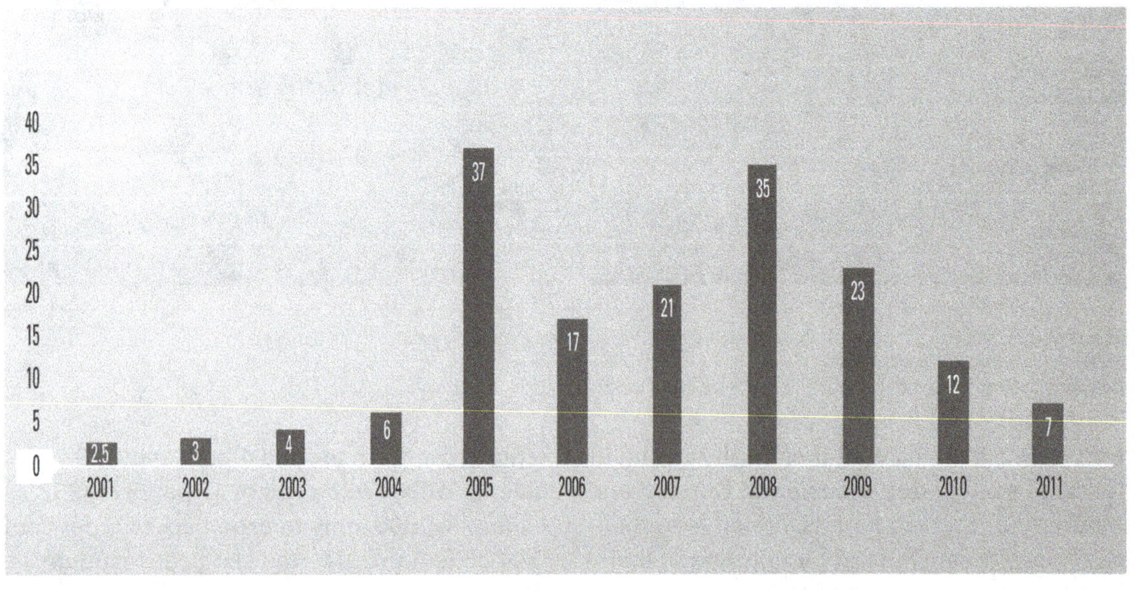

Source: Adapted from ESCWA, *Arab Integration: A 21st Century Development Imperative* (Beirut, 2013, E/ESCWA/OES/2013/3).

Intraregional direct investment grew from $2.5 billion in 2001 to $35 billion in 2008, but then dropped thereafter (figure 6.11). Arab intraregional investments remain meagre, not exceeding 11.2 per cent of total investments by Arab sovereign funds outside the region, which are estimated at around $1,600 billion.[22]

Tax and other incentives designed to attract FDI should be viewed with caution, as they

Figure 6.12. Net foreign direct investment, 2013 (current United States dollars - billions)

Source: World Bank, World Development Indicators.

Figure 6.13. Personal remittances received (current United States dollars - billions)

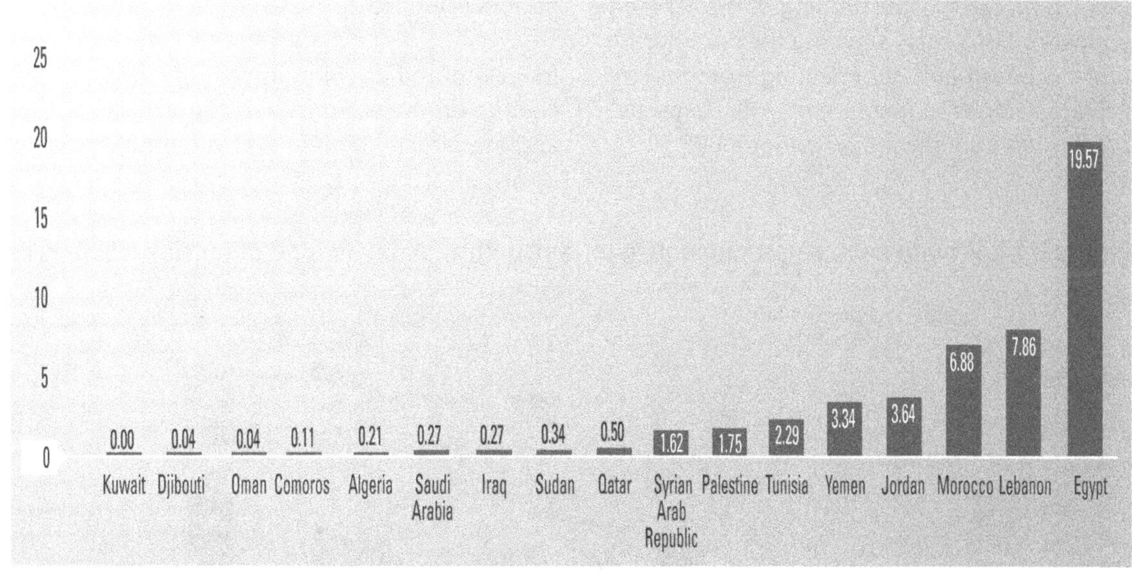

Source: World Bank, World Development Indicators.
Note: Last available years range from 2010 to 2014.

are sometimes used at the expense of generating public revenue. Their overall cost benefit should be analysed and a consistent policy on investment followed in order to foster a climate of stability. Rather than such incentives, emphasis should be placed on long-term measures that do not involve forgoing revenue, such as fighting corruption, facilitating the establishment of businesses and creating a friendly regulatory and even-handed judicial environment.[23]

Net FDI, which nets out inflows from foreign investors against FDI by the country to the rest of the world, is negative for most Arab economies in 2013 (figure 6.12). Competitiveness in the region's countries thus needs to be improved urgently in order to curb the outflow of domestic capital.

Remittances play a key role in the Arab region, both as a source of private sector income and in terms of outflows. Egypt, the world's sixth largest recipient of remittances, received $20 billion in 2014, while Lebanon, in tenth place, received $8 billion (figure 6.13). The region as a whole is expected to bring in $53 billion in 2015.[24] Remittances generally support private investment (such as education and housing) and consumption.

(c) Other financial flows

Public-private partnerships (PPP) traditionally involve private-sector funding of government-sponsored projects, allowing for risk-sharing and the possibility of benefiting from the private sector's management skills, expertise, innovation and efficiency. Under a PPP structure, efficiency gains can arise through competitive pressure on procurement, operation and maintenance costs when undertaken by private operators. PPP are relatively infrequent in Arab countries (figure 6.14), but it should be noted that data for the GCC countries were unavailable.

Data for developing Arab countries reveal a certain bias, in comparison with the world norm, towards use of PPP in certain less strategic and less regulated sectors that are more profitable for the private sector, thereby enabling the application of market or close-to-market rates, as in the case of energy, which is a rewarding industry from the perspective of the private investor (figures 6.15 and 6.16). Investment in transportation (box 6.2) and telecommunications also constituted a substantial share of the total during 1990-2013 (in terms of both the number and value of projects). By comparison, private-sector participation in the water and sewage sectors is limited.

In view of the growing impact of climate change on the region, Arab countries can and are already benefiting from multilateral

Figure 6.14. Private sector participation in infrastructure in developing countries, 1990-2013

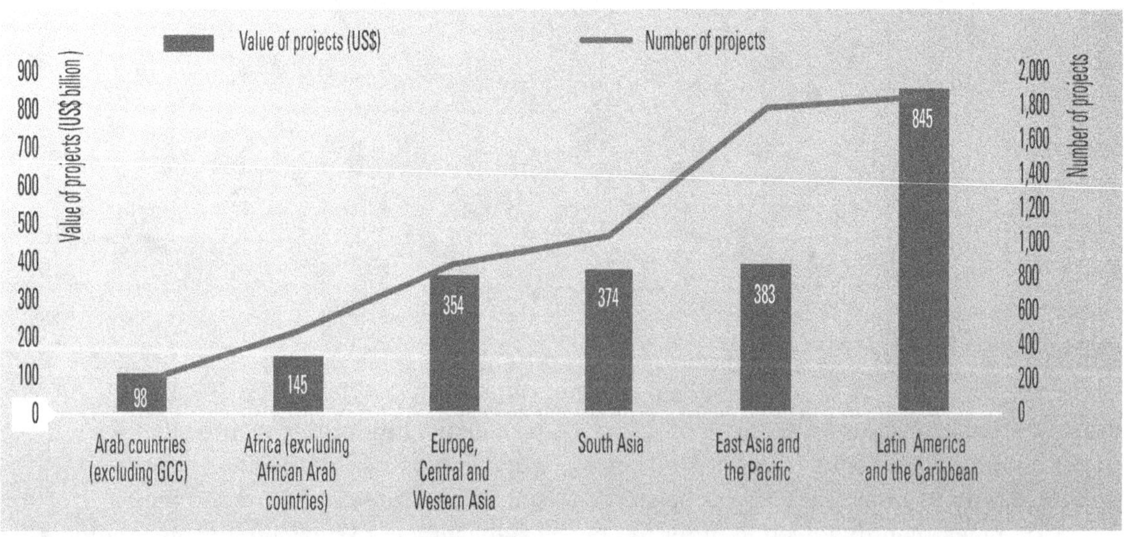

Source: World Bank, World Development Indicators; and World Bank and Public-Private Infrastructure Advisory Facility (PPIAF), Private Participation in Infrastructure database, available from http://ppi.worldbank.org/ (accessed 2 November 2015).

Box 6.2. Queen Alia International Airport project: A regional first

The $900 million project to overhaul Queen Alia International Airport in Jordan involved construction of a new terminal with capacity to handle 12 million passengers a year and operation of the airport. The challenges of being the first full airport concession in the Middle East and the first PPP finance deal compliant with sharia law, and foreign exchange risks, were considerable. They were surmounted by a well-prepared structure allowing for a project finance mechanism, asset security to all lenders through an inter-creditor agreement, and a pre-set formula for revenue adjustment in case of foreign exchange devaluation. The project achieved the highest revenue-sharing percentage among similar projects around the world, resulting in an increase in passenger traffic by 42 per cent in 2011 over 2007 and the creation of additional jobs. The project was awarded the PPP Gold Award for the Middle East and North Africa in 2013.

Source: Sherine El Sharkawy, "Financing sustainable development in the Arab region".

Figure 6.15. Distribution of projects in Arab countries with private sector participation, 1990-2013 (share in the number of projects)

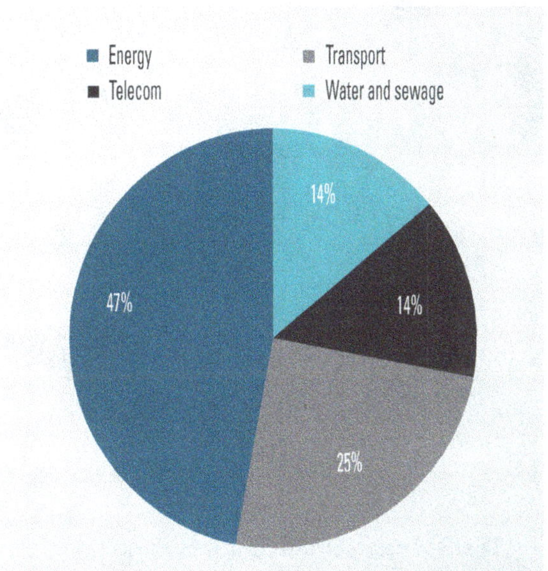

Source: World Bank and PPIAF, Private Participation in Infrastructure database (see figure 6.14).

Figure 6.16. Distribution of projects in Arab countries with private sector participation, 1990-2013 (share in the value of projects)

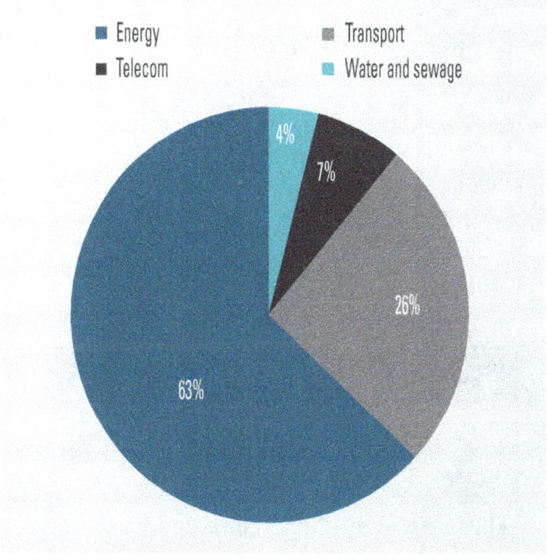

Source: World Bank and PPIAF, Private Participation in Infrastructure database.

climate-related funds, within and outside the United Nations Framework Convention on Climate Change (UNFCCC). Morocco and Egypt appear to have benefited the most in value terms and number of projects, while Jordan, Lebanon, Tunisia and Yemen have benefited from a relatively high number of smaller-scale projects (table 6.3).

Funds operating within the UNFCCC include several trust funds under the Global Environment Facility, which was established by the World Bank, the United Nations Development Programme (UNDP) and the United Nations Environment Programme (UNEP):

- The Global Environment Facility (GEF) Trust Fund (www.thegef.org) is the largest public

Table 6.3. Arab countries tapping climate funds by volume and number of projects, 1992-2014

Arab countries	GEF Trust Fund (1992 to date)		Special Climate Change Fund (2001 to date)		Least Developed Countries Fund (2002 to date)		Adaptation Fund (2009)		Clean Technology Fund		Strategic Climate Fund	
	Number of projects	millions of United States dollars	Number of projects	millions of United States dollars	Number of projects	millions of United States dollars	Number of projects	millions of United States dollars	Number of projects	millions of United States dollars	Number of projects	millions of United States dollars
Algeria	1	15.30										
Bahrain	1	0.33										
Egypt	11	79.69	2	11.81			1	6.90	2	300		
Iraq	1	2.20										
Jordan	8	11.20	1	2								
Kuwait	1	0.85										
Lebanon	5	5.56	1	7.14			1	7.86				
Morocco	9	58.5	3	17					3	388		
Syrian Arab Republic	1	4.07										
Tunisia	8	32.30	1	5.50								
Yemen	6	7.14			3	15.20					1	40.00
Total	52	217.14	8	43.45	3	15.20	2	14.76	5	688.00	1	40.00

Source: Sherif Arif and Fadi Doumani, "A strategic investment framework for green economy in Arab countries from an energy perspective".

climate change fund. Arab countries have received financial support for 52 projects totalling $217 million, or 23.8 per cent of the fund's climate change allocation since 1992. Egypt and Morocco are the largest beneficiaries, with $79.7 million and $58.5 million respectively.

- The Least Developed Countries Fund (www.thegef.org/gef/LDCF) supports climate change adaptation activities in developing countries that are party to the UNFCCC and facilitate technology transfer. Yemen has received $15.2 million since 2002.
- The Special Climate Change Fund finances climate change mitigation and adaptation activities that are complementary to the GEF and other bilateral and multilateral funding. Five Arab countries (Egypt, Jordan, Lebanon, Morocco and Tunisia) have received a total of $43.4 million from the fund since 2001.
- The Adaptation Fund (www.adaptation-fund.org) was established in 2009 to support adaptation projects in developing countries that are vulnerable to climate change. Egypt and Lebanon have received

a total of $14.8 million for agriculture and food security projects since 2009.

The World Bank operates two trust funds in collaboration with multilateral development banks:[25]

- The Clean Technology Fund (www-cif.climateinvestmentfunds.org/fund/clean-technology-fund) promotes the demonstration, deployment and transfer of low-carbon technologies in middle-income countries. It focuses on large infrastructure in a small number of countries, aiming to reduce technology costs, stimulate private-sector participation and promote replication in other countries. Egypt has received a $300 million grant and concessionary loans to establish a 250-megawatt build-own-operate wind energy project in the Gulf of Suez ($140 million) and a transport modal shift for developing new bus and rail infrastructure ($160 million). Morocco has received $388 million in grants and concessionary loans to develop wind and solar energy, including the Noor Ouarzazate Concentrated Solar Power Plant Project.
- The Strategic Climate Fund (www.climateinvestmentfunds.org/cif/node/3) has provided $40 million to Yemen to scale up renewable energy.

B. Science and technology

The role of science, technology and innovation in spurring economic development and employment is widely acknowledged. It is reaffirmed in the SDGs: explicit reference is made to science, technology and innovation in 10 of the 169 SDG targets, including three targets under goal 17 on means of implementation.

The Arab countries have gone some way towards developing science, technology and innovation, by striving to improve their education systems and acquire foreign expertise and technologies. However, the impact on industry has been limited due to an unfavourable business environment and weak links between science and industry. The Arab countries continue to be users, rather than generators, of technology. Technologies need to be deployed to foster more diversified economies. Unless a 'demand-pull' for technology is created through a vibrant economy, 'supply-push' will only lead to unemployment and brain drain. Instability in the region is an added impediment to achieving this supply-demand balance.

The following sections provide a brief analysis of the current situation. Note, however, that science, technology and innovation statistics for the region are hard to come by and may be outdated.

1. National science and technology capacities

The use of modern technology has expanded quickly in the Arab region. The number of Internet users and mobile cellular subscriptions rose significantly between 2000 and 2014, by which time there were 109 mobile telephone subscriptions for every 100 persons in the region, well above the global average of 96. In GCC countries, there are 179 subscriptions per 100 persons (figure 6.17).

Internet use (34.4 per cent of the population) for the region is below the global average (40.7 per cent) in 2014. It was higher than world average in the GCC countries only (72.3 per cent). Some Arab countries lag behind significantly: Somalia (1.6 per cent); Comoros (7 per cent); Mauritania and Djibouti (10.7 per cent).[26] Online government services are well developed in the Gulf countries, which score relatively well on the e-Government Development Index (GCC average of 0.65, compared with the global average of 0.49).[27] Morocco, Saudi Arabia and the United Arab Emirates, whose Governments strongly support the generation of Arabic digital content, account for 58 per cent of all web pages in Arabic. Egypt,

Figure 6.17. Mobile cellular subscriptions per 100 population

	2000	2014
Arab region	3.25	108.95
GCC	13.21	178.56
LDCs	0.26	68.62
Maghreb	3.44	116.44
Mashreq	2.16	103.10

Source: Authors' calculations based on World Bank, World Development Indicators.
Notes: Values are weighted against total population. The year 2000 was taken as base year because uptake in mobile cellular technology in the previous decade was slight.

Figure 6.18. Gross expenditure on research and development (percentage of GDP, most recent year)

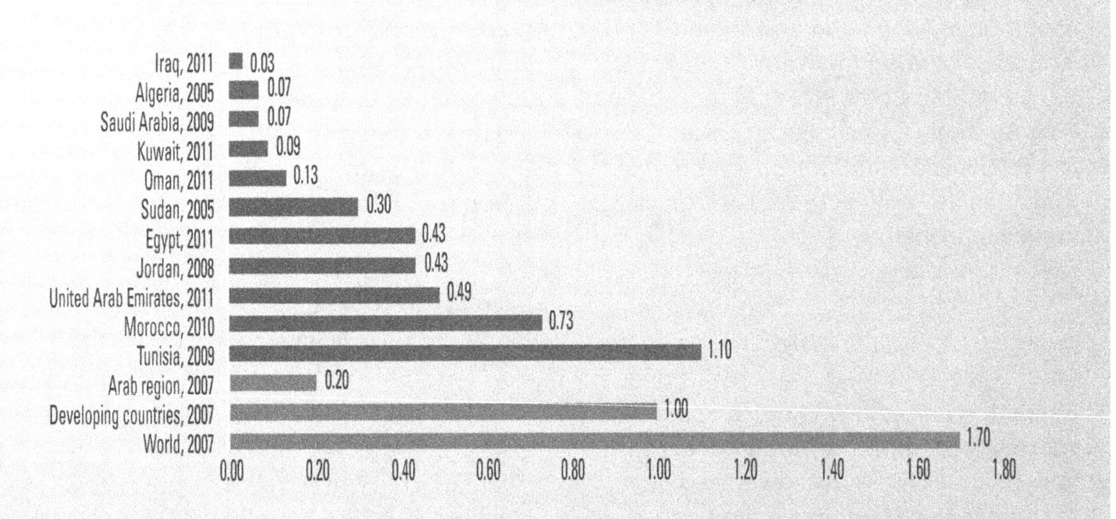

Sources: *UNESCO Science Report 2010: The Current Status of Science around the World* (Paris, 2010), pp. 3 and 8, available from http://unesdoc.unesco.org/images/0018/001899/189958e.pdf; and UNESCO Institute for Statistics (UIS) database, available from www.uis.unesco.org/Pages/default.aspx (accessed 23 July 2015).

Oman, Qatar and others are striving to digitize Arabic and Islamic cultural heritage.

In other areas, technological progress in the Arab region has been disappointing. What little manufacturing the region has tends to be low-technology.[28] Information and communications technology contributes a meagre percentage to exports from Arab countries, with Tunisia being the sole exception at 7 per cent of total

Figure 6.19. Researchers per million inhabitants (most recent year)

Saudi Arabia, 2009 47
Libya, 2009 77
Kuwait, 2011 132
Oman, 2011 160
Algeria, 2005 165
Palestine, 2010 327
Sudan, 2005 355
Iraq, 2011 426
Egypt, 2011 524
Morocco, 2011 864
Tunisia, 2008 1837
Jordan, 2008 1913
Arab region, 2007 373
Developing countries, 2007 580
World, 2007 1081
0 500 1000 1500 2000 2500

Sources: UNESCO Science Report 2010 and UIS database (see figure 6.18).
Note: For Saudi Arabia, Libya, the Sudan and Jordan, headcount rather than full-time equivalent (FTE) was reported.

Figure 6.20. Scientific and technical journal articles published per million inhabitants, 2011

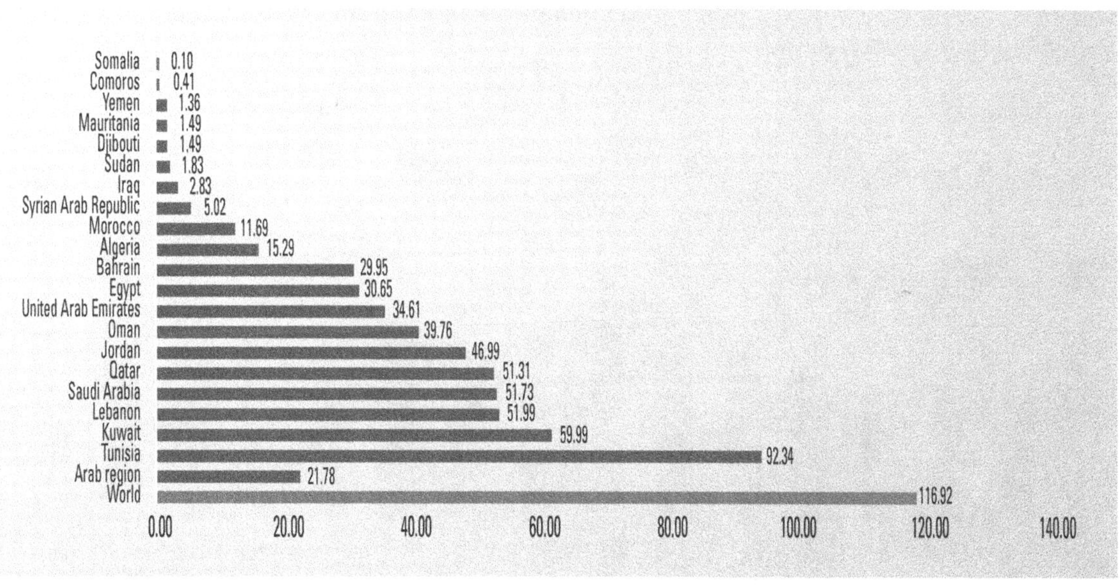

Source: World Bank, World Development Indicators.

exports. The share of business to consumer e-commerce in the region in 2013, estimated at 2.3 per cent of total trade, was very modest compared with the Asia-Pacific, European and North American regions.[29]

The capacity of the region to participate in modern science and technology will depend on human capacity and government incentives. Education systems in the region often fail to provide the basic skills needed for science and technology, and Governments and business pay scant attention to research and development.

Figure 6.21. Patent applications filed in selected Arab countries, 2013

Egypt	United Arab Emirates	Morocco	Saudi Arabia	Algeria	Tunisia	Jordan	Qatar	Syrian Arab Republic	Bahrain	Yemen	Sudan	Djibouti
2,057	1,426	1,144	931	840	549	392	332	257	170	80	16	3

Source: World Bank, World Development Indicators.

Figure 6.22. University/industry research collaboration, 2013-2014 (World Economic Forum Executive Opinion Poll Score)

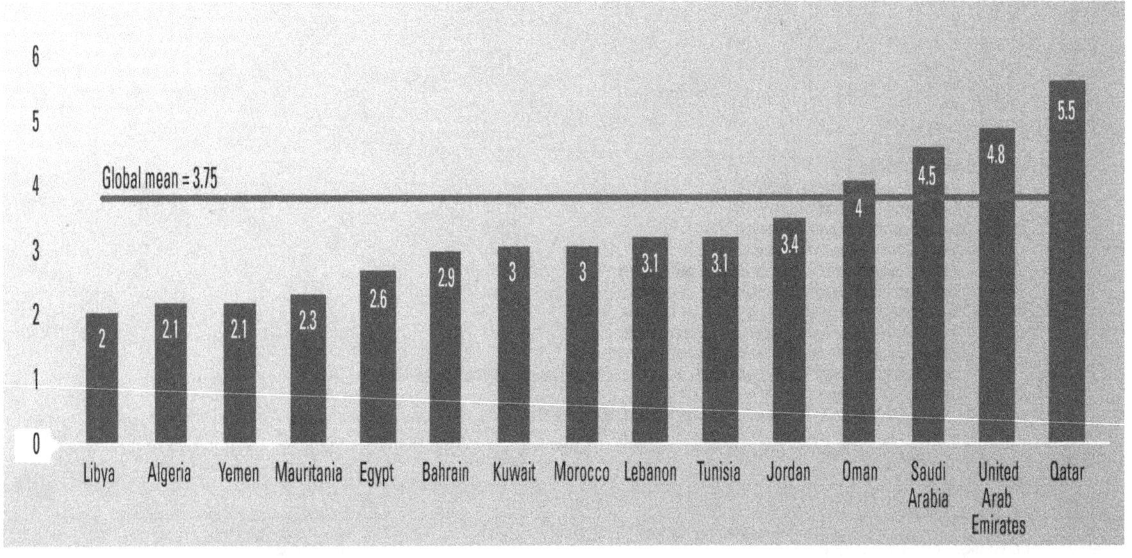

Source: Klaus Schwab (ed.), *The Global Competitiveness Report 2013-2014* (Geneva, World Economic Forum, 2013). Available from www3.weforum.org/docs/WEF_GlobalCompetitivenessReport_2013-14.pdf.

At only 0.2 per cent, average gross domestic expenditure on research and development in the region was one fifth of average spending by developing countries and 12 per cent of the global average (figure 6.18). Research and development spending tends to be dominated by the public sector in the Arab region.

Similarly, the average of 373 full-time researchers per million inhabitants in the

Arab region is below the global average for developing countries (580) and one third of the world average (1,081) (figure 6.19).[30]

Research and development output lags similarly. Around 7,800 scientific and technical journal articles were published in 2011 in the Arab region, amounting to 1.3 per cent of the world's total. On average, 22 articles were published per million inhabitants, compared with a global rate of 117 (figure 6.20). Similarly, 5,765 patent applications were filed in 2013 in 13 Arab countries, representing a mere 0.2 per cent of world applications (figure 6.21).[31]

The Arab region is handicapped by the inadequacy of links between universities, industry and the labour market. According to the World Economic Forum's Executive Opinion Survey for 2013/2014, Arab countries scored between 2.1 and 5.5 on a scale of 1 to 7 with respect to the level of university/industry research collaboration (figure 6.22). For most Arab countries, the score is below the global mean of 3.75.

2. Global and regional partnerships in technology

Progress on the transfer of environmentally sound technology has fallen short of the commitments made by the global community in the wake of the 1992 Rio Declaration on Environment and Development. To address this shortfall, the 2015 Addis Ababa Action Agenda provides for the establishment of a "technology facilitation mechanism". Moreover, the SDGs include targets regarding the said mechanism and the creation of a technology bank for LDCs in order to enhance science, technology and innovation cooperation (box 6.3).

Regional cooperation in the field of technology can help countries to tackle common challenges (especially those related to environmental degradation and natural resource scarcity) with fewer resources. However, the lack of regional cooperation between researchers is a serious handicap. Egypt, Jordan and Saudi Arabia maintain research partnerships between themselves and with countries outside the region, but other Arab countries appear to have done little to develop significant research partnerships.[32] The Arab Scientific Community Organization lists 126 scientific societies in various disciplines, of which only eight are regional. Efforts to mobilize renowned Arab researchers in the diaspora are multiplying and could be promising in the long term. One example is the Zewail City of Science and Technology in Egypt, inaugurated in 2011.[33]

Box 6.3. Global technology facilitation mechanism and a technology bank for LDCs

General Assembly resolution 66/288 of 27 July 2012, on "The future we want", calls for the creation of a "facilitation mechanism that promotes the development, transfer and dissemination of clean and environmentally sound technologies". It was concluded at the Third International Conference on Financing for Development, held in July 2015 in Addis Ababa, that such a mechanism would require a United Nations inter-agency task team on science, technology and innovation for the SDGs to enhance coordination of capacity-building initiatives, a multi-stakeholder forum on the subject and an online platform with information on available initiatives and programmes. Moreover, the Secretary-General of the United Nations appointed a high-level panel (see http://unohrlls.org/technologybank) in November 2014 to study the feasibility of a technology bank for LDCs and define its functions.

Figure 6.23. Arab region's share in global exports (percentage)

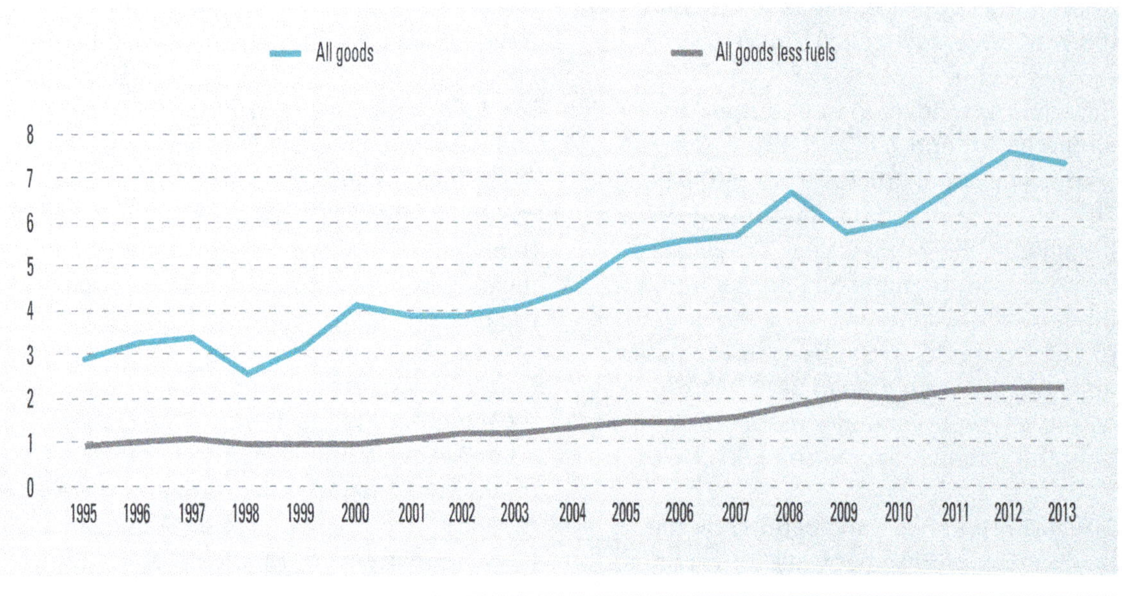

Source: UNCTADstat database (see figure 6.10).

C. Trade

The Arab region's share of world exports remains modest but doubled between 1995 and 2013 to reach 7.3 per cent (figure 6.23). That increase applies equally to fuel and other exports: the region's share of non-fuel exports increased from 1 per cent to 2 per cent between 1995 and 2013. Moreover, several Arab States have acceded to the World Trade Organization over the past two decades, while others have observer status and are negotiating accession.[34]

Several intraregional trade agreements operate. In 1957, members of the League of Arab States signed the Economic Unity Agreement. Commitment to Arab economic integration was renewed in 1980 and 1981 through the Charter for National Economic Action, the Strategy for Joint Arab Economic Action, and the Inter-Arab Trade Facilitation and Development Agreement. Other trade agreements include the Greater Arab Free Trade Area (GAFTA, 2005), the Gulf Cooperation Council Common Market (2008), and the Agadir Agreement (2004). The Arab Maghreb Union was established in 1989. Nevertheless, the Arab region remains one of the least economically integrated in the world, due in large part to the limited range of Arab country exports and weak and similar economic structures in most Arab countries (figure 6.24). Intraregional exports did not exceed 9 per cent of total exports in the region in 2012. Levels of intraregional trade in the Arab Maghreb Union and Gulf Cooperation Council are even lower in comparison with intraregional exports in the European Union (62 per cent of total exports) and the North American Free Trade Agreement zone (49 per cent).

Non-Arab developing countries represent the fastest growing market for Arab exporters (figure 6.25). Since 1995, Arab exports to other developing countries have grown by a factor of 15, followed by exports to developed countries (factor of about 6), and exports to other countries in the Arab region, which grew by a factor of just 5. Indeed, many Arab countries

Figure 6.24. Share of intra-group trade, 2012 (percentage)

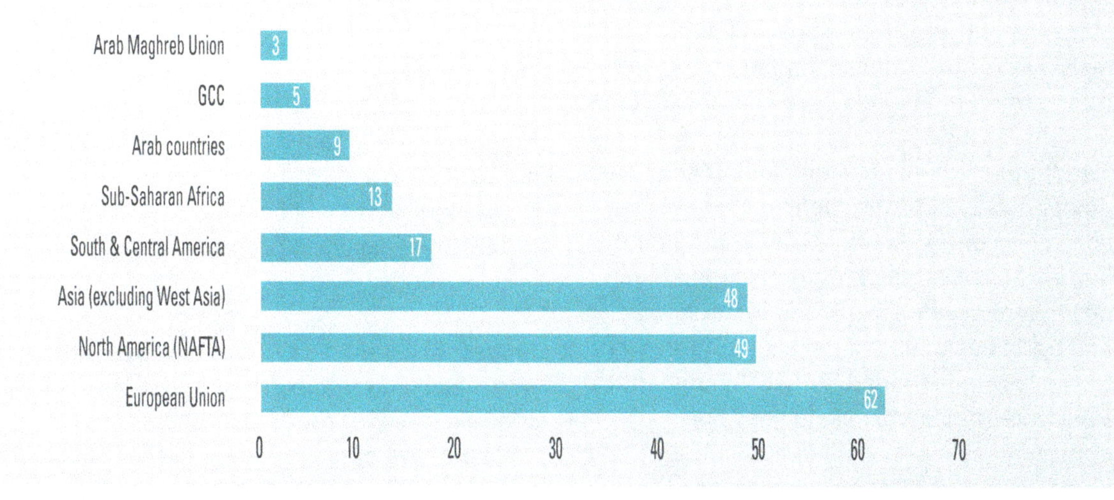

Source: UNCTADstat database.

Figure 6.25. Arab exports (percentage growth relative to 1995)

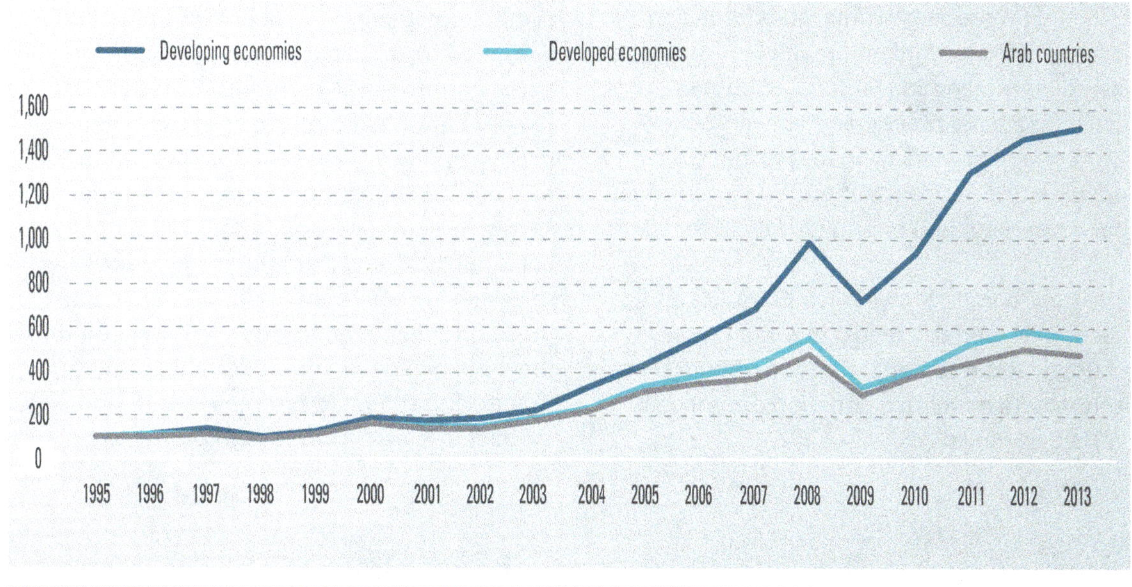

Source: UNCTADstat database.

have been quicker to conclude preferential arrangements with non-Arab parties than with each other, engaging in the deep economic commitments imposed by those arrangements and accepting commercial provisions that often surpass WTO requirements. As of January 2015, Arab States were parties to some 750 separate investment bilateral and international agreements.[35]

Recognizing that tariff reduction and elimination alone was ineffective in boosting intraregional trade, the League of Arab States announced in 2009 that a pan-Arab customs union and common market would be launched in 2015 and 2020 respectively. The long-term goal is to build new trade and investment partnerships in the Arab region by eliminating all forms of trade restrictions and quotas, and restrictions on residence, employment, and transportation between Arab countries.

Negotiations on the customs union have been postponed until further notice. It would be a natural second step after GAFTA, but first the impact of such a union on Arab economies, taking into account the specific characteristics and trade ties of each Arab economy, needs to be closely examined. ESCWA is preparing several reports on the challenges and opportunities associated with the union.

The failure to integrate trade and other economic policies, especially on investment, in the region has hampered the full development of trade. Institutions are failing to address intellectual property rights, standards and environmental regulations. The lack of regional coordination and inadequacy of human capacities have prevented the Arab States from presenting a strong and sound collective position in WTO negotiations. Arab countries have not benefited enough from aid for trade.

Capacity-building for parliamentarians, academics and the media in trade issues is needed, and a regional meeting should be held annually to develop a common approach to WTO trade talks.

D. Data and monitoring

High quality national statistics and flexibility in policymaking are critical for policy planning. Sound indicators will be a key to implementing the SDGs, measuring progress and ensuring accountability.

Statistical capacity in Arab countries remains weak, as illustrated by their inability to compile many of the MDG indicators. A review of the data contained in the global MDG database for six Arab countries reveals that they could only compile 42 per cent of the 45 MDG indicators that could be expected to be compiled by national Governments using their own official statistics. Of the remaining 58 per cent, statistics could be compiled from international agencies for some countries (24 per cent) or not at all (34 per cent). None of the selected countries produces official statistics for more than 27 of the MDG indicators. Many of the time series contain data points for only a few years between 1990 and 2014, limiting capacity to assess trends in the indicator. Based on these findings, it is possible to conclude that the evidence base and national capacity for monitoring the MDGs in the Arab region was modest at best.[36] That in turn points to one of

Box 6.4. Tunisia tackles statistical capacity issues in its MDGs report

Tunisia's 2013 MDGs report noted that the country's statistics system needed to provide more relevant and disaggregated data. The Tunisian National Statistics Council had already set up a working group on statistics reform with a view to improving reporting on MDGs as part of its National Statistics Programme for 2007-2011. The programme recommended that Tunisia adopt international definitions and methods and that statistics be compiled on specific MDGs, such as those related to sanitation.

Source: Taher Abdessalem and others, *Objectifs du Millénaire pour le Développement. Rapport National de Suivi 2013* (Tunisia and United Nations, 2014). Available from www.undp.org/content/dam/undp/library/MDG/english/MDG%20Country%20Reports/Tunisia/Rapport%20Suivi%202013%20OMD%20Tunisie%20Final.pdf.

Figure 6.26. Data gap analysis for 44 League of Arab States sustainable development indicators

	Arab region	LDCs	Mashreq	Maghreb	GCC
No data points	11%	17%	6%	9%	11%
1 data point	6%	9%	6%	3%	3%
2 data points	13%	14%	14%	13%	13%
3 or more data points	70%	60%	73%	75%	73%

Source: Cameron Allen and others, "Sustainable development indicators and the Arab region: gap analysis summary report", Expert Report for the Arab Sustainable Development Report (Beirut, 2014).

Figure 6.27. Level of statistical capacity, 2015

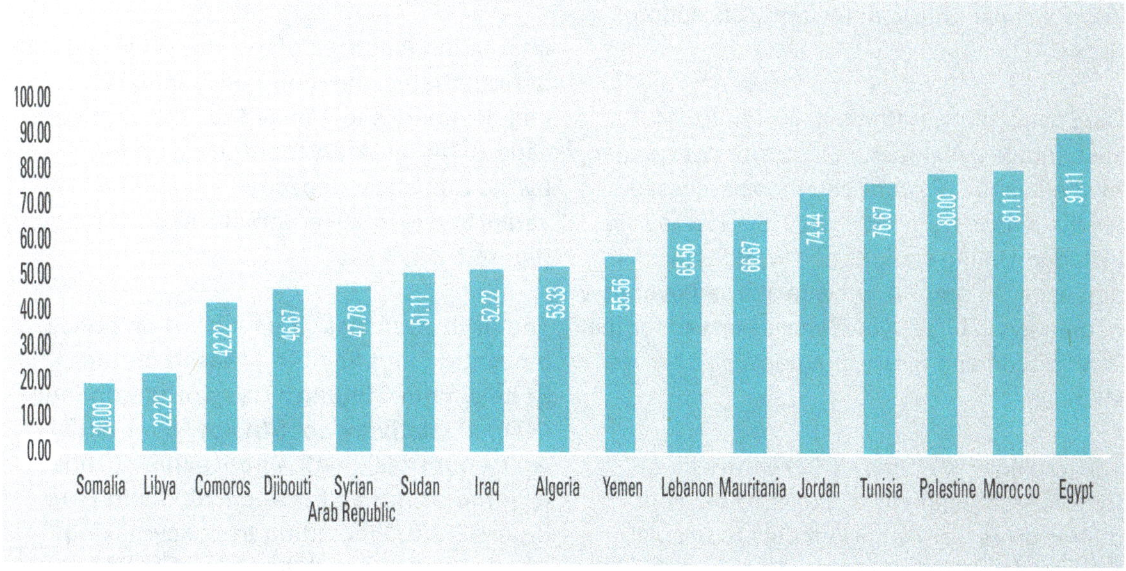

Source: World Bank, World Development Indicators.
Note: Scale from 0 (worst) to 100 (best).

the main challenges for improving the use of evidence in policymaking.

All countries in the region (except the Comoros and Libya) produced national MDG progress reports at least twice. They generally say little about statistics for monitoring and evaluation and the degree to which difficulties are discussed varies greatly. Some reports make no mention at all of such difficulties, while many confine themselves to general

Figure 6.28. BTI: Extent to which Government is innovative and flexible in policymaking

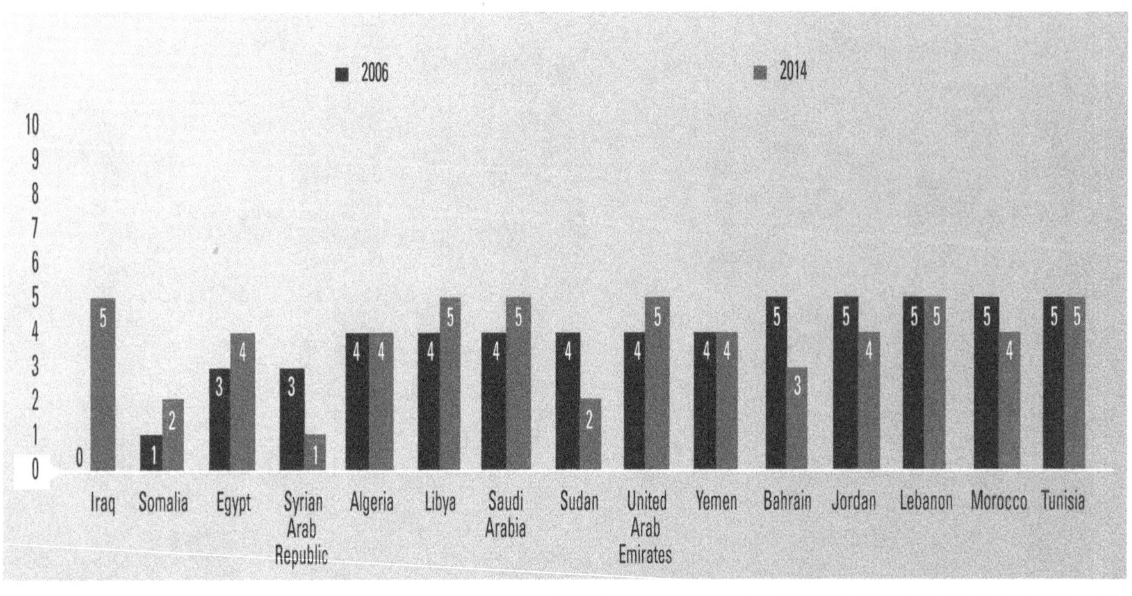

Source: Bertelsmann Stiftung, BTI. Available from http://www.bti-project.org/ (accessed 2 November 2015).
Note: Index ranges from 1 (worst) to 10 (best).

statements of the need to improve statistics. Tunisia constitutes a noteworthy exception (box 6.4).

Data availability in the Arab region for 44 sustainable development indicators developed by the League of Arab States was assessed for the period from 1990 to 2015.[37] The review included United Nations and World Bank databases in order to provide a broad overview of data availability, which was assessed for the Arab region and four subregions, and across all indicators.

The gap analysis (figure 6.26) shows that, for the Arab region as a whole, 83 per cent of indicators have sufficient data to enable the calculation of a basic trend (at least 2 data points). Of the remaining 17 per cent, data was either insufficient (6 per cent) or non-existent (11 per cent). Gaps are evident in all subregions. In the LDCs, 26 per cent of indicators had no data or a single data point. Data availability was highest in the Maghreb and Mashreq, with Egypt, Jordan, Morocco, Oman and Tunisia showing the highest levels (80 per cent or above).

International indices of the statistical capacity of Arab States and their policy innovation and flexibility show mixed results. Statistical capacity in the Arab countries, as reflected by the Statistical Capacity Indicator in 2015, varies between 20 in Somalia and 91 in Egypt (figure 6.27).[38]

The Arab countries' track record on policy innovation and flexibility, based on the Bertelsmann Stiftung's Transformation Index (BTI), is relatively poor (below 5 for all Arab countries), with a noticeable decline in some countries between 2006 and 2014 (figure 6.28). Innovation in policymaking often comes through learning from past experiences (effective monitoring and evaluation), observation and knowledge exchange (good practices, international cooperation) or consultancy (academic experts and practitioners). Flexibility refers to a Government's ability to adapt to and take advantage of developmental opportunities inherent in a given political situation. Assessments of several Arab countries find that States are "not particularly flexible or innovative, a fact that results more from an unwillingness to learn than from incapacity".[39]

Arab social development experts have identified several concerns about the region's monitoring experiences. One is that processes for compiling and reporting sustainable development indicators in Arab countries are not fully integrated into national and regional institutional structures. For example, each time a new indicator report is compiled, project teams must be created anew in both the agency responsible for the report and those that provide data. This limits opportunities for "learning-by-doing" and increases the burden of reporting. Access to data is another problem. Some data are simply unavailable, while in other cases data that are collected are not made available. Government agencies may, for a variety of reasons - including simple reluctance to share information – withhold information from citizens and even from other government agencies. Obliging users to pay for data is another impediment to access and may reflect a veiled desire to keep data secret. Strengthening laws governing access to information could help to resolve such problems.

In order to enhance data capacity and collection in the Arab region, the role of national statistical offices should be strengthened, and transparency of information enhanced to the fullest extent possible. A smaller set of the most relevant, or "headline", sustainable development indicators for the Arab region should be agreed upon and maintained over the years to allow for the identification of trends. In order to improve environmental data, a system of environmental-economic accounts[40] should be promoted in the Arab region. Following the Mediterranean example,[41] a regional partnership in the form of an observatory on sustainable development data, bringing together government and non-government stakeholders, could be established to fill knowledge gaps.

7. Achieving the 2030 Agenda for Sustainable Development in the Arab Region

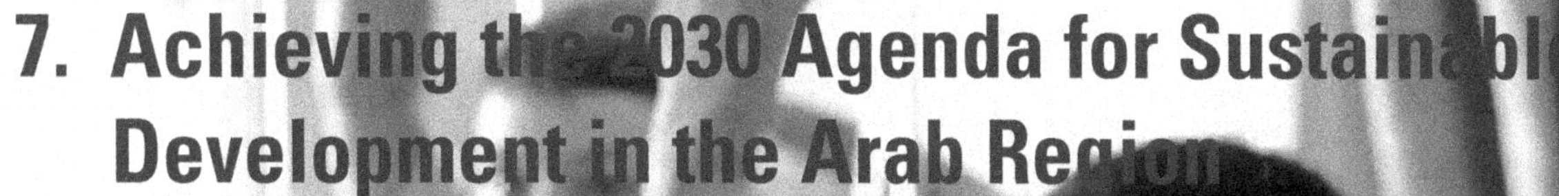

"There is no Plan B because we do not have Planet B. We have to work and galvanize our action."

United Nations Secretary-General Ban Ki-moon's press encounter at the People's Climate March (New York, 21 September 2014)

7. Achieving the 2030 Agenda for Sustainable Development in the Arab Region

The Arab region today is marked by conflict and instability. Amid the turmoil, it is difficult to focus on the long-term planning and investment required for sustainable development. Nevertheless, it would be a grave mistake to think that meeting pressing needs and planning for sustainable development are mutually exclusive. On the contrary, sustainable development strategies will be successful only if they address the root causes and effects of the instability, including its at times irreversible impact on cultural heritage and ecosystems, or the consequences of long-term displacement. The 2030 Agenda for Sustainable Development provides an opportunity to envisage a future for the region that is free from poverty and based on human rights, equality and sustainability, to embark on the road of sustainable development and peace, dignity and well-being for all.

Governments will need to provide equal access to the basic necessities of life and opportunities for all to contribute to, and benefit from, economic development. Particular efforts must be devoted to tackling poverty and unemployment, reducing gender disparities and addressing inequalities within and between countries. Quality education that is relevant to the labour market is a high priority. Special consideration should be given to vulnerable groups, especially refugees and internally displaced persons, the number of whom increases by the day.

Achieving sustainable and resilient societies will require policies and investments designed for tomorrow as well as today, especially in terms of natural resources and in order to address inherent risks. The Arab countries face increasingly dangerous water, food and energy issues that pose a threat to societies and development gains made to date. Consumption and production patterns need to be brought to sustainable levels. Cities and infrastructure must be made resilient to natural hazards and climate change. The opportunities opened up by technology for dealing with such issues have yet to be grasped in the Arab region.

Governments in the region need to acknowledge that peace, good governance and effective institutions are linked to one another, and that they are the prerequisites for, and guarantors of, sustainable development. The Arab countries need to work with the international community to enforce international humanitarian and human rights laws, and the right to self-determination. Good governance and effective institutions presuppose the unfettered participation by all in political life and the guarantee of safety from all forms of violence. That depends on the capacity of Governments to build consensus on a national vision and goals, engage stakeholders, and steer a process of major reforms while ensuring transparency and accountability. Sustainable development ultimately depends on the political will of those at the highest levels of the decision-making process.

Public and private investment will be needed to boost productive capacity while addressing environmental degradation. All the region's resources will need to be mustered. The capacity gap, including with regard to national statistics systems, needs to be resolved. Since bridging such gaps in means of implementation is beyond the capacities of any one Arab country, regional integration and a global partnership for sustainable development should be scaled up.

Achieving the SDGs will require urgent institutional action at the national, regional and global levels. Several crucial actions, common to all Arab countries, have been highlighted throughout the analysis and consultations for this report. The issues outlined in the following sections are general in nature and applicable to all Arab countries. Sectoral recommendations are beyond the scope of this report, but subsequent editions may look at specific subregions or thematic issues.

A. National action is at the core

In times of crisis, the State is the solution. To achieve the ambitious goals of the 2030 Agenda, national Governments are in the driver's seat. That said, the role of other development partners cannot be discounted. Parliamentarians, civil society, academia, the private sector, media and others can all contribute. Strong commitment and unwavering political will are critical. Actions need to be guided by the vital interest of peoples. The following action areas are crucial for achieving the 2030 Agenda:

Good governance: Governance deficits are a root cause for development failures worldwide. In the Arab region, they have proved to be existence-threatening. The impotence of Arab societies in the face of emerging challenges raises fundamental questions about governance in government, the private sector and civil society. Democratic, humanistic and moral governance models are essential in all sectors for coping with ongoing transformations. In Governments, they are especially needed in order to build trust in, and the legitimacy of, the State and its capacity to carry out the crucial tasks of shaping the future.

Integrated planning: Arab countries will need to translate the long-term SDGs into medium and short-term plans and initiatives. National strategies and policies need to be re-aligned and institutional coordination mechanisms improved. Countries need to build decision-support tools to enable integrated analysis, monitoring, accountability and follow-up. A shift from traditional policy assessment tools to sustainable development assessment instruments and modelling tools is already taking place in some countries. The systematic use of those instruments and regional exchange of experience and good practice could multiply the benefits. Multi-stakeholder engagement in sustainable development planning and implementation can be strengthened to ensure ownership at the national level. Periodic follow-up and review will help to ensure that plans and desired outcomes are aligned.

Aligning finance with sustainable development requirements: Financing needs for sustainable development are sizeable in the Arab countries. While domestic public finance remains the central resource, all sources, including foreign direct investment, remittances and public-private partnerships, need to be mobilized to bridge the financing gap. Official development assistance will remain a significant source of funding for some Arab countries, especially in a highly volatile and unpredictable political environment that limits economic opportunities and deters private investment. Global sources of financing, such as climate finance, need to be tapped more consistently.

Enhancing data capacity and collection: Countries need to set their own baselines and SDG targets, and strengthen their national statistical systems and review frameworks. To be most useful, national baselines and targets should be in harmony with the global indicators. Data quality, timeliness, disaggregation, accessibility and availability will require enhancement in many Arab countries to allow Governments to make informed decisions and improve transparency and accountability. International technical and financial support will be needed to develop statistical capacities, modernize and interconnect systems in the region.

Human resources capacity for effective public institutions: Credible and effective institutions thrive on the talent and values of public employees and the quality of their attitude, knowledge and skills. Entry to the civil service, especially at decision-making levels, should be on the basis of merit. It should not be used as a means of alleviating unemployment or to buy alliances. Investment in skills, leadership and management capacity is crucial. Developing strong financial management capacity and oversight is critical for the successful reform of public finances, which is a prerequisite for all other reforms.

Knowledge for sustainable development: Knowledge is a global good as well as an essential input in the modern economy. Quality education for all, improved research and development, and the ability to use scientific evidence in policymaking are central to moving towards a knowledge society. In order to bridge the knowledge-generation gap, and prevent it from broadening further, countries in the region will need to build on their own knowledge foundations and be open to global knowledge exchange opportunities.

Communication for sustainable development: Preparing a generation of youth educated and trained in the values and culture of sustainability should be a priority. This would involve a serious revision of school curricula and pedagogy, as well as capacity development of the media. Civil society can play a major role in disseminating knowledge and best practices.

B. Regional and global action to implement the 2030 Agenda

The Arab countries have much in common in terms of language and culture. In many ways, they are in the same boat, facing similar challenges. In others, they are different, and those differences offer room for complementarity. Both differences and similarities present a strong rationale for knowledge exchange, joint action and regional integration in the pursuit of sustainable development. In an interconnected and globalized world, where risks and opportunities are supranational, the Arab region cannot thrive in isolation. To strengthen its internal and external ties, it needs to embrace diversity and engage in open dialogue with other civilizations.

It is in the interest of the Arab region to advance a more effective global partnership that will help bridge its technology, finance and capacity gaps. The Arab countries can benefit from international cooperation on trade, halting illicit financial flows (and retrieving stolen assets), trade facilitation, climate change mitigation and climate finance, capacity development and green technology transfer. The global partnership must be harnessed in favour of the rule of international law, and to end the illegal occupation of Palestinian and other Arab lands.

Issues requiring collective action and cooperation include: security (and its spillover manifestations, such as refugees and terrorism); economic migration; water, energy and climate change; biodiversity, trade; transport; labour; and technology and knowledge. While the global institutional framework for sustainable development has been taking shape over the past few years, the time has come to build an effective regional institutional framework for sustainable development that addresses past challenges and weaknesses experienced with the MDGs. The following action areas are important elements for such a framework:

Regional follow-up and review mechanism for the 2030 Agenda: By boosting regional integration and promoting national action, a review mechanism can support implementation of the 2030 Agenda. Its legitimacy, coherence and accountability can be reinforced by:

- Developing an Arab 2030 Vision: A consolidated, long-term regional vision for sustainable development would allow the region to identify its own targets and means of implementation, and provide a basis for assessing progress, identifying lessons learned, highlighting common challenges and solutions, and promoting peer learning. The Arab Strategic Framework for Sustainable Development would need to be revisited in order to provide an umbrella for sectoral strategies in the region. The regional vision could also guide national strategies.
- Agreeing on a joint approach to measuring sustainable development: To allow for regular, long-term monitoring of progress, the sustainable development indicators developed for the Arab region need to be harmonized with those of the 2030 Agenda, thereby reducing the reporting burden and allowing for comparability.
- Institutionalizing the Arab Sustainable Development Report: The report should be seen as a tool for enhancing evidence-based policymaking, following the model of the Global Sustainable Development Report.
- Leveraging the Arab Forum on Sustainable Development: The forum is a central platform for regional consultations and voluntary reviews of progress, both horizontal and thematic, and at all levels. It supports regional preparations for the yearly sessions of the High-level Political Forum on Sustainable Development and mirrors its themes in its structure.[1] Future sessions of the Arab Forum should maintain its multi-stakeholder character and continue to bring together high-level participants representing economic, social, environmental and human rights concerns.

Regional financial cooperation: Despite the current conflicts, regional economic and financial cooperation can play a major role in supporting sustainable development. To be relevant to the 2030 Agenda, Arab financial institutions will need to adopt sustainable investment policies and focus their support on the countries that are most in need. A regional assessment of financing needs for achieving the SDGs in the Arab region will facilitate the identification of options for addressing those needs through existing or new initiatives and partnerships. Complementary strategies and initiatives, including a regional financing strategy, could be considered. The establishment of a regional bank for reconstruction and development needs to be further researched.

Regional technology cooperation: The region needs to grasp global opportunities, including those offered through the technology facilitation mechanism and the planned technology bank for LDCs. Transition of the Arab region to a knowledge economy requires the renegotiation of existing cooperation modalities for technology transfer, including North-South and South-South partnerships, to reduce the region's dependence on global markets. This should be complemented by a commitment to regional horizontal solidarity for sciences, technology and innovation, as well as knowledge-sharing between Arab countries. A regional research mechanism providing a vision for Arab research institutions is also highly recommended.

Annexes

Annex I. Preparatory Process

The Arab Sustainable Development Report is a joint publication of the United Nations Economic and Social Commission for Western Asia (ESCWA) and the United Nations Environment Programme (UNEP). Sister United Nations organizations and agencies, members of the Regional Coordination Mechanism for the Arab Region, and a range of regional and international experts and Governments have contributed. The names of the core team members and contributing authors are listed in the acknowledgements section.

The report has been informed by a wide range of documents as detailed below, including several expert reports on enablers and means of implementation for sustainable development, a suite of issues briefs on priority themes, national sustainable development assessment reports, statistical analyses (including on data gaps and trend analysis), and additional desk research. All documents can be accessed through the webpage of the Arab High-level Forum on Sustainable Development at www.escwa.un.org/information/meetingdetails.asp?referenceNUM=3572e.

Table A.1. Expert and statistical reports, 2015

Author	Title
Al-Jayyousi, Odeh	Role of technology in sustainable development in the Arab region
Allen, Cameron	The institutional framework of sustainable development in the Arab region: integrated planning for the post-2015 agenda
Allen, Cameron and Kamil Hamati	Trend analysis of selected sustainable development indicators for the Arab region
Allen, Cameron and others[a]	Sustainable development indicators and the Arab region: gap analysis summary report
Arif, Sherif and Fadi Doumani	A strategic investment framework for green economy in Arab countries from an energy perspective
Azzam, Fateh	A human rights approach to sustainable development in the Arab region
El Sharkawy, Sherine	Financing sustainable development in the Arab region
Mohamadieh, Kinda	Women's rights and gender equality for sustainable development: discussing the proposed SDGs within the context of the development problematique in the Arab region
Moubayed, Lamia	From government to governance: how will the Arab region meet the goals of sustainable development in the post-2015 period?
Naber, Nadine	The social pillar and the paradox of development in the Arab region
Smith, Robert	Measuring sustainable development in the Arab region: a review of country experiences and recommendations for monitoring and evaluation in the post-2015 era

[a] Issued in 2014.

Table A.2. Issues briefs prepared by the United Nations, 2015

Issues brief	Lead author
Economic growth, inequality and poverty in the Arab region	ESCWA
Food security and sustainable agriculture in the Arab region	FAO
Gender equality and women empowerment in the Arab region	UNFPA
Water and sanitation in the Arab region	ESCWA
Energy in the Arab region	ESCWA
Employment and decent work in the Arab region	ILO
Industrialization and innovation in the Arab region	UNIDO
Perspectives on inequality challenges in the Arab region	UNDP
Making cities and human settlements inclusive, safe, resilient and sustainable in the Arab region	UN-HABITAT
Sustainable consumption and production in the Arab region	UNEP
Climate change in the Arab region	UNEP
Marine resources in the Arab region	UNEP
Terrestrial ecosystems and biodiversity in the Arab region	UNEP
Disaster risk reduction for resilience and sustainable development in the Arab region	UNISDR
Strengthening regional and global partnerships for trade and investment in the Arab region	UNCTAD

1. Regional expert and statistical reports

Expert and statistical analysis reports were prepared by regional and international consultants (table A.1). Several were discussed at an expert meeting organized by ESCWA in December 2014 in Beirut.

2. Issues briefs on priority thematic issues

A key component of the report is the review of progress and trends across priority thematic issues contained in the SDGs. United Nations bodies and specialized agencies were therefore invited to prepare 15 short issues briefs on selected themes (table A.2).

3. National assessments

In addition to the top-down regional analysis, a bottom-up component was contributed in the form of several national assessments, which were undertaken in three phases: (a) a stocktaking report; (b) a multi-stakeholder meeting; and (c) preparation of a synthesis report. The research was undertaken by expert consultants under the guidance of a government focal point and with the support of ESCWA. The assessments focused on: sustainable development priorities, institutions and strategies; key obstacles to implementation; innovative success stories and best practices; and lessons learned and recommendations for building capacity. Assessments were commissioned for Jordan, Lebanon, Morocco, Tunisia and Yemen.

4. Regional consultations, expert meetings and review process

Internal and external consultations and expert workshops helped to shape the report. They included: scoping sessions and interdivisional coordination meetings with ESCWA focal points and experts; review of the concept note and draft report by the ESCWA Publications Committee; presentation and discussion of the approach at the Arab Consultative Meeting on an Accountability Framework for the Post-2015 Agenda (Tunisia, 15-16 September 2014); an expert group meeting to review draft issues briefs, expert reports and national assessments (Beirut, December 2014); and consultations in Arab countries as part of the national assessments.

A wide variety of stakeholders and experts from ESCWA and other United Nations agencies, Arab Governments, non-governmental organizations, academics and other experts reviewed the methodology and content of the report. Their contribution was essential. A technical summary of the report was presented at a side event of the Arab Forum on Sustainable Development (Manama, 5-7 May 2015). The final version of the report was subjected to formal peer review by selected experts, as well as internal review by ESCWA and United Nations agencies through the Regional Coordination Mechanism and the ESCWA Publications Committee.

Annex II. Statistical Methodology

1. Selection of indicators included in the snapshot

A set of sustainable development indicators was needed for the snapshot analysis (chapter 2). The Arab Sustainable Development Indicators (ASDIs) framework, adapted from global indicators established by the (now defunct) Commission for Sustainable Development and reworked under the Sustainable Development Initiative for the Arab Region by the League of Arab States, UNEP, ESCWA and the Abu Dhabi Global Environmental Data Initiative (AGEDI), is the most relevant set of indicators. It was agreed initially that implementation of the full set would be voluntary. Due to a lack of implementation, the set was subsequently reduced to a subset of 44 indicators that would be compulsory for all countries in the region. Although no country in the region regularly produces all of them, this short list was deemed an appropriate starting point.

The list was cross-checked against the 17 SDGs, a process that highlighted indicator insufficiencies in goals relating to issues such as gender, employment, peaceful societies, food security and climate change. Twelve more indicators were added to the short list in order to address those gaps. Terminology used in several indicators was adjusted slightly in order to account for differences in data sources. Some indicators were included under an SDG that is different from the theme under which they are categorized in the Arab list, where this was deemed to better suit the SDG framework.

2. Data collection and trend analysis

Based on this framework, and while acknowledging the limitations of non-nationally sourced statistics, data were then collected for the 22 Arab countries[1] from a range of official databases, mainly from the United Nations system (table A.3). Data covered the period from 1990 until 2015. Country official data were not sourced directly from national statistics offices due to issues regarding the availability of time series and comparability in most of the 22 countries.

The purpose of this report is to assess trends and progress in the Arab region over the past two decades across a selected set of sustainable development indicators. The aim of the data analysis was to establish a trend for each indicator based on two data points over two decades (approximately) at the regional level and subregional levels (GCC countries, LDCs, the Maghreb and the Mashreq). The evaluation of each indicator was based, as far as possible, on the evolution of the indicator between 1990 and the latest year of data available for the Arab region. For many indicators, data were available only for a few years, often without overlap between countries. In such cases, if data are available for at least two years, the analysis is made with reference to the earliest and the latest years for which data are available, as long as there is a minimum difference of five years between data points. Evaluations do not include projections.

Indicators used for analysis had at least one data point in the 1990s (base year of most of the indicators) and at least one in the 2000s (last year). The first data point was used as a proxy of the 1990s baseline and the last one available in the 2000s as a proxy for the current status. To establish a regional or subregional average for any indicator, at least 50 per cent of the population had to be represented in both years, regardless of the number of countries for which data are available. For example, availability of data for Algeria, Egypt, Iraq and the Sudan would be sufficient to establish a regional trend as the sum of their populations is more than half that of the Arab region as a whole.

Each indicator was then graphically represented to show its trend for the Arab region and each of the four subregions. The values calculated for each indicator are weighted averages, obtained by using the corresponding weighting factor specified in the United Nations Statistics Division (UNSD) metadata for MDG indicators[2] or, failing that, by a corresponding weighting factor. For example, for "access to improved water source (percentage of population)", a weighting factor of total population was used, as the indicator reflects a trend over the entire population for each country; whereas for the indicator "FDI net inflows as a percentage of GDP", GDP in constant 2005 United States dollars was used as the weighting factor. For some indicators, it was more intuitive to calculate a simple average. For others, cumulative totals were calculated rather than (or in addition to) weighted averages (for example, for total arable land and total number of displaced persons). The report indicates where cumulative totals were used rather than weighted or simple averages.

The formula used to calculate the regional and subregional weighted averages is the following:

For the 1990s:

$$\frac{\sum(\text{1990s value of indicator x 1990s weight value})}{\sum(\text{1990s weight value})}$$

For the 2000s:

$$\frac{\sum(\text{2000s value of indicator x 2000s weight value})}{\sum(\text{2000s weight value})}$$

Thus, the weighted average for "fixed telephone line subscribers (percentage of population)" in the Maghreb in 1990 is the sum of the values of the indicator for that year for each country multiplied by the corresponding weighting value for the same year for each country. The result is then divided by the sum of the weighting values for the same countries in 1990. The end result of this division is the corresponding weighted average of the Maghreb subregion in 1990. The regional average was also calculated for the Arab region overall using the same corresponding weighting factors and formula.

All decimal values were rounded to the nearest hundredth. Two average values represented each subregion, one reflecting the 1990s and another reflecting the 2000s results. The values for 1990s and 2000s were then used to plot a trend across the region for each indicator in the form of a clustered bar graph.

Table A.3. Data sources for the indicators in the snapshot

Indicator	Source
Population growth rate (total)	ESCWA calculations based on data from United Nations, Department of Economic and Social Affairs (DESA), *World Population Prospects: The 2015 Revision*, DVD Edition.
Goal 1	
Percentage of population below $1.25 (PPP) per day	United Nations and League of Arab States, *Arab Millennium Development Goals Report: Facing Challenges and Looking Beyond 2015* (Beirut, 2013, E/ESCWA/EDGD/2013/1).
Percentage of population living below national poverty line	

Indicator	Source
Goal 2	
Percentage of underweight children under 5 years old	ESCWA calculations based on WHO Global database on Child Growth and Malnutrition (available from www.who.int/nutgrowthdb/en), as taken from World Bank, World Development Indicators (accessed 28 September 2015) and DESA, *World Population Prospects*.
Percentage of undernourished population	ESCWA calculations based on UNSD, Millennium Development Goals Indicators Database (2015). Available from http://mdgs.un.org/unsd/mdg/Default.aspx. Accessed 28 September 2015.
Arable and permanent crop land area (cumulative total)	ESCWA calculations based on data from FAOSTAT. Available from http://faostat.fao.org. Aaccessed 29 September 2015.
Food production (average value of annual food production per capita)	ESCWA calculations based on data from FAO Suite of Food Security Indicators, available from http://faostat3.fao.org/browse/D/FS/E (accessed 29 October 2015); and World Development Indicators (accessed 10 September 2015).
Value of food imports (percentage of merchandise exports)	
Cereal imports dependency ratio	ESCWA calculations based on data from FAO Suite of Food Security Indicators (accessed 6 October 2015).
Goal 3	
Mortality rate under 5 years old	ESCWA calculations based on data from the United Nations Statistics Division (UNSD) and DESA, *World Population Prospects*.
Contraceptive prevalence rate	ESCWA calculations based on data from UNSD and DESA, Estimates and Projections of the Number of Women Aged 15-49 Who Are Married or in a Union: 2015 Revision. Available from http://www.un.org/en/development/desa/population/theme/marriage-unions/marriage_estimates.shtml. Accessed 10 September 2015.
Immunization against infectious childhood diseases (children 1 year old immunized against measles)	ESCWA calculations based on data from UNSD, and DESA, *World Population Prospects*.
Obesity among children	ESCWA calculations based on WHO Global Database on Child Growth and Malnutrition.
Goal 4	
Net enrolment rate in primary education	ESCWA calculations based on data from UNESCO Institute for Statistics (UIS) Database. Available from http://data.uis.unesco.org/Index.aspx?DataSetCode=EDULIT_DS. Accessed 22 September 2015.
Gross intake into last year of primary education	ESCWA calculations based on data from UIS.
Adult literacy rate	
Government expenditure on education (percentage of GDP)	
Pupil-teacher ratio, primary	
Goal 5	
Adult literacy rate (female)	ESCWA calculations based on data from UIS and DESA, *World Population Prospects*.
Adult literacy rate (male)	
Female employment to population ratio (above 15 years of age)	ESCWA calculations based on ILO estimates, as taken from the World Development Indicators (accessed 11 September 2015).
Male employment to population ratio (above 15 years of age)	

Indicator	Source
Seats held by women in national parliaments (percentage)	ESCWA calculations based on the World Development Indicators (accessed 17 September 2015).
Goal 6	
Access to an improved water source (percentage of population)	ESCWA calculations based on data from WHO/UNICEF Joint Monitoring Programme (JMP) for Water Supply and Sanitation. Available from www.wssinfo.org. Accessed 23 September 2015.
Access to improved sanitation (percentage of population)	ESCWA calculations based on data from JMP.
Annual withdrawals of ground and surface water as a percentage of available water	ESCWA calculations based on data from AQUASTAT and World Development Indicators.
Annual utilization or withdrawals of water – demand, all types	ESCWA calculations based on data from AQUASTAT.
Urban access to an improved water source (percentage of population)	ESCWA calculations based on data from JMP.
Rural access to an improved water source (percentage of population)	
Goal 7	
Share of consumption of renewable energy resources (excluding hydroelectricity)	ESCWA calculations based on data from World Development Indicators (accessed 23 October 2015); and IEA World Energy Statistics and Balances, available from: www.oecd-ilibrary.org/energy/data/iea-world-energy-statistics-and-balances_enestats-data-en (accessed 23 October 2015).
Energy consumption per capita	ESCWA calculations based on IEA statistics (2014), as taken from World Development Indicators (accessed 14 September 2015).
Access to electricity (percentage of population)	ESCWA calculations based on World Development Indicators (accessed 23 September 2015).
Goal 8	
GDP per capita	ESCWA calculations based on World Development Indicators (accessed 10 September 2015).
Gross capital formation (percentage of GDP)	
Employment to population ratio (total above 15 years of age)	ESCWA calculations based on modelled ILO estimates, as taken from World Development Indicators (accessed 10 September 2015).
Youth employment to population ratio (15-24 years)	ESCWA calculations based on modelled ILO estimates, as taken from World Development Indicators (accessed 14 September 2015).
Dependency ratio (young and old)	ESCWA calculations based on data from DESA, *World Population Prospects*.
Goal 9	
Manufacturing value added (percentage of GDP)	ESCWA calculations based on World Bank national accounts data, and OECD national accounts data files, as taken from World Development Indicators (accessed 9 November 2015).
Internet users (percentage of population)	ESCWA calculations based on International Telecommunication Union (ITU), World Telecommunication/ICT Development Report and database, and World Bank estimates, as taken from World Development Indicators (accessed 3 November 2015).
Telephone land line subscribers (percentage of population)	ESCWA calculations based on ITU, World Telecommunication/ICT Development Report and database.

Indicator	Source
Mobile telephone subscribers (percentage of population)	ESCWA calculations based on ITU, World Telecommunication/ICT Development Report.
Goal 11	
Deaths due to disasters (cumulative total)	ESCWA calculations based on data from EM-DAT disasters Database. Available from www.emdat.be. Accessed 7 October 2015.
Population growth rate – rural	ESCWA calculations based on data from DESA, *World Urbanization Prospects: The 2014 Revision* (custom data acquired via website).
Percentage of urban population from total	
Goal 12	
Passenger cars (per 1,000 people)	ESCWA calculations based on International Road Federation, World Road Statistics and data files, as taken from World Development Indicators (accessed 2 February 2015). Data update was not applicable to this indicator as it was discontinued from the World Development Indicators series.
Goal 13	
Emissions of greenhouse gases (kg per $1 GDP, PPP)	ESCWA calculations based on data from UNSD (accessed 9 October 2015) and World Development Indicators (accessed 22 October 2015).
Emissions of greenhouse gases (metric tons of CO_2 per capita)	ESCWA calculations based on data from UNSD (accessed 9 October 2015) and World Development Indicators (accessed 10 September 2015).
Goal 14	
Percentage of total population living in coastal areas	ESCWA calculations based on Center for International Earth Science Information Network (CIESIN), Place II dataset, as taken from World Development Indicators (accessed 23 October 2015).
Average annual fish catch (metric tons)	ESCWA calculations based on data from FAO annual fisheries and aquaculture statistics (accessed 2 November 2015).
Goal 15	
Protected area (terrestrial and marine as a percentage of total area)	ESCWA calculations based on UNEP and the World Conservation Monitoring Centre (compiled by the World Resources Institute, based on data from national authorities, national legislation and international agreements), as taken from World Development Indicators (accessed 2 November 2015), and FAO electronic files and website (accessed 2 November 2015).
Vegetation cover	ESCWA calculations based on data from FAOSTAT 2015 (accessed 1 November 2015).
Goal 16	
Refugee population by country of origin (total)	ESCWA calculations based on UNHCR databases, available from http://popstats.unhcr.org/en/time_series (accessed 26 October 2015); McGill Palestinian Refugee ResearchNet, available from http://prrn.mcgill.ca/background/table1.htm (accessed 26 October 2015); and UNRWA in figures 2015, available from www.unrwa.org/sites/default/files/unrwa_in_figures_2015.pdf (accessed 13 October 2015).
Refugee population by country of asylum (total)	
Index of political stability and absence of violence	ESCWA calculations based on data from FAO Suite of Food Security Indicators (accessed 29 October 2015).

Indicator	Source
Goal 17	
Net official development assistance received (percentage of GNI)	ESCWA calculations based on data from the Development Assistance Committee of the OECD, Geographical Distribution of Financial Flows to Developing Countries, Development Co-operation Report; and International Development Statistics database (www.oecd.org/dac/stats/idsonline), as taken from World Development Indicators (accessed 3 November 2015).
Foreign direct investments, net inflows (percentage of GDP)	ESCWA calculations based on International Monetary Fund, International Financial Statistics and Balance of Payments databases; World Bank, International Debt Statistics; World Bank and OECD GDP estimates, as taken from World Development Indicators (accessed 11 September 2015); and World Bank national accounts data; and OECD National Accounts data files, as taken from World Development Indicators (accessed 10 September 2015).

Annex III. Alternative Frameworks Considered

Analysis in the report, rather than simply addressing the 17 SDGs one by one, is framed in such a way as to group related issues together, thereby facilitating interpretation of results. The framework builds on the idea that sustainable development requires convergence between the three aspects of economic development, social equity and environmental protection (with governance often added as a fourth aspect).

The framework for the report is presented in chapter 1. Others that were caonsidered and which had an impact on the framework finally adopted included: the nested people-to-nature approach; the capital-based approach; the social foundations and environmental ceiling approach; the driver-pressure-State-response approach; and the "six elements" recently proposed by the Secretary-General (box A.1).

Box A.1. Alternative frameworks for sustainable development and the SDGs

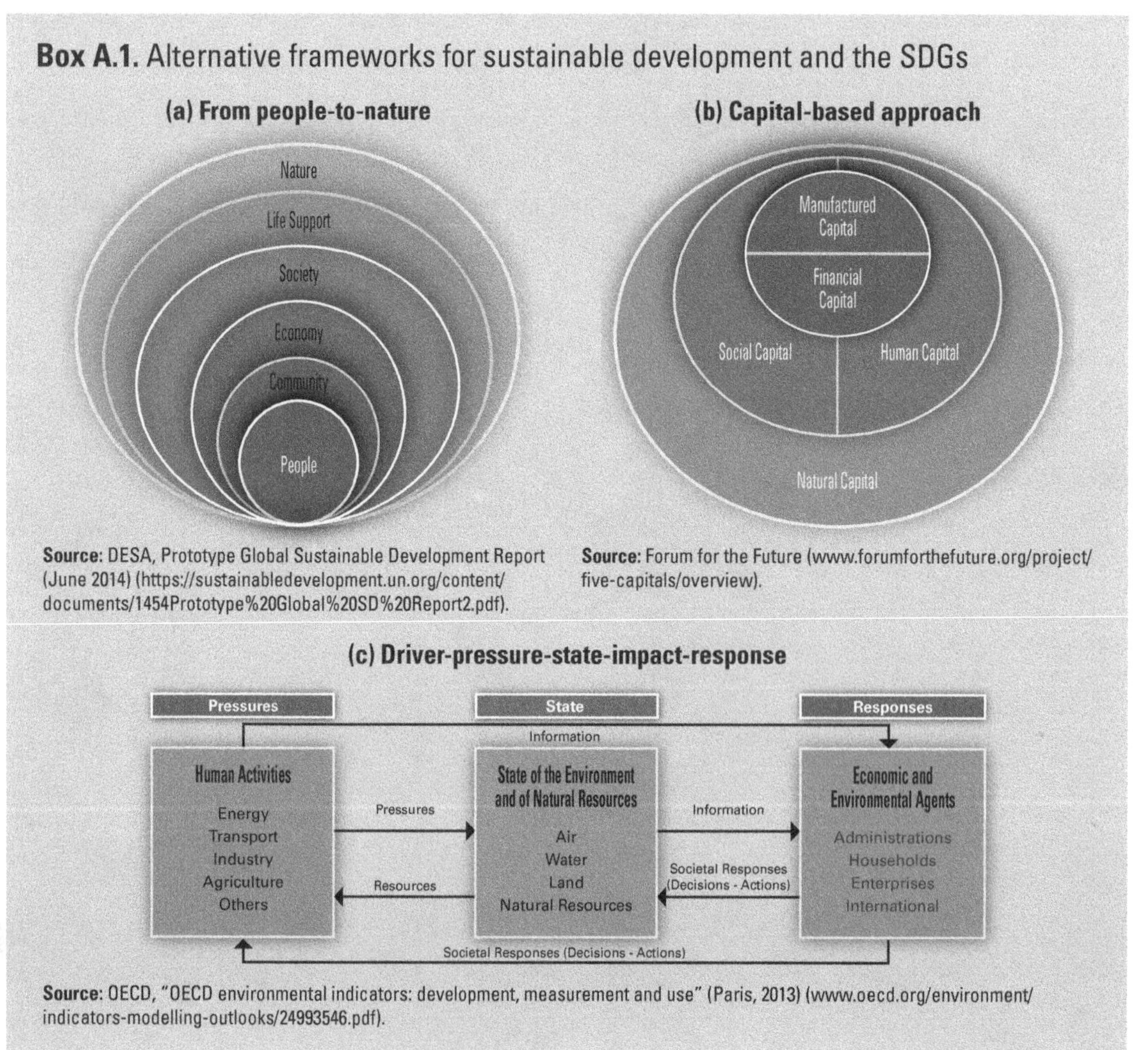

Source: DESA, Prototype Global Sustainable Development Report (June 2014) (https://sustainabledevelopment.un.org/content/documents/1454Prototype%20Global%20SD%20Report2.pdf).

Source: Forum for the Future (www.forumforthefuture.org/project/five-capitals/overview).

Source: OECD, "OECD environmental indicators: development, measurement and use" (Paris, 2013) (www.oecd.org/environment/indicators-modelling-outlooks/24993546.pdf).

Box A.1. Alternative frameworks for sustainable development and the SDGs

(d) Social foundations and environmental ceiling (doughnut)

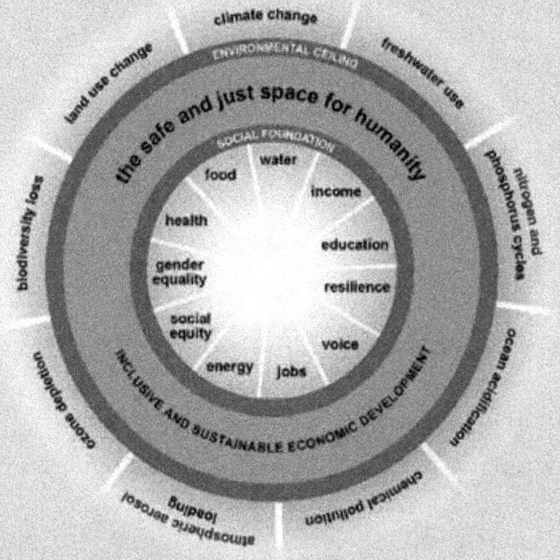

Source: Kate Raworth, "A safe and just space for humanity: can we live within the doughnut?", Oxfam Discussion Papers (Oxford, 2012). Available from www.oxfam.org/en/grow/policy/safe-and-just-space-humanity

(e) Six elements of the SDGs

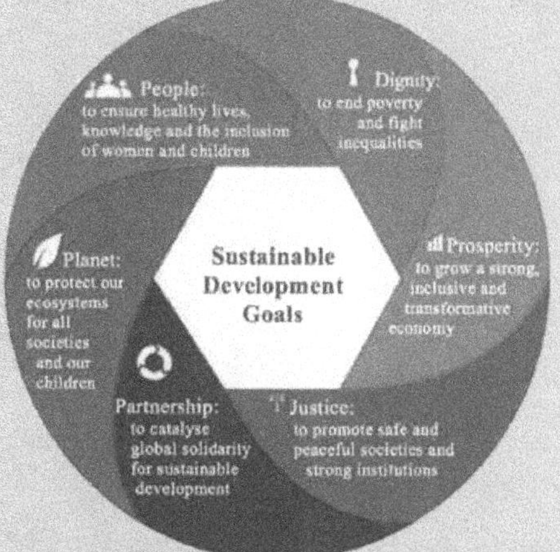

Source: The road to dignity by 2030: ending poverty, transforming all lives and protecting the planet, Synthesis report of the Secretary-General on the post-2015 agenda (2014, A/69/700).

Annex IV. Inventory of Major Global and Arab Regional Assessments, Publications and Databases of Relevance for Sustainable Development

Table A.4. Inventory

Sustainable development goal	Global assessments/reports	Regional assessments/reports	Sources of data
Goal 1. End poverty in all its forms everywhere	United Nations MDG Reports; World Bank-IMF Global Monitoring Reports; UNDP Human Development Reports; United Nations Research Institute for Social Development (UNRISD) Poverty Report; World Bank World Development Reports	United Nations and League of Arab States Arab MDG Reports; UNDP Arab Human Development Reports; ESCWA Arab Middle Class Report	World Bank World Development Indicators (WDIs); UNstats MDG Monitoring: UNdata; UNDP Human Development Report (HDR) Data
Goal 2. End hunger, achieve food security and improved nutrition and promote sustainable agriculture	United Nations MDG Reports; World Bank-IMF Global Monitoring Reports; FAO The State of the World Reports and State of Food Insecurity Reports; United Nations Convention to Combat Desertification (UNCCD) Reports; UNEP Global Environment Outlook (GEO) Reports; FAO Statistical Yearbooks	United Nations and League of Arab States Arab MDG Reports; International Food Policy Research Institute (IFPRI) 2010 Food Security in MENA Region; Corporate Equality Index (CEI) 2011: Food Security in MENA and Sub-Saharan Africa; UNEP Environment Outlook – Arab Region; World Bank/IFAD/FAO Improving Food Security in the Arab Region; AFED Ecological Footprint Report; AFED Food Security Report	FAOSTAT; UNdata; World Bank WDIs; UNStats MDG Monitoring: UNEP Geodata
Goal 3. Ensure healthy lives and promote well-being for all at all ages	United Nations MDG Reports; World Bank-IMF Global Monitoring Reports; WHO World Health Reports; OECD Environmental Outlook; World Happiness Report 2013; UNFPA: State of World Population; UNDP Human Development Reports	United Nations and League of Arab States Arab MDG Reports; UNDP Arab Human Development Reports	WHO Global Health Observatory; UNdata; World Bank WDIs; UNstats MDG Monitoring: UNICEF Global Databases; UNDP HDR data; UNFPA Data

Sustainable development goal	Global assessments/reports	Regional assessments/reports	Sources of data
Goal 4. Ensure inclusive and equitable quality education and promote lifelong learning opportunities for all	United Nations MDG Reports; World Bank-IMF Global Monitoring Reports; UNESCO Global Monitoring Reports	United Nations and League of Arab States Arab MDG Reports; Arab Knowledge Reports; Arab World Literacy Reports; Arab World Learning Barometer (Brookings Institute); UNESCO Education For All Regional Report for Arab States; UNDP Knowledge Report	UNdata; World Bank WDIs; UNstats MDG Monitoring: UNICEF Global Databases; UNESCO Data Centre; UNDP HDR data
Goal 5. Achieve gender equality and empower all women and girls	UN-Women: Progress of the World's Women; United Nations MDG Reports; DESA: The World's Women; Save the Children: State of the World's Mothers Report	United Nations and League of Arab States Arab MDG Reports; UN-Women Status of Arab Women Report; UNFPA-Arab States Policy Briefs; UNDP Arab Human Development Reports	Word Bank GenderStats; World Bank WDIs; UNstats MDG Monitoring: UNICEF Global Databases; UNdata; UNDP HDR data
Goal 6. Ensure availability and sustainable management of water and sanitation for all	United Nations MDG Reports; World Bank-IMF Global Monitoring Reports; United Nations World Water Development Report; UNEP GEO Reports; OECD Environmental Outlook; UNICEF and WHO: Drinking Water and Sanitation 2014 Update; UNESCO: Global Water Futures 2050; United Nations World Water Development Report	United Nations and League of Arab States Arab MDG Reports; ESCWA Water Development Reports; ESCWA: Inventory of Shared Water Resources in Western Asia; UNEP Environment Outlook – Arab Region; World Bank: Water in the Arab World; AFED Water Report; World Bank MENA Water Outlook; IFAD Water Security Report; UNDP Water Governance Report	UNdata; World Bank WDIs; UNStats MDG Monitoring: UNEP Geodata
Goal 7. Ensure access to affordable, reliable, sustainable and modern energy for all	Global Tracking Framework Report; International Institute for Applied Systems Analysis (IIASA) Global Energy Assessment; IEA World Energy Outlooks; Intergovernmental Panel on Climate Change (IPCC) Working Group III Reports; UNEP GEO Reports; REN21 Renewables Reports; Global Trends in Renewable Energy Investment; United Nations World Water Development Report - Water and Energy Report	IRENA Renewable Energy in MENA; AFED Sustainable Energy Report; Arab Union of Electricity Statistical Bulletins, REN21 MENA Renewable Energy Status Report; RCREEE Arab Future Energy Index; League of Arab States Pan-Arab Renewable Energy Strategy 2030	World Bank WDIs; UNEP Geodata; Arab Union of Electricity

Sustainable development goal	Global assessments/reports	Regional assessments/reports	Sources of data
Goal 8. Promote sustained, inclusive and sustainable economic growth, full and productive employment and decent work for all	DESA World Economic and Social Survey; World Bank World Development Reports; IMF World Economic Outlooks; UNDP Human Development Reports; ILO Global Employment Trends; World Bank Development Reports; World Tourism Organization (UNWTO): Tourism Highlights	Arab Monetary Fund Joint Arab Economic Report; ESCWA 2013 Arab Integration Report; ESCWA Surveys of Economic and Social Developments; UNDP Arab Human Development Reports; IMF MENA Economic Outlook; UNDP Arab Human Development Reports; World Bank MENA Economic Developments & Prospects; World Bank MENA Quarterly Economic Briefs; ILO & UNDP Rethinking Economic Growth Report	ILOSTAT; World Bank WDIs; UNstats MDG Monitoring: UNdata; UNWTO; IMF; Arab Monetary Fund
Goal 9. Build resilient infrastructure, promote inclusive and sustainable industrialization and foster innovation	UNIDO Industrial Development Report; UNISDR Global Assessment Report; UNESCO: Status of Science Around the World; Reuters Science Watch Reports; International Federation of Red Cross and Crescent World Disasters Report	Science Watch Global Research Report: Middle East; Reuters Science Watch Middle East Report; UNDP Knowledge Report	World Bank WDIs; UNSD; UNESCO Data Centre; UNIDO; UNdata
Goal 10. Reduce inequality within and among countries	UNDP Human Development Reports; United Nations MDG Reports; Credit Suisse Global Wealth Databook; Oxfam Equality Reports	United Nations and League of Arab States Arab MDG Reports; UNDP Arab Human Development Reports; Economic Research Forum Equity and Equality Report; World Bank Economic Inequality in the Arab Region	World Bank Findex; World Bank WDIs; UNstats MDG Monitoring: UNdata; UNDP HDR Data
Goal 11. Make cities and human settlements inclusive, safe, resilient and sustainable	UN-Habitat: Global Reports on Human Settlement; IEA World Energy Outlook; DESA World Urbanization Prospects; UNISDR Global Report on Disaster Risk Reduction (DRR)	UN-Habitat State of Arab Cities Reports; UNEP Environment Outlook – Arab Region; Arab Strategy for Disaster Risk Reduction 2020; UNEP Atlas of Our Changing Environment	World Bank WDIs; UNstats MDG Monitoring: UNSD; UNdata
Goal 12. Ensure sustainable consumption and production patterns	United Nations Trends Reports: Towards Sustainable Consumption and Production; World Business Council for Sustainable Development: Vision 2050 Report; UNEP: The Marrakech Process Progress Report; IRENA Renewable Energy Reports; International Resource Panel: Decoupling Report	IRENA Renewable Energy in MENA; AFED Green Economy Report; AFED Ecological Footprint Report; World Bank Centre for Mediterranean Integration (CMI) Green Growth Report	World Bank WDIs; UNEP Geodata

Sustainable development goal	Global assessments/reports	Regional assessments/reports	Sources of data
Goal 13. Take urgent action to combat climate change and its impacts	IPCC Assessment Reports; UNFCCC Independent Reports; UNEP: Emission Gap Reports; World Bank: Turn Down the Heat Reports; UNISDR Global Assessment Report; UNEP GEO Reports; OECD Environmental Outlook	UNEP Environment Outlook – Arab Region; ESCWA: RICCAR; UNDP 2010 Mapping Climate Change Threats and Human Development Impacts in the Arab Region; AFED Climate Change Report	World Bank WDIs; UNEP Geodata; World Bank Open Climate Data; UNdata; IPCC Climate Data Distribution Centre
Goal 14. Conserve and sustainably use the oceans, seas and marine resources for sustainable development	United Nations World Ocean Assessment (Regular Process for Global Reporting and Assessment of the State of the Marine Environment, including Socioeconomic Aspects); UNEP Keeping Track Reports; UNEP GEO Reports; Assessment of Assessments on Oceans; FAO State of the World's Fisheries	UNEP Environment Outlook – Arab Region; UNEP Regional Seas Reports	UNEP Geodata
Goal 15. Protect, restore and promote sustainable use of terrestrial ecosystems, sustainably manage forests, combat desertification, and halt and reverse land degradation and halt biodiversity loss	Convention on Biological Diversity (CBD) Global Biodiversity Outlooks United Nations Forest Forum Reports; FAO Global Forest Resources Assessments; UNEP GEO Reports; UNCCD Reports; FAO The State of the World Reports; OECD Environmental Outlook	UNEP Environment Outlook – Arab Region; UNEP Atlas of Our Changing Environment	World Bank WDIs; UNEP Geodata; AGEDI Geoportal
Goal 16. Promote peaceful and inclusive societies for sustainable development, provide access to justice for all and build effective, accountable and inclusive institutions at all levels	Human Security Report; UNDP Human Development Reports; World Bank: World Development Reports; Centre for Systemic Peace Global Governance Reports; UNHCR Global Trends Reports; United Nations Office on Drugs and Crime (UNODC) World Drugs and Crime Reports	United Nations Arab MDG Reports; UNDP Arab Human Development Reports; ESCWA 2013 Arab Integration Report	World Bank WGIs; UNHCR Population Statistics; Centre for Systemic Peace; UNdata

Sustainable development goal	Global assessments/reports	Regional assessments/reports	Sources of data
Goal 17. Strengthen the means of implementation and revitalize the Global Partnership for Sustainable Development - Finance	MDG Gap Task Force Reports; World Bank World Development Reports; Secretary-General's Report on Implementation of Action for the LDCs; United Nations Office of the High Representative for the Least Developed Countries, Landlocked Developing Countries and Small Island Developing States (UN-OHRLLS) Reports on LDCs, LLDCs and SIDS; Climate Policy Initiative: Global Landscape of Climate Finance; DESA World Economic and Social Survey 2012 - In Search of New Development Finance; UNICEF (2014) Financing for Development; United Nations System Task Team (UNTT) Working Group on Sustainable Development Financing; World Bank: Financing for Development Post-2015	United Nations Arab MDG Reports; ESCWA 2013 Assessing the Financing Gap in the Arab Region Report; Arab Monetary Fund Joint Arab Economic Report; ESCWA 2012 Progress Towards Monterrey Consensus Report; International Finance Corporation (IFC) Sustainable Investment in MENA Report	World Bank WDIs; IMF; UNdata; Arab Monetary Fund
Goal 17. Strengthen the means of implementation and revitalize the Global Partnership for Sustainable Development - Technology	World Intellectual Property Organization (WIPO) Annual Reports; UNESCO: Status of Science Around the World; DESA World Economic and Social Survey 2011 – Green Tech Transformation; Reuters Science Watch Reports	Reuters Science Watch Report: Middle East	World Bank WDIs; UNESCO Data Centre
Goal 17. Strengthen the means of implementation and revitalize the Global Partnership for Sustainable Development - Trade	UNCTAD Trade and Investment Reports; IMF World Economic Outlooks	Arab Monetary Fund Joint Arab Economic Report; ESCWA 2013 Arab Integration Report	World Bank WDIs; IMF; UNSD; Arab Monetary Fund

Endnotes

Chapter 1

1. A/RES/70/1.
2. Available from www.escwa.un.org/divisions/sd/pubs/index.asp?PubNUM=SDI-2011.
3. See resolution number 2 of the Council of Arab Ministers Responsible for the Environment at its 15 June 2014 extraordinary session, and ESCWA resolution 314 (XXVIII) of 18 September 2014.
4. Robert Smith, "Measuring sustainable development in the Arab region: a review of country experiences and recommendations for monitoring and evaluation in the post-2015 era", Expert Report for the Arab Sustainable Development Report (Beirut, 2015, E/ESCWA/SD/2015/Technical Paper.1). Available from http://css.escwa.org.lb/SDPD/3572/7-Statistics.pdf. According to this review, around one third of the MDG indicators could be measured in the region using only official statistics. Their quality is medium at best and only medium-low in some countries.
5. World Bank, World Development Indicators. Averages in other regions in 2014: Latin America and the Caribbean (80 per cent); Europe and Central Asia (71 per cent); and sub-Saharan Africa (37 per cent).
6. United Nations Development Programme (UNDP), *Water Governance in the Arab Region: Managing Scarcity and Securing the Future* (New York, 2013).
7. Renewable energy desalination in the region has been tested and there are plans for larger plants. For example, construction in the city of Al Khafji, Saudi Arabia, of a photovoltaic desalination plant capable of supplying 60,000 cubic metres of desalinated water a day was announced in 2015. See www.water-technology.net/projects/al-khafji-solar-saline-water-reverse-osmosis-solar-swro-desalination-plant.
8. Report of the Expert Group Meeting on the Water-Energy-Food Security Nexus in the Arab Region, Amman, 24-25 March 2015 (E/ESCWA/SDPD/2015/WG.2/2/Report), p. 3.
9. Harvard Hegre and others, "Forecasting armed conflict along 'the shared socioeconomic pathways'", paper presented at the International Studies Association, Toronto, Canada, 26-29 March 2014.
10. See www.unocha.org/syria.
11. United Nations High Commissioner for Refugees (UNHCR), 2015 UNHCR Country operations profile - Somalia. Available from www.unhcr.org/pages/49e483ad6.html (accessed 12 September 2015).
12. United Nations Relief and Works Agency for Palestine Refugees in the Near East (UNRWA), "UNRWA in figures as of 1 January 2015". Available from www.unrwa.org/sites/default/files/unrwa_in_figures_2015.pdf.

Chapter 3

1. Issues briefs and expert reports are available from www.escwa.un.org.lb/information/meetingdetails.asp?referenceNum=3572E.
2. World Bank, World Development Indicators. Available from http://data.worldbank.org/products/wdi (accessed 30 August 2015).
3. The dependency ratio reflects the ratio of number of children (0-14 years old) and older persons (65 years or over) to the working-age population (15-64 years old).
4. World Bank, World Development Indicators.
5. World Bank, *Confronting Poverty in Iraq* (Washington, D.C., 2010).
6. World Bank, World Development Indicators.
7. Middle East is the regional grouping adopted in the Global Findex Database of the World Bank.
8. Asli Demirguc-Kunt and others, "The Global Findex Database 2014", Policy paper No. 7255 (Washington, D.C., World Bank, 2015). Available from www.worldbank.org/en/programs/globalfindex.
9. Azza Morssy, "Industrialization and Innovation in the Arab Region", Issues Brief for the Arab Sustainable Development Report (2015). Available from http://css.escwa.org.lb/SDPD/3572/Goal9.pdf.
10. Not only is the civil service oversized, it also costs too much. The region has the highest civil service wage bill in the world, at 9.8 per cent of GDP, compared with a world average of 5.4 per cent. In Lebanon, the cost of central government personnel is believed to have more than doubled in a decade (2000-2010). Civil servants in the region are paid on average 30 per cent more than their private sector counterparts. In contrast, average public service wages around the world are 20 per cent lower than those of the private sector. Bloated State structures distort the job market by impeding the development of a dynamic and prosperous private sector. See Masood Ahmed and others, "Youth unemployment in the MENA region: determinants and challenges" (International Monetary Fund, 2012). Available from https://www.imf.org/external/np/vc/2012/061312.htm; and Lamia Moubayed, "Why civil service reform is an inevitable choice in times of crisis" (Beirut, Institut des Finances Basil Fuleihan, n.d.). Available from www.institutdesfinances.gov.lb/english/loadFile.aspx?pageid=2002&phname=PDF.
11. Lida Bteddini, "Governance and public sector employment in the Middle East and North Africa", Voices and Views: Middle East and North Africa (World Bank, 2012). Available from http://blogs.worldbank.org/arabvoices/governance-and-public-sector-employment-middle-east-and-north-africa.
12. Employment-to-population ratio is defined by the International Labour Organization (ILO) as the proportion of a country's working age population that is employed. Ages 15 and older are generally considered the working-age population. The indicator reflects the ability of an economy to create employment. See http://kilm.ilo.org/2011/download/kilm02EN.pdf.
13. World Bank, World Development Indicators database, based on modeled ILO data. Available from http://data.worldbank.org/indicator/SL.EMP.TOTL.SP.ZS/countries/1W-1A?display=graph (accessed 30 August 2015).
14. ILO, *Global Employment Trends for Youth 2013: A Generation at Risk* (Geneva, 2013). Available from http://www.ilo.org/wcmsp5/groups/public/---dgreports/---dcomm/documents/publication/wcms_212423.pdf.
15. ILO, *Rethinking Economic Growth: Towards Productive and Inclusive Arab Societies* (Geneva, 2012).
16. The wage share has declined in practically all regions since the early 1990s. What makes the Arab region different is the speed and depth of the decline.
17. Niranjan Sarangi and Khaled Abu-Ismail, "Economic growth, inequality and poverty in the Arab region".

18. ESCWA and others, *2015 Situation Report on International Migration: Migration, Displacement and Development in a Changing Arab Region* (Beirut, 2015, E/ESCWA/SDD/2015/1).
19. See for example E/C.12/1/Add.98, paras. 15-18; CEDAW/C/OMN/CO/1, paras. 27 and 42; CEDAW/C/SAU/CO/2, paras. 23-24; and CEDAW/C/ARE/CO/1, para. 36.
20. Nadia Belhaj Hassine, "Economic inequality in the Arab region", Policy Research Working Paper, No. 6911 (Washington, D.C., World Bank, June 2014). Available from www-wds.worldbank.org/external/default/WDSContentServer/WDSP/IB/2014/06/09/000158349_20140609130102/Rendered/PDF/WPS6911.pdf.
21. The Gini Index measures inequality based on differences in income and expenditures. Higher values reflect higher inequality.
22. United Nations and League of Arab States, *Arab Millennium Development Goals Report*.
23. Calculated as a ratio of income share held by the richest 20 per cent to the share held by the poorest 20 per cent.
24. ESCWA, *Arab Middle Class: Measurement and Role in Driving Change* (Beirut, 2014, E/ESCWA/EDGD/2014/2).
25. Heba El Laithy, "Inequality in the southern Mediterranean: a survey of selected countries", MEDPRO Technical Report, No. 23 (Mediterranean Prospects, December 2012). Available from www.medpro-foresight.eu/system/files/MEDPRO%20TR%20No%2023%20WP7%20El%20Laithy.pdf.
26. For a list of reservations by country, see www.un.org/womenwatch/daw/cedaw/reservations-country.htm.
27. In Algeria, article 2 of the 2012 law on representation of women to elected bodies stipulates that variable quotas of between 20 per cent and 50 per cent of candidates for parliament be set aside for women (Law No. 12-03 of 12 January 2012, available in Arabic from http://www.joradp.dz/ftp/jo-arabe/2012/a2012001.pdf.)
28. United Nations and League of Arab States, *Arab Millennium Development Goals Report*. In South Asia the ratio of females to males in vulnerable employment is 111, in South-East Asia and the Pacific the ratio is 113, in East Asia it is 117, in Latin America and the Caribbean it is 102, and in Sub-Saharan Africa it is 121.
29. Data are from the World Bank, World Development Indicators and based on modelled ILO estimates.
30. ILO, "Jobs and employment in the Post-2015 Development Agenda", paper presented to the League of Arab States Conference on Arab Sustainable Development Priorities in the Post-2015 Agenda, Amman, May 2014.
31. World Health Organization (WHO), "Violence against women: intimate partner and sexual violence against women", Factsheet No. 239 (2014). Available from www.who.int/mediacentre/factsheets/fs239/en.
32. World Bank, World Development Indicators.
33. United Nations and League of Arab States, *Arab Millennium Development Goals Report*.
34. UNESCO, "The hidden crisis: armed conflict and education", 2011 Education for All Global Monitoring Report (Paris, 2011). Available from: http://unesdoc.unesco.org/images/0019/001907/190743e.pdf.http://www.unesco.org/new/en/education/themes/leading-the-international-agenda/efareport/reports/2011-conflict/
35. Global Coalition to Protect Education from Attack. *Education Under Attack 2014* (New York, 2013). Available from http://www.protectingeducation.org/sites/default/files/documents/eua_2014_full.pdf.
36. ESCWA, *Palestine, the Occupation and the Fourth Geneva Convention: Facts and Figures* (Beirut, 2014, E/ESCWA/ECRI/2014/Booklet.1).
37. World Bank, World Development Indicators.
38. Klaus Schwab, ed., *The Global Competitiveness Report 2013-2014* (Geneva, World Economic Forum (WEF), 2013). Available from www.weforum.org/reports/global-competitiveness-report-2013-2014.
39. Liesbet Steer and others, *Arab Youth: Missing Educational Foundations for a Productive Life?* (Washington, D.C., Center for Universal Education at Brookings, February 2014). Available from www.brookings.edu/~/media/research/files/interactives/2014/arab-world-learning-barometer/arabworld_learningbarometer_en.pdf.
40. E4E Arab Youth, *Education for Employment: Realizing Arab Youth Potential* (Washington, D.C., Education for Employment, Islamic Development Bank and the International Finance Corporation (IFC), April 2011). Available from http://mckinseyonsociety.com/downloads/reports/Education/IFCBook_A4_Online_Complete.pdf.
41. Nadine Naber, "The social pillar and the paradox of development in the Arab region", Expert Report for the Arab Sustainable Development Report (Beirut, 2015, E/ESCWA/SDD/2015.WP.2). Available from http://css.escwa.org.lb/SDPD/3572/4-Social.pdf.
42. World Health Organization (WHO) and UNICEF, *Progress on Sanitation and Drinking Water: 2015 Update and MDG Assessment* (Geneva, 2015). Available from www.wssinfo.org/fileadmin/user_upload/resources/JMP-Update-report-2015_English.pdf.
43. Ibid. In 1990, the percentage of the Arab rural population with access to an improved water source was 71 per cent, compared to a global average of 62 per cent. In 2015, the percentages were 74 and 84, respectively.
44. Ibid. In 1990, the percentage of the Arab urban population with access to an improved water source was 92 per cent, compared to a global average of 95 per cent. In 2015, the percentages were 91 and 96, respectively.
45. Palestinian Water Authority, "Status report of water resources in the occupied State of Palestine – 2012" (2013), p.1. Available from http://www.pwa.ps/userfiles/file/%D8%AA%D9%82%D8%A7%D8%B1%D9%8A%D8%B1/%D8%AA%D8%B5%D9%86%D9%8A%D9%81%201/WR%20STATUS%20Report-final%20draft%202014-04-01.pdf.
46. Palestinian Water Authority, "Gaza water resources status report, 2013/2014" (2014), p.5. Available from http://www.pwa.ps/userfiles/file/%D8%AA%D9%82%D8%A7%D8%B1%D9%8A%D8%B1/%D8%AA%D8%B5%D9%86%D9%8A%D9%81%201/Gaza%20water%20Resources%20status%20report%20%202013-2014.pdf.
47. WHO and UNICEF, *Progress on Sanitation and Drinking Water*.
48. ESCWA, *Water Supply and Sanitation in the Arab Region: Looking beyond 2015* (Beirut, 2015, E/ESCWA/SDPD/2015/BOOKLET.1).
49. World Bank, World Development Indicators.
50. Ibid.
51. Jana el-Baba, "The sustainable development framework in Lebanon: a national assessment", Country Report for the Arab Sustainable Development Report (2015). Available from http://css.escwa.org.lb/SDPD/3572/Lebanon.pdf.
52. FAO, *Regional Overview of Food Insecurity - Near East and North Africa: Strengthening Regional Collaboration to Build Resilience for Food Security and Nutrition* (Cairo, June 2015).
53. Severity of malnutrition by stunting: low (below 20 per cent); medium (20-29 per cent); high (30-39 per cent); very high (>= 40 per cent).
54. World Bank, World Development Indicators.
55. Ibid.
56. Ibid.
57. WHO, Global Infobase. Available from www.who.int/infobase (accessed 30 August 2015).
58. World Bank, World Development Indicators.
59. Ibid.
60. Ali H. Mokdad and others, "The state of health in the Arab world, 1990–2010: an analysis of the burden of diseases, injuries, and risk factors", *The Lancet*, vol. 383 (25 January 2014), pp. 309-320. Available from

www.thelancet.com/pdfs/journals/lancet/PIIS0140-6736(13)62189-3.pdf.

61. Ibid.
62. In LDCs, lower-respiratory infections, diarrhea, and malaria continue to take their toll, while rates of heart disease and stroke are much lower. For middle- and higher-income countries in the Arab region, the most widespread non-communicable diseases include heart disease, depression and anxiety, chronic back and neck pain and diabetes. These have risen steadily since 1990, driven largely by changes in lifestyle and population increases.
63. Ali H. Mokdad and others, "The state of health in the Arab world".
64. Hissa Al Thani, "Disability in the Arab region: current situation and prospects", *Behinderung und Dritte Welt (Journal for Disability and International Development)*, vol. 3 (2006), pp. 4-9. Available from http://www.iiz-dvv.de/index.php?article_id=137&clang=1.
65. United Nations and League of Arab States, *Arab Millennium Development Goals Report.*
66. World Bank, World Development Indicators.
67. Ibid.
68. Ibid.
69. United Nations and League of Arab States, *Arab Millennium Development Goals Report.*
70. Ali H. Mokdad and others, "The state of health in the Arab world".
71. Samer Jabbour and others (eds.), *Public Health in the Arab World* (Cambridge, Cambridge University Press, 2012).
72. Nadine Naber, "The social pillar and the paradox of development in the Arab region".
73. Ibid.
74. United Nations Office for the Coordination of Humanitarian Affairs (OCHA), Syrian Arab Republic. Available from www.unocha.org/syria (accessed 12 September 2015).
75. Thalif Deen, "Syrian crisis threatens development in Arab world", 17 January 2014. Available from http://www.ipsnews.net/2014/01/syrian-crisis-threatens-development-arab-world.
76. ESCWA, *Palestine, the Occupation and the Fourth Geneva Convention.*
77. United Nations Human Settlements Programme (UN-Habitat), *The State of Arab Cities 2012: Challenges of Urban Transition* (Nairobi, December 2012).

Chapter 4

1. These issues briefs are available from www.escwa.un.org.lb/information/meetingdetails.asp?referenceNum=3572E.
2. International Fund for Agricultural Development (IFAD), "Fighting water scarcity in the Arab countries", fact sheet (Rome, March 2009). Available from www.ifad.org/operations/projects/regions/pn/factsheets/WWF_factsheet.pdf.
3. UNESCO, *The United Nations World Water Development Report 2015: Water for a Sustainable World.* (Paris, 2015), chapter 13. Available from http://unesdoc.unesco.org/images/0023/002318/231823E.pdf.
4. UNDP, *Water Governance in the Arab Region.*
5. ESCWA, "Chapter 33: Arab region and Western Asia", in *The United Nations Word Water Development Report 4* (Paris, UNESCO, 2012). Available from http://www.unesco.org/new/en/natural-sciences/environment/water/wwap/wwdr/wwdr4-2012/.
6. Total annual volume of groundwater and surface water withdrawn from their sources for human use, expressed as a percentage of the total volume of water available annually through the hydrological cycle (total renewable water resources).
7. UNDP, *Water Governance in the Arab Region.*
8. *ESCWA Water Development Report 5: Issues in Sustainable Water Resources Management and Water Services in the Arab Region* (Beirut, 2013, E/ESCWA/SDPD/2013/4).
9. IFAD, "Fighting water scarcity in the Arab countries".
10. Author's calculations based on FAO, AQUASTAT and DESA, World Population Prospects. The four Arab countries above the 1,000 cubic meters per person water scarcity line in 2014 are: the Comoros, Iraq, Mauritania and Somalia.
11. Mohamed El-Ashry and others (eds.), *Arab Environment: Water - Sustainable Management of a Scarce Resource* (Arab Forum for Environment and Development (AFED), 2010).
12. Author's calculations based on FAO, AQUASTAT; and DESA, World Population Prospects.
13. Ibid.
14. FAO, AQUASTAT, 2013 data.
15. UNDP, *Water Governance in the Arab Region.*
16. Arab Organization for Agricultural Development (AOAD), *Arab Agricultural Statistics Yearbook* (Khartoum, 2006). Available from http://www.aoad.org/Agricultural_%20Statistical_Book_Vol32.pdf; and IFAD, "Fighting water scarcity in the Arab countries".
17. UNDP, *Water Governance in the Arab Region.*
18. International Desalination Association (IDA) and Global Water Intel (GWI), *The 27th Worldwide Desalting Plant Inventory* (2014).
19. UNDP, *Water Governance in the Arab Region.*
20. International Energy Agency - Energy Technology Systems Analysis Programme (IEA-ETSAP) and International Renewable Energy Agency (IRENA), "Water desalination using renewable energy", Technology Brief, No. 112 (March 2012). Available from www.irena.org/DocumentDownloads/Publications/IRENA-ETSAP%20Tech%20Brief%20I12%20Water-Desalination.pdf.
21. World Bank, *Renewable Energy Desalination: An Emerging Solution to Close the Water Gap in the Middle East and North Africa* (Washington, D.C., 2012). Available from http://water.worldbank.org/sites/water.worldbank.org/files/publication/water-wpp-Sun-Powered-Desal-Gateway-Meeting-MENAs-Water-Needs_2.pdf.
22. World Bank and others, *Water Reuse in the Arab World: From Principle to Practice - Voices from the Field* (Dubai, May 2011). Available from http://water.worldbank.org/sites/water.worldbank.org/files/publication/Water-Reuse-Arab-World-From-Principle%20-Practice.pdf.
23. FAO, Suite of Food Security Indicators; and ESCWA, *Pathways towards Food Security in the Arab Region: An Assessment of Wheat Availability* (Beirut, 2015, E/ESCWA/SDPD/2015/1).
24. ESCWA and others, "Background paper on addressing new and emerging challenges to secure renewed political commitment to sustainable development in the Arab region" (Beirut, October 2011, E/ESCWA/SDPD/2011/WG.5/6).
25. ESCWA, *Land Degradation Assessment and Prevention: Selected Case Studies from the ESCWA Region* (Beirut, 2007 E/ESCWA/SDPD/2007/4).
26. World Bank, World Development Indicators.
27. Ibid.
28. Land Portal Foundation data. Available from http://landportal.info (accessed 30 August 2015).
29. See World Bank, World DataBank. Available from http://databank.worldbank.org/data/reports.aspx?source=2&country=&series=AG.YLD.CREL.KG&period= (accessed 30 August 2015).
30. Calculated based on FAOSTAT 2015 data.
31. Hussein Abaza and others (eds.), *Arab Environment 4: Green Economy – Sustainable Transition in a Changing Arab World* (AFED, 2011). Available from http://afedonline.org/Report2011/PDF/En/Full-eng.pdf.
32. Ibid.
33. IFAD, "Fighting water scarcity in the Arab countries".
34. Ibid.; and AOAD, *Arab Agricultural Statistics Yearbook.*
35. Abdoul-Karim Sadik and others (eds.), *Arab Environment 7: Food Security – Challenges and Prospects* (AFED, 2014).

36. FAO, *Food Wastage Footprint: Impacts on Natural Resources* (Rome, 2013). Available from www.fao.org/docrep/018/i3347e/i3347e.pdf.
37. FAO, "Reducing food losses and waste in the Near East & North Africa region" (Rome, February 2014, NERC/14/7 Rev.1).
38. Ibid.
39. Habib El-Andaloussi and Lara Geadah, "Energy in the Arab region", Issues Brief for the Arab Sustainable Development Report (Beirut, ESCWA, 2015). Available from http://css.escwa.org.lb/SDPD/3572/Goal7.pdf.
40. World Bank, World Development Indicators; and International Energy Agency (IEA) data.
41. IEA data. Algeria, Lebanon, Morocco and Tunisia witnessed a fall in energy intensity between 2000 and 2010, as noted in a report by MEDENER, *Energy Efficiency Indicators for Mediterranean Countries* (April 2014).
42. IEA data.
43. IEA, "Energy snapshot of the week", 19 August 2014. Available from www.iea.org/newsroomandevents/graphics/2014-08-19-energy-consumption-per-capita-and-energy-intensity.html.
44. Habib El-Andaloussi and Lara Geadah, "Energy in the Arab region". In 2015, the United Arab Emirates and Kuwait announced plans to reduce fuel subsidies.
45. World Bank, World Development Indicators; and IEA data.
46. ESCWA estimation based on the targets of member States.
47. The number of deaths caused by natural disasters in the Arab region may be underreported.
48. UNEP and others, *Environment Outlook for the Arab Region - Environment for Development and Human Well-being* (2010). Available from http://eoar.cedare.int/report/EOAR_Full%20Report%20(EN).pdf.
49. See www.arabclimateinitiative.org.
50. Algeria, the Comoros, Djibouti, Jordan, Lebanon, Mauritania, Morocco, Oman, Tunisia and the United Arab Emirates. See www4.unfccc.int/submissions/indc/Submission%20Pages/submissions.aspx.
51. Averages for East Asia and the Pacific and Latin America and the Caribbean were 5.9 and 2.9 respectively. See http://data.worldbank.org/indicator/EN.ATM.CO2E.PC/countries/1W-Z4-ZJ?display=graph.
52. UNEP, "Marine resources in the Arab region", Issues Brief for the Arab Sustainable Development Report (2015). Available from http://css.escwa.org.lb/SDPD/3572/Goal14.pdf.
53. A syndrome of ecosystem responses to human activities that fertilize bodies of water with nitrogen and phosphorus, often leading to changes in animal and plant populations and degradation of water and habitat quality.
54. UNEP and others, *Environment Outlook for the Arab Region.*
55. UNEP, *2005 Annual Report* (2006).
56. Richard Mackay, *The Atlas of Endangered Species* (Oxon, Earthscan, 2009).
57. 2008 data from International Union for Conservation of Nature (IUCN). Available from www.iucnredlist.org (accessed 2 November 2015).
58. UNEP, "State of biodiversity in West Asia" (2010). Available from http://www.unep.org/delc/portals/119/Stateofbiodiv-westasia.pdf.
59. UNEP and others, *Environment Outlook for the Arab Region,* p. 185.
60. Hedi Hadri and Mustapha Guellouz, *Forest and Rangelands in the Near East Region - Facts and Figures* (Cairo, FAO Office for the Near East, 2011).
61. UNEP and others, *Environment Outlook for the Arab Region,* p. 181.
62. World Bank, Data – Terrestrial protected areas. Available from http://data.worldbank.org/indicator/ER.LND.PTLD.ZS/countries?display=graph (accessed 30 August 2015).

Chapter 5

1. Expert reports are available from http://www.escwa.org.lb/information/meetingdetails.asp?referenceNum=3572E.
2. German Federal Ministry for Economic Cooperation and Development, "Development for peace and security: development policy in the context of conflict, fragility and violence", BMZ Strategy Paper 4 (BMZ, 2013). Available from www.bmz.de/en/publications/topics/peace/Strategiepapier333_04_2013.pdf.
3. Unless otherwise stated, the figures in this section were taken from ESCWA, *Palestine, the Occupation and the Fourth Geneva Convention: Facts and Figures* (Beirut, 2014, E/ESCWA/ECRI/2014/Booklet.1).
4. Foundation for Middle East Peace, Settlements. Available from http://fmep.org/issues/settlements (accessed 23 September 2015).
5. Limor Yehuda and others, "One rule, two legal systems: Israel's regime of laws in the West Bank" (The Association for Civil Rights in Israel (ACRI), October 2014).
6. Palestinian Water Authority, "Status report of water resources in the occupied State of Palestine – 2012" (October 2013).
7. Report on UNCTAD assistance to the Palestinian people: developments in the economy of the Occupied Palestinian Territory (TD/B/62/3).
8. Ibid., pp. 2-3.
9. Ibid.
10. More than two million other refugees registered with UNRWA live in the West Bank and Gaza Strip. See "UNRWA in figures as of January 2015". Available from www.unrwa.org/sites/default/files/unrwa_in_figures_2015.pdf.
11. Jad Chaaban and others, *Socioeconomic Survey of Palestinian Refugees in Lebanon* (Beirut, American University of Beirut and UNRWA, 2010).
12. ESCWA, "Beyond governance and conflict: measuring the impact of the neighbourhood effect in the Arab region", Working Paper (Beirut, 2014, E/ESCWA/ECRI/2014/WP.1)
13. Fateh Azzam, "A human rights approach to sustainable development in the Arab region", Expert Report for the Arab Sustainable Development Report (Beirut, 2015). Available from http://css.escwa.org.lb/SDPD/3572/8-AzzamSD.pdf.
14. Slight improvements were measured in Tunisia (due to the successful conclusion of parliamentary and presidential elections in 2014) and Egypt (due to a reduction in violent crime, "reflecting the effectiveness of the security apparatus"). See Institute for Economics and Peace, *Global Peace Index 2015: Measuring Peace, Its Causes and Its Economic Value* (June 2015), pp. 15 and 17. Available from http://static.visionofhumanity.org/sites/default/files/Global%20Peace%20Index%20Report%202015_0.pdf.
15. The three other countries are Niger, South Sudan and Ukraine.
16. The Global Terrorism Index, published by the Institute for Economics and Peace, calculates the direct and indirect effects of terrorism globally. It is a composite index that consists of four indicators: number of accidents; number of fatalities; number of injuries and total harm to buildings (accidents weighted 1, fatality 3, injury 0.5 and the damage from 0 to 3 depending on harshness). Data is compiled from the Global Terrorism Database (www.start.umd.edu/gtd/).
17. UNHCR, Syria Regional Refugee Response. Available from http://data.unhcr.org/syrianrefugees/regional.php (accessed 18 August 2015).
18. "UNRWA in Figures as of 1 January 2015".
19. The initial reaction of Governments to the 2011 Arab uprisings was to increase salaries and jobs in the public sector as a short-term response to social discontent. The Government of Egypt announced a 15 per cent wage rise for all civil servants (estimated at 5.8 million) and incentives schemes for the lowest-paid. Tunisia's transitional Government also announced an employment plan that included the creation of 20,000 jobs in the public sector. Such

measures present large financial risks over the long term (see Lamia Moubayed, "From government to governance: how will the Arab region meet the goals of sustainable development in the post-2015 period").

20. Daniel Kaufmann, "Governance and the Arab world transition: reflections, empirics and implications for the international community", The 2011 Brookings Blum Roundtable Policy Briefs (Brookings Institute, 2011).
21. Dev Kar and others, *The Absorption of Illicit Financial Flows from Developing Countries: 2002-2006* (Washington, D.C., Global Financial Integrity, 2010).
22. See Corruption Watch, available from www.corruptionwatch.org.za/learn-about-corruption/what-is-corruption/we-are-all-affected; and Sofia Wickberg, "Literature review on costs of corruption for the poor", 16 May 2013, available from www.u4.no/publications/literature-review-on-costs-of-corruption-for-the-poor.
23. CPI ranges from 10 (highly "clean") to 0 (highly corrupt). Available from www.transparency.org/cpi2011. CPI scores from the years prior to the Arab uprisings show similar results.
24. The BTI evaluates whether and how developing countries and countries in transition are steering social change towards democracy and a market economy. Guided by a standardized codebook, country experts assess (on a scale of 1 to 10) the extent to which 17 criteria have been met. A second country expert then reviews those assessments and scores. The 49 individual scores given per country are then subjected to processes of regional and interregional calibration for the sake of consistency.
25. *Public Sector Transparency and Accountability in Selected Arab States: Policies and Practices* (United Nations publication, ST/ESA/PAD/SER.E/71).
26. Promotion and protection of all human rights, civil, political, economic, social and cultural rights, including the right to development (A/HRC/7/23).
27. UNHCR, "Background note on gender equality, nationality laws and statelessness 2014". Available from www.unhcr.org/4f5886306.html.
28. A/RES/34/169.
29. ESCWA, *An Overview of the Arab Security Sector amidst Political Transition: A Reflection on Legacies, Functions and Perceptions* (Beirut, 2013, E/ESCWA/ECRI/2013/2).
30. The Global Competitiveness Index and similar indices are based on perceptions and the details of how they are calculated require analysis before a proper assessment of scores and rankings can be made.
31. Robert Beschel and Mark Ahern, "Public financial management reform in the Middle East and North Africa: an overview of regional experience", Report No. 55061-MNA (Washington, D.C., World Bank, 2010) Available from http://go.worldbank.org/B4V6K2F140.
32. The IMF 2010 analysis was carried out in 72 countries (including Egypt, Jordan, Morocco, Palestine, the Sudan and Yemen in the Arab region) and assessed and compared the quality of budget institutions. For further discussion, see Cameron Allen, "The institutional framework of sustainable development in the Arab region".
33. The findings are similar to those produced by the Freedom House measures of voice and accountability, the World Governance Indicators, and Barclay's Capital's Emerging Markets Research. See Lamia Moubayed, "From government to governance: how will the Arab region meet the goals of sustainable development in the post-2015 period" for a discussion of the various indices.
34. Martin Greeley, "Synthesis report: findings and recommendations from a seven country study of UN engagement in poverty reduction and national development strategies" (New York, UNDP, March 2008).
35. Darren Swanson and others, "GovernAbilities: The nexus of sustainability, accountability and adaptability – Essential tools for successful governance in the 21st century" (Winnipeg, International Institute for Sustainable Development, May 2014).
36. Many review tools are available: (a) national peer reviews; (b) internal peer reviews; (c) external auditing; (d) parliamentary reviews; (e) budgetary reviews; (f) public and local monitoring; and (g) international and regional monitoring. See Barry Dalal-Clayton and Steve Bass, "A review of monitoring mechanisms for national sustainable development strategies", *Environmental Planning Issues, No. 27* (International Institute for Environment and Development (IIED), July 2006).
37. Article 2 of the Pact of the League of Arab States, 22 March 1945 (an unofficial English translation is available from http://avalon.law.yale.edu/20th_century/arableag.asp).
38. Membership of the RCM: Joint United Nations Programme on HIV/AIDS (UNAIDS); United Nations Conference on Trade and Development (UNCTAD); United Nations Development Programme (UNDP); United Nations Development Operations Coordination Office (UNDOCO); United Nations Environment Programme (UNEP); United Nations Educational, Scientific and Cultural Organization (UNESCO); Food and Agriculture Organization of the United Nations (FAO); United Nations Population Fund (UNFPA); United Nations Human Settlements Programme (UNHABITAT); United Nations High Commissioner for Refugees (UNHCR); United Nations Information Centre (UNIC); United Nations Children's Fund (UNICEF); United Nations Industrial Development Organization (UNIDO); United Nations Entity for Gender Equality and the Empowerment of Women (UNWOMEN); United Nations Relief and Works Agency for Palestine Refugees in the Near East (UNRWA); United Nations Office of the High Commissioner for Human Rights (UNOHCHR); United Nations Office on Drugs and Crime (UNODC); United Nations Office for Project Services (UNOPS); United Nations University (UNU); United Nations Economic and Social Commission for Western Asia (ESCWA); International Civil Aviation Organization (ICAO); International Fund for Agricultural Development (IFAD); International Telecommunications Union (ITU); International Labour Organization (ILO); International Organization for Migration (IOM); International Monetary Fund (IMF); League of the Arab States; United Nations Office for the Coordination of Humanitarian Affairs (OCHA); Universal Postal Union (UPU); World Food Programme (WFP); World Health Organization (WHO); World Bank.
39. All Forum documents may be accessed at www.escwa.un.org/information/meetingdetails.asp?referenceNum=3572E.

Chapter 6

1. The Agenda was adopted at the Third International Conference on Financing for Development in July 2015. Available from http://www.un.org/esa/ffd/wp-content/uploads/2015/08/AAAA_Outcome.pdf.
2. The papers and issues briefs are available from www.escwa.un.org.lb/information/meetingdetails.asp?referenceNum=3572E.
3. ESCWA, "Sustainable development: financing gap in the Arab region" (Beirut, 2015, E/ESCWA/EDID/2015/IG.1/5).
4. Najib Saab (ed.), *Arab Environment 5: Survival Options - Ecological Footprint of Arab Countries* (AFED, 2012).
5. ESCWA calculations.
6. Richard Dobbs and others, *Infrastructure Productivity: How to Save $1 Trillion a Year* (McKinsey & Company, 2013).
7. International Energy Agency, *World Energy Outlook Report 2014* (Paris, Organisation for

Economic Co-operation and Development/ IEA, 2014).

8. The IEA includes Iran in its definition of the Middle East, but in the absence of figures on the Arab countries alone, this estimate is useful as an order of magnitude.
9. Sherine El Sharkawy, "Financing sustainable development in the Arab region", Expert Report for the Arab Sustainable Development Report (Beirut, ESCWA, 2015, E/ESCWA/SDPD/2015/ Technical Paper.2).
10. Since there is no forecast of principal repayments and disbursements of private debt, the historical average between 2009 and 2013 was used. Net equity flows, including portfolio and net foreign direct investment, were projected as a ratio to GDP based on the average for the historical period.
11. Tax effort is an index of a country's tax collection performance relative to its potential. How much a country should be collecting is determined by a number of factors, including its stage of economic development and the share of trade and agriculture in economic activity.
12. Harald Finger and others, *Toward New Horizons: Arab Economic Transformation amid Political Transitions* (Washington, D.C., IMF, 2014). Available from www.imf.org/ external/pubs/ft/dp/2014/1401mcd.pdf.
13. Ricardo Fenochietto and Carola Pessino, "Understanding countries' tax effort", IMF Working Paper, No. 13/244, (Washington, D.C., IMF, November 2013). Available from www.imf.org/external/pubs/ft/wp/2013/ wp13244.pdf.
14. Bob Rijkers and others, "Political connections and tariff evasion: evidence from Tunisia", Policy Research Working Paper, No. 7336 (Washington, D.C., World Bank, June 2015). Available from http:// documents.worldbank.org/curated/ en/2015/06/24697879/political-connections-tariff-evasion-evidence-tunisia.
15. Roberta Gatti and others, "Striving for better jobs: the challenge of informality in the Middle East and North Africa", MENA Knowledge and Learning Quick Notes Series, No. 49 (Washington, D.C., World Bank, 2011). Available from http:// documents.worldbank.org/curated/ en/2011/12/15572235/striving-better-jobs-challenge-informality-middle-east-north-africa-region.
16. Sherine El Sharkawy, "Financing sustainable development in the Arab region".
17. Shir Hever, "How much international aid to Palestinians ends up in the Israeli Economy?" (Aid Watch, September 2015). Available from http://www.aidwatch.ps/ sites/default/files/resource-field_media/ InternationalAidToPalestiniansFeeds TheIsraeliEconomy.pdf.
18. Khaled Hussein and others, "Reinforcing the role of Arab development funds: the financing gap", Office of the ESCWA Executive Secretary Working Paper Series (Beirut, 2013, E/ESCWA/OES/2013/WP.6).
19. World Bank, *Arab Development Assistance: Four Decades of Cooperation* (Washington, D.C., June 2010). Available from http:// siteresources.worldbank.org/INTMENA/ Resources/ADAPub82410web.pdf.
20. Khaled Hussein and others, "Reinforcing the role of Arab development funds".
21. Sherine El Sharkawy, "Financing sustainable development in the Arab region".
22. ESCWA, *Arab Integration: A 21st Century Development Imperative* (Beirut, 2013, E/ ESCWA/OES/2013/3).
23. Sherine El Sharkawy, "Financing sustainable development in the Arab region".
24. Dilip Ratha and others, "Migration and remittances: recent developments and outlook", Migration and Development Brief No. 24 (Washington, D.C., World Bank, 2015). Available from http://siteresources. worldbank.org/INTPROSPECTS/ Resources/334934-1288990760745/ MigrationandDevelopmentBrief24.pdf.
25. The African Development Bank (AfDB), the African Development Fund (ADF), the Asian Development Bank (ADB), the European Bank for Reconstruction and Development (EBRD), and the Inter-American Development Bank (IDB).
26. World Bank, World Development Indicators.
27. ESCWA, *Regional Profile of the Information Society in the Arab Region* (Beirut, 2013, E/ ESCWA/ICTD/2013/6).
28. Only 1.5 per cent of manufactured exports in the Arab countries in 2008 were considered to fit into the high-technology category, compared with a global average of 17 per cent (data from the World Development Indicators).
29. ESCWA, *Regional Profile of the Information Society.*
30. *UNESCO Science Report 2010: The Current Status of Science around the World* (Paris, 2010), p. 8. Available from http://unesdoc.unesco.org/ images/0018/001899/189958e.pdf.
31. World Bank, World Development Indicators.
32. UNDP and Mohammed bin Rashid Al Maktoum Foundation, *Arab Knowledge Report 2014: Youth and Localisation of Knowledge* (Dubai, 2014). Available from http://www.arabstates.undp.org/content/ dam/rbas/report/UNDP-GENERAL-REPORT-ENG.pdf.
33. See www.zewailcity.edu.eg.
34. Arab member States of WTO are: Bahrain, Djibouti, Egypt, Jordan, Kuwait, Mauritania, Morocco, Oman, Qatar, Saudi Arabia, Tunisia, United Arab Emirates and Yemen. Those with observer status are: Algeria, the Comoros, Iraq, Lebanon, Libya, the Sudan and the Syrian Arab Republic.
35. UNCTAD, International Investment Agreements database. Available from http://investmentpolicyhub.unctad.org/IIA (accessed 27 October 2015).
36. Robert Smith, "Measuring sustainable development in the Arab region". Egypt, Iraq, Jordan, Morocco, Saudi Arabia and Tunisia were selected for this review because they: are geographically representative of the Arab region; are relatively developed economically and socially and, therefore, could be expected to have reasonably good capacity to undertake MDG and sustainable development monitoring; and have all produced MDG and sustainable development indicator reports of some kind.
37. The indicators are largely based on the global set of indicators of the United Nations Commission on Sustainable Development. One of the criteria for the choice of those indicators was in fact data availability in the Arab countries, regardless of their relevance to the region's development issues. Available from www.escwa.un.org/divisions/sd/pubs/ index.asp?PubNUM=SDI-2011.
38. The Statistical Capacity Indicator scores the capacity of a country's statistical system. It is based on a diagnostic framework assessing methodology, data sources, and periodicity and timeliness. Countries are scored against 25 criteria in those areas, using publicly available information and/or country input. The overall score is then calculated as a simple average of all three area scores on a scale of 0-100.
39. Bertelsmann Stiftung, Transformation Index BTI 2014. Available from www.bti-project. org/reports/country-reports/index.nc (accessed 25 September 2015).
40. See http://unstats.un.org/unsd/ envaccounting/default.asp.
41. Monia Braham, "Regional integration and the post-2015 development agenda: towards a follow-up and review mechanism of sustainable development policies in the Mediterranean Arab countries", *CIHEAM Watch Letter*, No. 34 (September 2015).

Chapter 7

1. See General Assembly resolution 67/290 of 9 July 2013 on the format and organizational aspects of the high-level political forum on sustainable development.

Annex II

1. Algeria, Bahrain, the Comoros, Djibouti, Egypt, Iraq, Jordan, Kuwait, Lebanon, Libya, Mauritania, Morocco, Oman, the State of Palestine, Qatar, Saudi Arabia, Somalia, the Sudan, the Syrian Arab Republic, Tunisia, the United Arab Emirates and Yemen.
2. See UNSD, Series Metadata. Available from http://mdgs.un.org/unsd/mdg/PrintableMetadata.aspx (accessed 28 September 2015).

www.ingramcontent.com/pod-product-compliance
Lightning Source LLC
Chambersburg PA
CBHW081434270326
41932CB00019B/3205

* 9 7 8 9 2 1 1 2 8 3 8 8 4 *